Edition KWV

Die „Edition KWV“ beinhaltet hochwertige Werke aus dem Bereich der Wirtschaftswissenschaften. Alle Werke in der Reihe erschienen ursprünglich im Kölner Wissenschaftsverlag, dessen Programm Springer Gabler 2018 übernommen hat.

Weitere Bände in der Reihe http://www.springer.com/series/16033

Eva I. Hoppe-Fischer

Essays on Contract Design and Incentive Provision

Springer Gabler

Eva I. Hoppe-Fischer
Wiesbaden, Germany

Bis 2018 erschien der Titel im Kölner Wissenschaftsverlag, Köln
Dissertation Universität zu Köln, 2011

Edition KWV
ISBN 978-3-658-24132-2 ISBN 978-3-658-24133-9 (eBook)
https://doi.org/10.1007/978-3-658-24133-9

Library of Congress Control Number: 2019933863

Springer Gabler

Originally published by Kölner Wissenschaftsverlag, Köln, 2011

This Springer Gabler imprint is published by the registered company Springer Fachmedien Wiesbaden GmbH part of Springer Nature
The registered company address is: Abraham-Lincoln-Str. 46, 65189 Wiesbaden, Germany

To my family

To my family

Acknowledgements

After my joy over the acceptance of this thesis by the faculty of Management, Economics and Social Sciences of the University of Cologne in February 2011, it is time to look back and thank all those who have contributed to my work by encouraging me and giving me scientific and personal support.

First of all, I would like to thank my supervisor Patrick Schmitz for his extraordinary guidance. Already in the final years of my undergraduate studies he raised my interest in contract theory so much that I was very happy about the chance to intensify my studies as a research assistant at his seminar. I am especially grateful for his strong encouragement to start our first joint research paper (later published in the Journal of Public Economics) only shortly after the beginning of my postgraduate studies. The countless inspiring discussions with Patrick Schmitz helped me to develop a profound understanding of contract theory and perhaps even more important, led to my enthusiasm for doing research.

Moreover, I am very grateful to my second supervisor Oliver Gürtler. He paid detailed attention to my thesis and made very helpful comments and valuable suggestions.

Furthermore, I was glad that Achim Wambach agreed to be the chairman of my disputation. I would like to thank him very much for leading it to an interesting and vital discussion.

I enjoyed working together with my coauthor David Kusterer. I like to remember our fruitful discussions and the days in the lab. I thank him for helping me to finalize the figures for this thesis.

I have benefitted from inspiring discussions at numerous conferences and seminars and from valuable comments made by several editors and anonymous referees. I would like to thank Bruno Biais, Florian Englmaier, Maija Halonen-Akatwijuka, Oliver Hart, Timo Henckel, Elisabetta Iossa, Bernd Irlenbusch,

Kai Konrad, Andrea Leuermann, David Martimort, Warwick McKibbin, Wanda Mimra, Gerard Pfann, Andreas Roider, Stéphane Saussier, Anja Schöttner, and Dirk Sliwka.

I also thank our secretary Kristin Pfeiffer who always provided friendly assistance and our student assistants Jana Boes and Felix Meickmann who were very supportive in programming and conducting the experiments.

Many thanks to Anne Bissels for designing the cover of this book.

I am deeply grateful to my family and friends. Especially my parents and Markus Fischer gave me strength and motivation in all possible ways.

Cologne, February 2011 Eva Isabel Hoppe

Contents

1

Introduction

The economic theory of contracts, i.e. the theory of incentives, asymmetric information, and institutional design, has been a highly active field of research in microeconomics in the last three decades. Emphasizing the importance of unverifiable actions and privately held information, contract theory provides formal tools to analyze various aspects of the organization of economic activities and relationships. For instance, issues as diverse as the allocation of property rights (e.g., the pros and cons of vertical and lateral integration or the trade-offs between public and private ownership), the design of selling and procurement mechanisms, the provision of investment incentives in trading relationships, the design of wage schemes, and the assignment of different tasks within firms, have all been fruitfully studied from a contract-theoretic perspective.[1]

In traditional contract theory, it is typically assumed that decision makers are interested in their own monetary payoffs only. Moreover, they have unlimited cognitive abilities and behave in a perfectly rational way. Yet, in practice people often do not behave this way. While empirical research is very difficult in contract theory,[2] since the focus is on asymmetric information

[1]For surveys see Salanié (1997), Schweizer (1999), and Bolton and Dewatripont (2005).

[2]For literature reviews on empirical tests of contract theory, see Prendergast (1999), Masten and Saussier (2002), and Chiappori and Salanié (2003).

E. I. Hoppe-Fischer, *Essays on Contract Design and Incentive Provision*,
Edition KWV, https://doi.org/10.1007/978-3-658-24133-9_1

which means that there are inherent data availability problems, controlled laboratory experiments have recently turned out to be an important source of data in contract-theoretic contexts. In particular, laboratory experiments are not only useful to test the assumptions and predictions of existing theories, but they can also generate new insights that may lead to novel psychological hypotheses to explain economic behavior.[3]

This collection of essays on the theory of contract design and incentive provision is divided into two parts. Part I consists of three chapters that study traditional contract-theoretic models, while Part II consists of three chapters that report about experimental investigations.

In particular, the three theoretical studies that form Part I are motivated by the classic procurement problem of a principal who wants a certain good or service to be delivered by an agent. A procurement context brings up many interesting research questions. For example, who should own the assets required to provide the good or service to be procured? How should the relevant tasks be allocated between the principal and the agent? What should the payment scheme look like? Should the principal create incentives for the agent to gather information about the production costs?

In **Chapter 2**, the principal represents the government; i.e., we consider a public procurement setting.[4] The government wants a certain good or service (e.g., public education, medical services, or public transportation) to be provided. Should the required assets (e.g., the school building, the hospital, or the railroad network) be publicly or privately owned or should a public-private partnership be formed? Our theoretical framework builds on the incomplete contracting approach, according to which it is impossible to write complex

---

[3] For a comprehensive introduction to the history, methods, and controversy of experimental economics see Bardsley et al. (2010). For surveys on experimental methods see also Friedman and Sunder (1994) and Friedman and Cassar (2004). Camerer (2003) provides an extensive survey of experimental and theoretical work on strategic interaction focusing on behavioral and psychological aspects.

[4] This chapter is based on Hoppe and Schmitz (2010a).

and detailed contracts conditioned on all possible future contingencies.[5] We show that the initially specified quantity of an ex ante describable basic good can have important effects on investment incentives, which has been neglected in the literature so far. We also study how the conflicting tasks of investing in quality improvements and cost reductions should be assigned. It turns out that the optimal contracts and governance structures crucially depend on the exogenous parameters of the model such as the nature of the investments and the parties' bargaining powers. Our findings are in line with the empirical observation that privatization is typically not a pure choice between merely public or private institutions, but it often involves more complex governance structures where the responsibility for certain tasks is vested in private hands and the responsibility for other tasks is vested in public hands.

In **Chapter 3**, we study a sequential public procurement model that consists of two stages.[6] The government agency wants a facility (such as a hospital or a toll road) to be built and subsequently to be managed to provide a public service. We consider two different modes of provision. In a public-private partnership, the tasks of building and managing are bundled, while under traditional procurement, these tasks are delegated to separate private contractors.[7] The two modes of provision strongly differ in their incentives to innovate and to gather private information about future costs to adapt the service provision to changing circumstances. We assume that initially only the basic features of the good or service can be described in a contract, but after some time has passed, i.e. when the provision stage is reached, it be-

[5] The model in Chapter 2 extends Hart, Shleifer, and Vishny's (1997) work, which studies privatization from an incomplete contracting perspective. The incomplete contracting approach was pioneered by Grossman and Hart (1986) and Hart and Moore (1990). See Hart (1995) for a comprehensive textbook exposition and see Schmitz (2001) for a non-technical survey on the incomplete contracting approach.

[6] This chapter is based on Hoppe and Schmitz (2010b).

[7] We follow Hart (2003), who argues that a key property of a public-private partnership is the fact that building the infrastructure and subsequent service provision are bundled. On public-private partnerships, see also Grimsey and Lewis (2004) and Yescombe (2007).

comes clear how the good or service can be improved by adapting it. For instance, advances in the field of medical research may require hospitals to meet growing service standards, e.g. to adapt to new medical equipment or to enlarge the number of operating rooms. It turns out that, depending on the potential benefits of such adaptations, the government agency's preferred mode of provision may be different from the one that should be chosen from a welfare perspective.

In **Chapter 4**, we consider a principal who wants an agent to produce a specific good.[8] At the outset, no one knows the agent's production costs. But after the principal has offered a contract, the agent can engage in costly information gathering.[9] We consider two different scenarios. In both scenarios, costly information gathering at the contracting stage is a pure rent-seeking activity, because it is commonly known that the ex post efficient trade decision does not depend on the state of nature. In the first scenario, if the agent does not acquire information before the contract is signed, he will not learn the state of nature before trade can take place. In contrast, in the second scenario, if the agent has not gathered information before signing the contract, he costlessly learns the state of nature before trade can take place. The model has surprising implications. We show that there are circumstances under which the agent's expected rent is smaller in scenario II than in scenario I; i.e., the agent is worse off when more information becomes available to him over time. In contrast, the principal's expected profit is always weakly larger in scenario II; i.e., she can only benefit from the fact that the agent becomes costlessly informed before trade takes place.

In Part II, three experimental studies are presented. The first two studies investigate contract-theoretic problems that were brought up in Part I. Specifically, we explore whether suitable contracts can mitigate underinvest-

[8] This chapter is based on Hoppe and Schmitz (2010c).

[9] Also in Crémer and Khalil (1992) and Crémer, Khalil, and Rochet (1998a), costly information gathering can occur after the principal's contract offer. In contrast, Crémer, Khalil, and Rochet (1998b) analyze information gathering before the contract is offered.

ment problems and how conflicting tasks should be allocated between different decision makers. We find that central contract-theoretic insights are corroborated by the data. However, the data also suggests that social preferences and bounded rationality clearly affect the subjects' behavior. While social preferences have been studied extensively in the experimental literature in the last few years, limited cognitive abilities appear to have received less attention. The short experimental study in the final chapter explores the relationship between cognitive abilities and the susceptibility to behavioral biases.

Chapter 5 is motivated by the vital debate in the contract-theoretic literature about whether contracts can mitigate or even solve the hold-up problem, i.e. the underinvestment problem that arises when investments are relationship-specific and non-contractible.[10] Ultimately, this question has to be answered empirically. As a first step in that direction, we have conducted a laboratory experiment with 960 participants. We consider investments that directly benefit the non-investing party. In this setting, according to standard contract-theoretic reasoning, a simple fixed-price contract cannot improve investment incentives compared to a no-contract benchmark. In contrast, a suitable option contract can solve the hold-up problem, provided that renegotiation can be prevented. If renegotiation cannot be ruled out, according to standard theory, contracting is useless.[11] Indeed, we find that in the experiment fixed-price contracts cannot mitigate the hold-up problem, while option contracts are very effective when renegotiation can be prevented. However, we also find that even when renegotiation cannot be prevented, option contracts still significantly improve investment incentives compared to a no-contract treatment. This finding may be attributed to Hart and Moore's (2008) recent idea that contracts can serve as reference points.

[10] This chapter is based on Hoppe and Schmitz (2011). See Hart and Moore (1988, 1999), Rogerson (1992), and Maskin and Tirole (1999) for important theoretical investigations whether contracts can solve the hold-up problem.

[11] In particular, Maskin and Moore (1999) and Che and Hausch (1999) have shown that in the case of investments that directly benefit the non-investing party there exists no contractual solution at all to mitigate the hold-up problem if renegotiation cannot be prevented.

Chapter 6 studies a multi-task principal-agent problem in which tasks can be in direct conflict with each other.[12] For example, consider a merchant (principal) who wants to sell two products. The merchant may hire either one or two sales representatives (agents) who can exert non-contractible effort to promote the products, so that the wages can depend only on which products are sold. If the products are imperfect substitutes, then promotion effort in one task increases the probability of sale of the promoted product, but at the same time it lowers the probability of sale of the other product. In theory, it is then difficult to induce a single agent to exert efforts in the two conflicting tasks, so that the principal is better off by hiring two different agents.[13] In contrast, if there is no conflict between the tasks, the principal prefers to have one agent in charge of both tasks. In the experiment, even though the wages are more generous than predicted by standard theory (which may be attributed to social preferences), we find that in the presence of conflict subjects indeed choose two efforts significantly less often when both tasks are assigned to a single agent than when there are two agents each in charge of one task. In the absence of conflict, it turns out that the principal is significantly better off when only one agent is in charge of both tasks.

Chapter 7 contributes to the recently brought up line of research that investigates the impact of cognitive ability on judgement and decision making.[14] Frederick (2005) introduced the cognitive reflection test (CRT), which is a simple three-item test to measure a person's mode of reasoning and cognitive ability. He showed that people with high CRT scores are generally more patient and more willing to gamble in the domain of gains. In our experiment, we investigate whether the incidence of behavioral biases is related to cognitive abilities. Specifically, we study the base rate fallacy, the conservatism

---

[12] This chapter is based on Hoppe and Kusterer (2009).

[13] The agents are then "advocates" in the wording of Dewatripont and Tirole (1999). Our model extends Bolton and Dewatripont's (2005) complete-contracting formalization of Dewatripont and Tirole's (1999) ideas.

[14] This chapter is based on Hoppe and Kusterer (2011). See also Oechssler, Roider, and Schmitz (2009) for a related study.

bias, overconfidence, and the endowment effect.[15] We find that individuals with lower cognitive abilities are significantly more likely to exhibit both, the base rate fallacy and the conservatism fallacy. With regard to overconfidence, we find that subjects with higher CRT scores have a significantly more precise self-assessment. Finally, test scores do not affect the occurrence of the endowment effect, which is striking in both, low and high CRT groups.

[15] When people are asked to judge the probability of an event, they exhibit the base rate fallacy if they overweight specific evidence and do not sufficiently take into account the base rate probability, while they exhibit the conservatism bias if they do not sufficiently adapt prior probabilities to new evidence. People are overconfident if they have excessive confidence in their own answers to questions. The endowment effect refers to the fact that people often demand more to give up an object than they would be willing to pay to buy the object.

Part I

Contract Design and Incentive Provision: Theoretical Studies

Part I

2

Public versus Private Ownership: Quantity Contracts and the Allocation of Investment Tasks

2.1 Introduction

This chapter offers a new perspective on the boundaries between public and private firms. Suppose the government wants a certain good or service to be provided. According to the property rights approach to the theory of the firm, ownership structures (i.e., the allocation of control rights over the non-human assets that are required to provide the good) matter when only incomplete contracts can be written. However, in the light of the high complexity involved in the provision of public goods or services, focusing on property rights only might be too narrow. Instead, a richer set of contractual arrangements encompassing various task assignments and hybrid governance structures seems to be relevant. Indeed, in the public debate, privatization frequently refers to providing private parties with governing authority or managerial responsi-

E. I. Hoppe-Fischer, *Essays on Contract Design and Incentive Provision*,
Edition KWV, https://doi.org/10.1007/978-3-658-24133-9_2

bilities, but it is not necessarily associated with transferring asset ownership.[1] For instance, in the context of museum privatization, Schuster (1998, p. 128) argues that "it is highly unlikely that privatization will entail a choice between pure forms of public institutions and private institutions; rather, it will entail a complex set of arrangements, each one slightly different from the next, with responsibility for certain elements of the cultural institution's operations being vested in private hands but with responsibility for others vested in public hands." Similarly, contracts on the privatization of infrastructure projects do not only specify the transfer of ownership rights, but also assign the responsibilities regarding design, construction, maintenance, and modernization (see e.g. Gilroy et al., 2007, and Samuel, 2005).

In order to study how the assignment of investment tasks and the decision between private and public ownership interact, we extend Hart, Shleifer, and Vishny's (1997) seminal work on incomplete contracts and privatization. Society, represented by the government G, writes a contract with a manager M who is supposed to provide a good or service. After the contract which specifies the characteristics of a basic version of the good has been written, two kinds of observable but unverifiable investments can be made. First, it is possible to invest in the development of a quality innovation which (if implemented) increases the government's benefit from the good. Yet, the quality innovation also has the side effect of increasing the costs of provision. Second, it is possible to invest in a cost innovation which (if implemented) reduces the manager's costs, but also lowers the quality of the provided good. Hence, the implementation of an innovation leads to an (ex ante non-contractible) modification of the good actually provided. Both kinds of innovations are efficient. This means their desired effects outweigh their negative side effects; i.e., both innovations increase the total surplus (defined as the sum of the two parties' payoffs). However, the implementation of innovations requires access

[1] See e.g. Kosar (2006), who emphasizes that privatization is not an either/or decision, but rather a matter of degrees and there are myriad means through which the private sector may participate in the provision of a good or service.

to the essential assets. Under public ownership, the government controls the assets, so that it has the right to approve or veto the implementation of innovations, while under private ownership the manager can decide whether or not innovations are implemented.

It has been pointed out by Hart (2003, p. C71) that the model of public versus private ownership by Hart, Shleifer, and Vishny (1997) differs from the standard private-sector property rights model in two ways. First, the focus is on investments affecting the cost-versus-quality trade-off that has often been emphasized in the debate on privatization.[2] Second, a long-term contract between government and manager is of crucial relevance, while in the standard property rights model contracts are assumed to be sufficiently incomplete to be useless. In our model, in accordance with the complex arrangements governing the provision of public goods and services in practice, we develop these two specific aspects further and argue that their implications may have been seriously underestimated.

In particular, we extend Hart, Shleifer, and Vishny's (1997) analysis in three important ways. First, we follow their assumption that "G and M are able to write a long term contract specifying some aspects of the good or service to be provided" (p. 1132). Yet, while they assume that the quantity specified in the contract is always the ex post efficient one, we show that ex ante the parties may actually prefer to agree on a smaller quantity, which will later be renegotiated to its first-best level.[3] Indeed, in practice it is often observed that the government systematically ends up paying a larger price due to an increase in the number of items being procured, a larger project size, or additional features required by the government ex post. For example, referring to the transportation sector in a number of countries, Flyvbjerg

[2]See e.g. Melese (2005) for a discussion of privatization in the context of hospitals or Texas Center for Policy Studies (2002) regarding water privatization. See also Shleifer (1998) for a literature survey.

[3]The fact that for strategic reasons parties might deliberately agree on ex post inefficient clauses in an initial contract that will be renegotiated later has also been pointed out by Huberman and Kahn (1988) in a different context. See also Nöldeke and Schmidt (1995).

(2004, p. 39) states that "an important cause for cost increases is that the scope or ambition level for a given project changes significantly during its development and implementation."[4]

Second, we depart from the standard property rights approach by assuming that the investment tasks are "contractible control actions" in the sense of Aghion, Dewatripont, and Rey (2002, 2004); i.e., while the investment levels are non-contractible, it is possible to contractually specify who is in charge of which task and hence bears the investment costs. This assumption is in the spirit of the privatization debate where, as has been pointed out above, it is a central issue which responsibilities remain in the public hand and which ones are delegated to the private sector. Schuster (1998, p. 130) argues that "what is most important is the recognition that the management and operation of the museum can be separated into its constituent parts and those parts can be vested separately in a wide variety of responsible authorities." For instance, in the context of museum privatization, it is plausible that in order to achieve a cost-efficient provision, the responsibility to maintain and operate the museum may be assigned to a private party, while due to quality concerns the care for the designated collections and the restoration of old paintings may remain in public responsibility.[5]

---

[4] As an illustration, the US Department of Transportation had to pay $30 million more for the Interstate 39/USH 51 (Wausau beltline) project due to "a decision to upgrade the design speed of an interchange to 60 miles per hour, which resulted in five bridges being added to the project and several other bridges being lengthened" (Department of Transportation, 2003, p. 4). Bolten et al. (2008) analyze the reasons for procurement cost growth of the US Department of Defense. One striking example is "the Global Broadcast System, which had a more than 400 percent increase in quantity" (p. 42). See also Kaeser (2008) for related examples from the US Navy.

[5] Examples for cost-reducing investments that may be undertaken by the government directly abound in the context of the recent debate on public sector accountability, where central as well as local governments face the challenge to develop performance auditing systems (Sevilla, 2005). In order to meet the growing expectations for transparency, the public sector will have to invest in human capital and new technology and to re-engineer processes so that they become more cost efficient (Economist Intelligence Unit, 2005).

Third, in addition to public and private ownership, we consider two kinds of public-private partnerships where the parties are in more symmetric positions. In particular, either both parties can veto the implementation of innovations (i.e., there is joint ownership), or they have no veto power; i.e., the government has the right to implement quality innovations and the manager has the right to implement cost innovations.[6] Indeed, according to the European Investment Bank (2004), a public-private partnership is a generic term for relationships formed between the private sector and public bodies which includes a wide variety of working arrangements from formal joint venture companies to loose and informal partnerships.[7]

As we combine four different ownership structures with four possible task assignments, there are altogether 16 governance structures which we analyze. It will turn out that only five governance structures can actually be optimal.

Under private ownership, the manager should always be in charge of the investment in cost innovation, while it depends on the parties' relative bargaining powers who will be responsible for the quality investment. Similarly, under public ownership the government should be in charge of the investment in quality innovation, while the responsibility for the cost investment depends on the bargaining powers. Finally, if the parties agree on a partnership, then no one will have veto power and they assign the cost investment to the manager and the quality investment to the government.

---

[6] Shared authority and joint ownership have recently also been studied by Francesconi and Muthoo (2006) in the framework of Besley and Ghatak (2001), where a nongovernmental organization directly benefits from the provision of a public good. See also Bös and De Fraja (2002), Hart (2003), Bentz, Grout, and Halonen (2005), Bennett and Iossa (2006a,b), Martimort and Pouyet (2008), and Chen and Chiu (2010) who discuss other aspects of public-private partnerships from an incomplete contracts perspective.

[7] Note that the OECD (2008, p. 21) defines a public-private partnership "as an agreement between the government and one or more private partners [...] according to which the private partners deliver the service in such a manner that the service delivery objectives of the government are aligned with the profit objectives of the private partners." A partnership in which the parties agree on no veto power, so that both of them are free to pursue their main objectives, seems to be also in the spirit of this definition.

Different allocations of ownership rights imply markedly different patterns of investments. In particular, under private ownership the investment in cost reduction is at its first-best level, while there is underinvestment in the development of quality improvements. Hart, Shleifer, and Vishny (1997) argue that private ownership leads to overinvestment in cost reduction, because the manager disregards the side effect of the cost innovation (as she has the right to implement the innovation without having to compensate the government for the reduced quality). Yet, the overinvestment result crucially relies on their implicit assumption that the ex ante specified quantity of the basic good is the ex post efficient one. In general, the manager's investment in cost reduction is an increasing function of the quantity specified in the initial contract. If the ex ante specified quantity is small, then the investment yields only a small return in the absence of renegotiation. When the parties renegotiate, the manager will get only a fraction of the additional total return (cost savings net of benefit reduction) generated by her investment. Hence, if the parties initially specify a sufficiently small quantity, there is underinvestment, while a suitably chosen intermediate quantity leads to the first-best investment level. In contrast, the quality investment is independent of the ex ante specified quantity, because under private ownership the manager would not implement the quality innovation in the absence of renegotiation. This means that the quality investment is carried out only because successful renegotiation of the implementation decision is anticipated (and as a consequence, the incentives to invest in quality depend on the parties' bargaining powers in the renegotiations).

Similarly, under public ownership first-best investments in quality improvement are attainable by specifying the appropriate quantity of the basic good in the initial contract, while there is always underinvestment in cost reduction.

In a partnership where no party has veto power, both kinds of innovations are implemented even in the absence of renegotiations, because the manager chooses to implement the cost innovation and the government implements the quality innovation. Hence, renegotiation will occur only with regard to the quantity. The manager's incentives to invest in cost reduction are the same as under private ownership, while the government's incentives to invest in quality are the same as under public ownership. This means that now both investments depend on the ex ante specified quantity. However, in general the quantity that induces first-best cost investments will be different from the one that induces first-best quality investments. In other words, there are two goals that the parties must try to attain with only one instrument. It will turn out that the parties then agree on a quantity which induces overinvestment with regard to one task and underinvestment with regard to the other task.

Which governance structure is the optimal one depends on the importance of the cost innovation, its adverse effect on quality, the importance of the quality innovation, its cost-increasing side effect, and the parties' bargaining powers. Roughly speaking, if one party has a sufficiently large bargaining power, then the extent of the underinvestment in one task (which is the only disadvantage of ownership by a single party) becomes arbitrarily small, so that a partnership cannot be optimal. In contrast, if the parties' bargaining powers are almost equal, then the underinvestment problem under single ownership will turn out to be most severe, which makes ownership by a single party less attractive. Whether private or public ownership will be preferred depends on the relative strengths of the side effects caused by the innovations. If the side effect of the cost (quality) innovation becomes very large, so that inducing cost (quality) investment is relatively unimportant, then public (private) ownership is optimal (because then the first-best investment in the important innovation is induced). In contrast, if the side effects of both innovations almost disappear, then a partnership with no veto power must be optimal, because overinvestment (which is the partnership's drawback compared to single ownership) is no longer a problem.

This chapter brings together different strands of literature. First, there is by now a huge literature on the pros and cons of privatization. For surveys, see e.g. Vickers and Yarrow (1988), Shleifer (1998), and Martimort (2006). Second, our study contributes to the growing literature on the property rights approach to the theory of the firm based on incomplete contracting as pioneered by Grossman and Hart (1986) and Hart and Moore (1990); see Hart (1995) for a comprehensive survey.[8] While several authors have investigated the issue of privatization from an incomplete contracts perspective, many of these papers rely on informational asymmetries (e.g., Shapiro and Willig, 1990, Laffont and Tirole, 1991, and Schmidt, 1996a,b). In contrast, following Hart, Shleifer, and Vishny (1997), we assume throughout that there is symmetric information between the government and the manager. Third, to the best of our knowledge, the present study is the first one that analyzes an incomplete contracting model of privatization when the investments are "contractible control actions" in the sense of Aghion, Dewatripont, and Rey (2002, 2004). In standard models of the property rights approach, only ownership rights (i.e., the control over ex post decisions) can be allocated ex ante, while in addition we consider how the investment tasks should be assigned to the parties.[9]

The remainder of the chapter is organized as follows. In the following section, the model is introduced. In Section 2.3, we analyze the investment incentives for all assignments of the investment tasks and for all ownership structures, taking into account that quantity contracts are feasible. In Section 2.4, we characterize circumstances under which different governance structures are optimal. Concluding remarks follow in Section 2.5. Most proofs have been relegated to the appendix.

---

[8] For discussions of the foundations of incomplete contracting, see Hart and Moore (1999), Che and Hausch (1999), and Tirole (1999). See also Roider (2004), who studies the interaction of organizational form and quantity contracts in this framework.

[9] Aghion, Dewatripont, and Rey (2002) argue that in traditional moral hazard models, actions are pre-assigned. In contrast, in their "partial contracting" approach they consider contractible control actions which have the property that while their level is noncontractible, it is possible to contractually specify who is in control of such an action. Note that their approach is closely related to the literature on multi-task principal-agent analyses and job design in the tradition of Holmström and Milgrom (1991). See also Halonen-Akatwijuka (2010), who studies how organizational design and technology choice interact with the allocation of ownership.

2.2 The model

Consider the following model of the public or private provision of a good (or service). At date 0, the government (G) and a manager (M) write a contract that specifies a quantity $q \in [0,1]$ of a basic good (whose characteristics can be described ex ante) and a payment P_0 from the government to the manager. When the manager provides the basic good, she incurs costs qC_0, while the government's benefit is given by qB_0, where $B_0 > C_0$. The parties also agree on an ownership structure and on an investment task assignment.

Specifically, the ownership structure $o \in \{M, G, J, N\}$ determines who is in control of the essential assets needed to provide the good. Under private ownership ($o = M$), the manager has the right to modify the assets in order to implement innovations that may improve quality or reduce her provision costs (and thus may influence the ex ante non-contractible characteristics of the actually provided good). Under public ownership ($o = G$), the government controls the essential assets. Moreover, we consider two kinds of partnerships. Under $o = J$, both parties have veto power, so that no one can implement any innovations without the partner's consent, while under $o = N$ each party has the right to modify the assets to implement innovations.

The task assignment $A \in \{M, G, MG, GM\}$ determines who is in charge of the two types of non-contractible investments that can be made at date 1. The investments are denoted by e and i and they are measured by their costs. The investment $e \in [0, \bar{e})$ aims at developing an innovation to reduce the costs of providing the good. If implemented, such an innovation reduces the manager's costs per unit by $c(e)$, but at the same time it also lowers the quality and thus reduces the government's benefit per unit by $b(e)$. The investment $i \in [0, \bar{i})$ results in an innovation that can improve the good's quality, so that the government's benefit per unit is increased by $\beta(i)$, but at the same time the manager's costs per unit are increased by $\gamma(i)$. The assignment $A = M$ (resp. $A = G$) means that the manager (resp. the government) is in charge of both investments. The assignment $A = MG$ (resp. $A = GM$) means that the manager (resp. the government) is in charge of investment task e and the government (resp. the manager) is responsible for investment task i.[10] Note that the party in charge of an investment task has to bear the associated investment costs.

Finally, at date 2 the parties may renegotiate the quantity of the good to be provided, the decisions whether or not to implement the innovations, and the payment. Following the standard incomplete contracting approach, the negotiations are modelled using the Nash bargaining solution. The time structure of the model is illustrated in Figure 2.1.

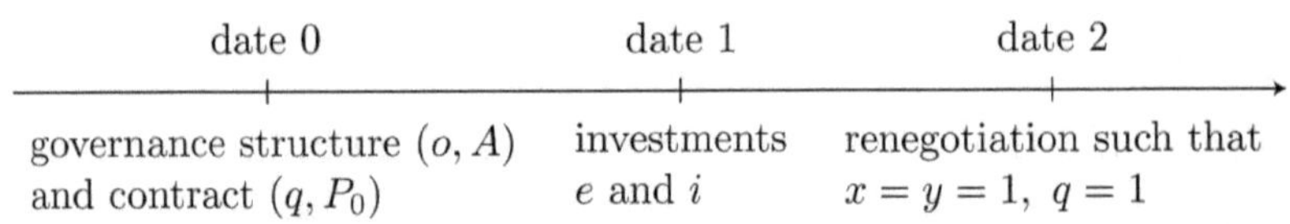

Figure 2.1. The sequence of events.

The manager's per unit costs of providing the good are given by

$$C(x, y, e, i) = C_0 - xc(e) + y\gamma(i),$$

where $x \in \{0, 1\}$ (resp. $y \in \{0, 1\}$) denotes the decision whether or not the cost innovation (resp. the quality innovation) is implemented. Similarly, the government's per unit benefit from provision of the good is given by

$$B(x, y, e, i) = B_0 + y\beta(i) - xb(e).$$

Following Hart, Shleifer, and Vishny (1997), we assume throughout that it is ex post efficient to implement both kinds of innovations. Formally, we make the following assumption for all investment levels $e > 0$ and $i > 0$.

Assumption 2.1 $c(e) > b(e)$ and $\beta(i) > \gamma(i)$.

[10] Following Aghion and Tirole's (1994) work on the management of innovation, we assume that an innovation once made becomes known to both parties. Hence, a party that has the right to implement an innovation can do so regardless of who developed it.

For simplicity, let all functions be twice differentiable and let the following technical assumptions be satisfied.

Assumption 2.2 $c(0) = 0$, $\lim_{e\to 0} c'(e) = \infty$, $c'(\bar{e}) = 0$, $c''(e) < 0$, $b(0) = 0$, $0 < b'(e) < c'(e)$, $b''(e) \geq c''(e)$.

Assumption 2.3 $\beta(0) = 0$, $\lim_{i\to 0} \beta'(i) = \infty$, $\beta'(\bar{i}) = 0$, $\beta''(i) < 0$, $\gamma(0) = 0$, $0 < \gamma'(i) < \beta'(i)$, $\gamma''(i) \geq \beta''(i)$.

The first-best benchmark. Assume for a moment that every decision were contractible. Then the parties would always implement both innovations ($x^{FB} = y^{FB} = 1$). They would agree on the efficient quantity $q^{FB} = 1$ and they would choose the investment levels e^{FB} and i^{FB} that are given by

$$c'(e^{FB}) - b'(e^{FB}) = 1,$$
$$\beta'(i^{FB}) - \gamma'(i^{FB}) = 1.$$

In the remainder of the chapter, we return to the second-best world in which the class of feasible contracts is restricted as described above.

Ex post bargaining. As the parties are symmetrically informed, in accordance with the Coase Theorem they will always agree on the ex post efficient quantity and implementation decisions. Assuming that the negotiations at date 2 lead to the Nash bargaining solution, each party gets its default payoff (i.e., what it would get in the absence of renegotiation) plus a fraction of the renegotiation surplus (i.e., the additional surplus generated by the ex post efficient decisions). In the absence of renegotiation, quantity q is provided and the characteristics of the good depend on the ownership structure as the owner can decide which innovations are implemented. Specifically, let x^o and y^o denote the implementation decisions in the absence of renegotiation. Hence, the manager's date-2 payoff is

$$U_M^o(e, i) = P_0 - qC(x^o, y^o, e, i) + \alpha\Delta,$$

and the government's date-2 payoff is

$$U_G^o(e,i) = qB(x^o, y^o, e, i) - P_0 + (1-\alpha)\Delta,$$

where $\Delta = [B(1,1,e,i) - C(1,1,e,i)] - q\,[B(x^o, y^o, e, i) - C(x^o, y^o, e, i)]$ is the renegotiation surplus and $\alpha \in (0,1)$ denotes the manager's bargaining power.

Consider $o = M$. In the absence of renegotiation, the manager will implement the cost innovation ($x^M = 1$), which improves her default payoff $P_0 - q[C_0 - x^M c(e) + y^M \gamma(i)]$, while she will not implement the quality innovation ($y^M = 0$), because she would suffer from the cost increase without profiting from the improved quality. Analogously, if $o = G$, then in the case of disagreement the government would implement the quality innovation only ($x^G = 0$, $y^G = 1$). Next, consider $o = J$, so that each party has veto power. In this case, the manager would veto the implementation of the quality innovation, while the government would not approve the implementation of the cost innovation ($x^J = y^J = 0$). Finally, under $o = N$, where each party is free to implement any innovation, the manager would implement the cost innovation and the government would implement the quality innovation ($x^N = y^N = 1$).

Given a governance structure (i.e., an ownership structure o and a task assignment A), we can now characterize the equilibrium investment levels e_A^o and i_A^o, which may depend on the contractually specified quantity q of the basic good.

Since the parties are symmetrically informed, at date 0 they agree on a governance structure (o, A) and a quantity q which maximizes the total surplus

$$S_A^o = B_0 + \beta(i_A^o) - b(e_A^o) - [C_0 - c(e_A^o) + \gamma(i_A^o)] - i_A^o - e_A^o,$$

where successful renegotiation is anticipated. By choosing a suitable lump sum payment P_0 the parties can arbitrarily divide the total surplus.

2.3 Quantity contracts and investments

2.3.1 Only the manager has investment tasks

Suppose first that it is exogenously given that the manager is responsible for both investment tasks, $A = M$. Then the date-1 investment levels under ownership structure o are characterized by

$$(e^o_M, i^o_M) = \arg\max_{(e,i)} U^o_M(e,i) - e - i.$$

Consider first the case of privatization ($o = M$), where $x^M = 1$ and $y^M = 0$. In this case, the manager's date-2 payoff reads

$$U^M_M(e,i) = P_0 - qC_0 + qc(e) + \alpha\left[\beta(i) - \gamma(i) + (1-q)(B_0 - C_0 + c(e) - b(e))\right].$$

Hence, at date 1 the manager chooses e^M_M and i^M_M to maximize $U^M_M(e,i) - e - i$, so that the investment levels can be characterized by the first-order conditions

$$\begin{aligned} qc'(e^M_M) + \alpha(1-q)[c'(e^M_M) - b'(e^M_M)] &= 1, \\ \alpha\left[\beta'(i^M_M) - \gamma'(i^M_M)\right] &= 1. \end{aligned}$$

Note that the quality investment i^M_M is always below its first-best level i^{FB}, because the manager can obtain a fraction α of the marginal return of this investment only through renegotiations. In contrast, observe that the manger's investment e^M_M in the development of a cost innovation is a function of the contractually specified quantity q.[11] In particular, when q is increased, then the manager gets a larger fraction of the marginal return generated by her investment in cost innovation, $q[(1-\alpha)c'(e^M_M)+\alpha b'(e^M_M)]+\alpha[c'(e^M_M)-b'(e^M_M)]$. For this reason, the manager has increased incentives to invest when q becomes larger. Observe that if q were zero, then there would be underinvestment compared to the first-best. In this case, the investment would generate no returns in the

[11] To simplify the notation, we suppress the dependence of the investments on q whenever appropriate.

absence of renegotiation, and the manager will get only the fraction α of the returns when the quantity is renegotiated to its efficient level. In contrast, if the parties agreed on the efficient quantity $q = 1$ at date 0 already, then there would be overinvestment. In this case, the manager would ignore the negative side effect that the cost innovation has on the benefit of the government. It follows that there is an intermediate quantity $\bar{q}$ such that the manager will invest e^{FB}.

Lemma 2.1 *(i) The investment level $e_M^M(q)$ is increasing in q.*

(ii) There exists a quantity $\bar{q} \in (0,1)$ such that $e_M^M(\bar{q}) = e^{FB}$, which is given by

$$\bar{q} = \frac{1-\alpha}{c'(e^{FB}) - \alpha}.$$

Proof. See the appendix. ■

It is straightforward to see that the investment level $e_M^M(q)$ is increasing in α for any given q. In particular, if the manager's bargaining power α is relatively large, then the investment is only slightly below the first-best level even for $q = 0$. Hence, specifying a small quantity q ex ante is sufficient to generate the additional investment incentives such that the manager invests e^{FB}. Therefore, the larger is α, the smaller will be the optimal date-0 quantity $\bar{q}$.

Moreover, it is intuitively clear that if the marginal side effect of the cost innovation becomes larger, then the first-best investment level e^{FB} decreases. However, the manager does not take into account the full change of the marginal side effect and hence does not reduce her investment e_M^M sufficiently when the quantity level is not adjusted. For this reason, the optimal quantity must go down when $b'(e)$ becomes larger.

Remark 2.1 *(i) The quantity $\bar{q}$ is decreasing in the manager's bargaining power α.*

(ii) The quantity $\bar{q}$ goes down if the marginal side effect of the cost innovation, $b'(e)$, increases.

Proof. See the appendix. ■

Consider next public ownership, $o = G$. In this case the default decisions are $x^G = 0$ and $y^G = 1$, so that the manager's date-2 payoff is

$$U_M^G(e,i) = P_0 - qC_0 - q\gamma(i) + \alpha\left[c(e) - b(e) + (1-q)(B_0 - C_0 + \beta(i) - \gamma(i))\right].$$

Hence, at date 1 the manager chooses the investment levels e_M^G and i_M^G that maximize $U_M^G(e,i) - e - i$. Both kinds of investments are always below their first-best levels. In particular, the cost investment is implicitly defined by the first-order condition

$$\alpha\left[c'(e_M^G) - b'(e_M^G)\right] = 1.$$

The quality investment i_M^G now depends on the contractually specified quantity. Note that if the parties agreed on the efficient quantity $q = 1$ at date 0, then the manager would not invest in quality at all, because she would have to suffer from the negative side effect of the quality innovation (i.e., she would have to incur larger costs) without profiting from the enhanced benefit of the government. In contrast, if q is zero, then the investment yields no returns without renegotiation, and the manager gets the fraction α of the returns when the quantity is renegotiated. As there is always underinvestment and the total surplus $B(1,1,e,i) - C(1,1,e,i) - e - i$ is concave in i, the parties will ex ante specify the quantity $q = 0$, because $i_M^G(0)$ is the largest level of quality investment that can be induced under $o = G$.[12]

Lemma 2.2 *Under G-ownership, $i_M^G(q) < i_M^M$ for all $q > 0$ and $i_M^G(0) = i_M^M$.*

Proof. See the appendix. ■

Next, consider $o = J$, where $x^J = y^J = 0$. The manager's date-2 payoff then is

$$U_M^J(e,i) = P_0 - qC_0 + \alpha\left[\beta(i) - \gamma(i) + c(e) - b(e) + (1-q)(B_0 - C_0)\right].$$

[12] Notice that this result is in the spirit of Maskin and Moore (1999) and Che and Hausch (1999), who show that it may be optimal to write no contract at all if a party's investment can improve the bargaining position of the other party only.

Under this ownership regime, the manager chooses

$$\left(e_M^J, i_M^J\right) = \arg\max_{(e,i)} U_M^J(e,i) - e - i.$$

Inspection of the first-order conditions immediately reveals that now both investment levels are independent of the quantity q. In the absence of renegotiation, the manager does not get any returns from her investments. The manager thus gets only a fraction α of the returns through renegotiation. In particular, $e_M^J = e_M^G$ and $i_M^J = i_M^M = i_M^G(0)$. Hence, $o = J$ leads to the same investment levels as $o = G$ when under G-ownership the quantity is optimally chosen.

Finally, consider $o = N$ so that renegotiations occur only with regard to the quantity (as $x^N = y^N = 1$). Then the manager's date-2 payoff reads

$$U_M^N(e,i) = P_0 - qC_0 + qc(e) - q\gamma(i) + \alpha(1-q)\left[B_0 - C_0 + \beta(i) - \gamma(i) + c(e) - b(e)\right].$$

At date 1, the manager chooses

$$\left(e_M^N, i_M^N\right) = \arg\max_{(e,i)} U_M^N(e,i) - e - i.$$

Since now both innovations are implemented without renegotiation, both investment levels depend on the specified quantity q. Thus, $e_M^N(q) = e_M^M(q)$ and $i_M^N(q) = i_M^G(q)$. Recall that $e_M^M(q)$ is increasing in q, whereas $i_M^G(q)$ is at its largest attainable level for $q = 0$. But this means that creating efficient investment incentives by choosing the optimal quantity for one investment task will have adverse effects on the other task.

Proposition 2.1 *If quantity contracts are taken into account and the manager is in charge of both investment tasks, then $o = M$ is always optimal.*

Proof. See the appendix. ■

Note that this result is in stark contrast to Hart, Shleifer, and Vishny (1997). In their model, the parties do not explicitly specify a quantity in the initial contract. They implicitly assume that the date-0 contract is based on the ex post efficient quantity $q^{FB} = 1$, so that under M-ownership there is always overinvestment in cost innovation (while there is underinvestment in quality innovation). The overinvestment effect can be so strong that G-ownership (which leads to underinvestment in both tasks) may be superior even when the manager is in charge of both investment tasks. In contrast, we argue that if it is possible to write a contract on the provision of a basic good as assumed by Hart, Shleifer, and Vishny (1997), then it is also reasonable to specify in this contract the quantity that is optimal from an ex ante perspective. By choosing a suitably small quantity (which will be renegotiated ex post), the parties can ensure that the manager has just the right incentives to invest in cost reduction.[13] As a consequence, G-ownership can be optimal only if the government has to make an investment decision itself, as we will see in the next subsections.

2.3.2 Only the government has investment tasks

Suppose now that the government is responsible for both investment tasks, $A = G$. Then, the investment levels under ownership structure o are characterized by

$$(e_G^o, i_G^o) = \arg\max_{(e,i)} U_G^o(e,i) - e - i.$$

Consider first public ownership ($o = G$), so that $x^G = 0$ and $y^G = 1$. In this case, at date 1 the government chooses the investments e_G^G and i_G^G that maximize $U_G^G(e,i) - e - i$. The investment levels are implicitly defined by

$$(1-\alpha)\left[c'(e_G^G) - b'(e_G^G)\right] = 1,$$

[13]Note that Hart, Shleifer, and Vishny's (1997) model also differs from the present one in that they assume that under public ownership a fraction of the gains from innovations can be realized by hiring another manager from a competitive market, while we assume that the parties are locked in; i.e., their relationship has undergone Williamson's (1985) "fundamental transformation." However, it is straightforward to show that also in their original model private ownership is always optimal when the suitable quantity of the basic good is contractually specified.

$$q\beta'(i_G^G) + (1-\alpha)(1-q)[\beta'(i_G^G) - \gamma'(i_G^G)] = 1.$$

Note that this case is similar to M-ownership when the manager is in charge of both tasks. Yet, in contrast to that case, now there is always underinvestment regarding e, while it is the investment i in quality innovations that is increasing in q and for which the first-best level can be implemented by specifying a suitable quantity ex ante.

Lemma 2.3 *(i) The investment level $i_G^G(q)$ is increasing in q.*

(ii) There exists a quantity $\tilde{q} \in (0,1)$ such that $i_G^G(\tilde{q}) = i^{FB}$. Specifically,

$$\tilde{q} = \frac{\alpha}{\beta'(i^{FB}) + \alpha - 1}.$$

The comparative statics properties of the quantity $\tilde{q}$ are analogous to the properties of $\bar{q}$. In particular, when the government's bargaining power or the marginal side effect of the quality innovation become small, then the quantity $\tilde{q}$ must increase.

Remark 2.2 *(i) The quantity $\tilde{q}$ is increasing in the manager's bargaining power α.*

(ii) The quantity $\tilde{q}$ goes down if the marginal side effect of the quality innovation, $\gamma'(i)$, increases.

Consider next the case of privatization, $o = M$. At date 1, the government chooses the investment levels $\left(e_G^M, i_G^M\right) = \arg\max_{(e,i)} U_G^M(e,i) - e - i$. There is always underinvestment. The quality investment is given by

$$(1-\alpha)\left[\beta'(i_G^M) - \gamma'(i_G^M)\right] = 1,$$

while the cost investment e_G^M depends on the contractually specified quantity.

Lemma 2.4 *Under M-ownership, $e_G^M(q) < e_G^G$ for all $q > 0$. Moreover, $e_G^M(0) = e_G^G$.*

Hence, given private ownership, the parties will ex ante specify the quantity $q = 0$.

Next, consider $o = J$, so that the government chooses $\left(e_G^J, i_G^J\right) = \arg\max_{(e,i)} U_G^J(e,i) - e - i$. As is clear from the first-order conditions, the investment levels satisfy $e_G^J = e_G^G = e_G^M(0)$ and $i_G^J = i_G^M$. Hence, $o = J$ leads to the same investments as $o = M$ when under M-ownership the quantity zero is specified.

Finally, consider $o = N$, where the government chooses the investments $\left(e_G^N, i_G^N\right) = \arg\max_{(e,i)} U_G^N(e,i) - e - i$. Thus, $e_G^N(q) = e_G^M(q)$ and $i_G^N(q) = i_G^G(q)$. In analogy to Proposition 2.1, we can now state the following result.

Proposition 2.2 *If quantity contracts are taken into account and the government is in charge of both investment tasks, then $o = G$ is always optimal.*

2.3.3 Both parties have investment tasks

Suppose first that the government is responsible for the investment in cost reduction and the manager is in charge of the investment in quality improvement ($A = GM$). In this case, the investment levels under ownership structure o are characterized by $e_{GM}^o = \arg\max_e U_G^o(e,i) - e$ and $i_{GM}^o = \arg\max_i U_M^o(e,i) - i$. As the payoffs are additively separable, the government's investment in cost innovation does not depend on the level of the investment in quality. This means that different task assignments concerning the investment in quality do not affect the government's choice of the investment in cost reductions. Hence, for any given quantity, $e_{GM}^o = e_G^o$ must hold. Similar arguments apply to the manager's investment in quality improvement, so that $i_{GM}^o = i_M^o$ must hold for any given level of quantity q.

Proposition 2.3 *The task assignment $A = GM$ is never optimal.*

Proof. See the appendix. ■

The task assignment $A = GM$ is always inferior, because it means that a party can never improve its bargaining position by investing. In the absence of renegotiation, the government would never invest in cost reduction (which could only reduce its benefit), while the manager would never invest in quality (which could only increase her costs). The best the parties can do is either to agree on $o = J$ or to specify a quantity of zero, so that their disagreement payoffs are independent of the investments. The parties will then invest only because they get a fraction of the returns through renegotiation, so that there is always underinvestment. In contrast, as we have seen above, if one party is the single owner and responsible for both investments, then this party can improve its bargaining position by investing and it will even choose a first-best investment level for one task if the appropriate quantity is specified ex ante.

Suppose next that the manager is in charge of the cost investment and the government is in charge of the quality investment ($A = MG$). The investment levels under ownership structure o are then given by $e^o_{MG} = \arg\max_e U^o_M(e, i) - e$ and $i^o_{MG} = \arg\max_i U^o_G(e, i) - i$. Because of additive separability, it is immediately clear that $e^o_{MG} = e^o_M$ and $i^o_{MG} = i^o_G$ must hold for any given quantity q. If there is M-ownership, then $e^M_{MG}(q) = e^M_M(q)$ and $i^M_{MG} = i^M_G$. Since the latter investment does not depend on q, it is straightforward to see that it is optimal for the parties to specify $q = \bar{q}$, because then the investment in cost reduction is at its first-best level. Similarly, under G-ownership, it is optimal to set $q = \tilde{q}$.

Proposition 2.4 *If $A = MG$, then $o = J$ cannot be optimal.*

Proof. Since $e^M_M(\bar{q}) = e^{FB} > e^J_M$ and $i^J_G = i^M_G$, $o = M$ is better than $o = J$. ■

Finally, consider $o = N$, so that $q = \bar{q}$ induces first-best investment in cost reduction, while $q = \tilde{q}$ leads to first-best quality investment. Hence, in the special case $\bar{q} = \tilde{q}$, the first-best outcome can be attained. Now consider $q = \bar{q} < \tilde{q}$, so that $e = e^{FB}$ and $i < i^{FB}$. Increasing q slightly above $\bar{q}$ leads only to a second-order loss regarding e, but it implies a first-order gain with regard to i. Therefore, the optimal quantity $q = \hat{q}$ must lie strictly between $\bar{q}$ and $\tilde{q}$. A similar argument holds if $\bar{q} > \tilde{q}$.

Lemma 2.5 *Consider the case $A = MG$.*

(i) Suppose that $\bar{q} = \tilde{q}$. Then the parties agree on $o = N$ and they specify the quantity $\hat{q} = \bar{q} = \tilde{q}$, so that the first-best outcome is achieved.

(ii) Suppose that $\bar{q} \neq \tilde{q}$. If the parties choose the ownership structure $o = N$, then they specify the quantity $\hat{q}$, where $\min\{\bar{q}, \tilde{q}\} < \hat{q} < \max\{\bar{q}, \tilde{q}\}$.

Proof. See the appendix. ■

Lemma 2.5 implies that if $\bar{q} \neq \tilde{q}$, then one of the two investments is above and the other investment is below the first-best level when the parties agree on the optimal quantity $\hat{q}$. In particular, the following result holds.

Remark 2.3 *There is a critical level of the manager's bargaining power,*

$$\hat{\alpha} = \frac{\beta'(i^{FB}) - 1}{c'(e^{FB}) + \beta'(i^{FB}) - 2} \in (0, 1),$$

such that $\tilde{q} = \bar{q}$.

(i) If $\alpha < \hat{\alpha}$, then $\hat{q} \in (\tilde{q}, \bar{q})$, so that $e^N_{MG}(\hat{q}) < e^{FB}$ and $i^N_{MG}(\hat{q}) > i^{FB}$.

(ii) If $\alpha > \hat{\alpha}$, then $\hat{q} \in (\bar{q}, \tilde{q})$, so that $e^N_{MG}(\hat{q}) > e^{FB}$ and $i^N_{MG}(\hat{q}) < i^{FB}$.

Proof. See the appendix. ■

To conclude, under $o = N$ and $A = MG$, there is exactly one bargaining power for which the first-best outcome can be achieved. Otherwise, consider the case in which the manager's bargaining power α is small, so that the quantity $\tilde{q}$ that is required to induce first-best quality investments is smaller than the quantity $\bar{q}$ that is required to induce first-best cost investments. In this case, if the optimal quantity $\hat{q} \in (\tilde{q}, \bar{q})$ is chosen, there is underinvestment in cost innovation and overinvestment in quality innovation.

Figure 2.2 shows how the quantities $\bar{q}$ and $\tilde{q}$ behave as functions of the manager's bargaining power α. Note that $\hat{q}$ must always lie between these two curves, as is illustrated in the displayed example.[14] Notice that the critical bargaining power $\hat{\alpha}$ will go up if the marginal side effect of the quality innovation increases (which makes $\tilde{q}$ smaller according to Remark 2.2, while $\bar{q}$ remains unchanged). Similarly, an increase in the marginal side effect of the cost innovation decreases $\hat{\alpha}$.

[14] In all examples that we illustrate in the subsequent figures, we assume that $c(e) = 2e^{1/2} - e$ and $\beta(i) = 2i^{1/2} - i$, where $\bar{e} = \bar{i} = 1$. In Figure 2.2 and in Figure 2.3, we depict the case $b(e) = 0.4c(e)$ and $\gamma(i) = 0.5\beta(i)$, so that $\hat{\alpha} = 0.6$.

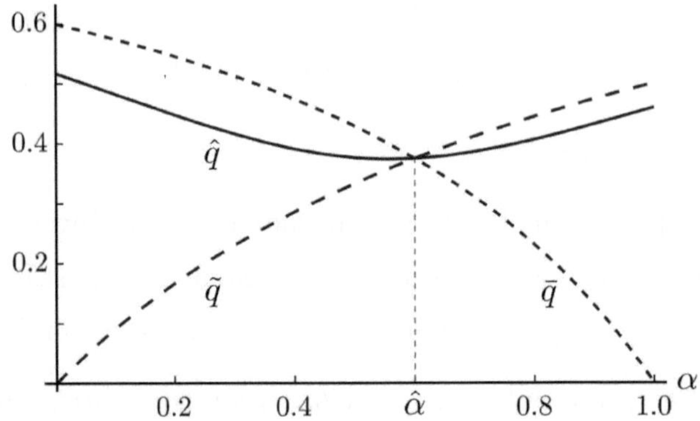

Figure 2.2. Optimal quantities.

To summarize the analysis so far, consider Table 2.1, which illustrates the optimal quantities for all potentially optimal governance structures. Note that a priori there are 16 governance structures resulting from all conceivable combinations of the four ownership structures and the four different task assignments. The preceding analysis implies that only five governance structures can potentially be optimal.

Specifically, $A = GM$ can never be optimal according to Proposition 2.3. Propositions 2.1 and 2.2 show that if both tasks are assigned to one party, then this party should be the owner. Proposition 2.4 then implies that $o = J$ can never be optimal. It also follows that $o = N$ can be optimal only if the government chooses the quality investment and the manager chooses the cost investment.

	$o = M$	$o = G$	$o = J$	$o = N$
$A = M$	$\bar{q}$			
$A = G$		$\tilde{q}$		
$A = GM$				
$A = MG$	$\bar{q}$	$\tilde{q}$		$\hat{q}$

Table 2.1. Five governance structures can be optimal.

The remaining five governance structures can turn out to be optimal. The investment levels associated with these governance structures are illustrated in Figure 2.3.

For instance, consider the investment in cost reduction, which is displayed in the left panel of Figure 2.3. Under $o = M$, the parties specify the quantity $\bar{q}$ at date 0, so that the investment is always at its first-best level, regardless of whether the manager or the government is in charge of the quality investment, $e^M_{MG}(\bar{q}) = e^M_M(\bar{q}) = e^{FB}$. Under $o = G$, if the manager (resp. the government) is responsible for the cost investment, then it is increasing (resp. decreasing) in the manager's bargaining power α. Moreover, note that under $o = N$ the manager has always stronger incentives to invest in cost reduction than she would have under $o = G$. In accordance with Remark 2.3, if the quantity $\hat{q}$ is specified, then she overinvests relative to the first-best level whenever her bargaining power α is larger than $\hat{\alpha}$.

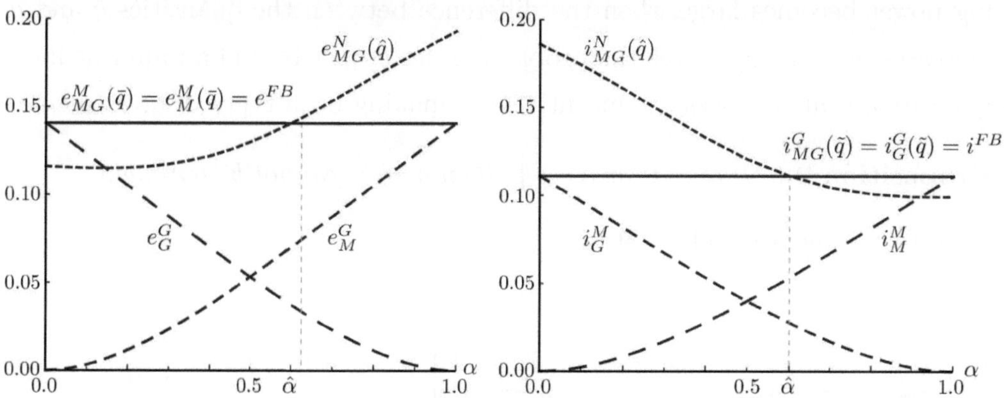

Figure 2.3. Investments in cost and quality innovations.

2.4 Optimal governance structures

In this section we characterize the specific circumstances favouring each of the possibly optimal governance structures. Under sole ownership by one party, the optimal investment task assignment depends on who has the larger bargaining power, as is stated in the following proposition.

Proposition 2.5 *(i) Consider $o = M$. If $\alpha > 1/2$, then both investments should be assigned to the manager ($A = M$). If $\alpha < 1/2$, then the manager should be responsible for the cost investment and the government for the quality investment ($A = MG$).*

(ii) Consider $o = G$. If $\alpha > 1/2$, then the manager should be responsible for the cost investment and the government for the quality investment ($A = MG$). If $\alpha < 1/2$, then both investments should be assigned to the government ($A = G$).

Proof. See the appendix. ■

Note that if both parties happen to have the same bargaining power, then $e^G_{MG} = e^G_G$ and $i^M_{MG} = i^M_M$, so that the parties are indifferent between the task allocations mentioned in Proposition 2.5.

A partnership with no veto power can be optimal only if the parties' bargaining strengths do not become too asymmetric. When one party's bargaining power becomes large, then the difference between the quantities $\bar{q}$ and $\tilde{q}$ increases, which aggravates the problem under $o = N$ to find an intermediate quantity $\hat{q}$ that balances the incentives for making both types of investments.

Proposition 2.6 *If $\alpha \to 0$ or $\alpha \to 1$, then $o = N$ cannot be optimal.*

Proof. See the appendix. ■

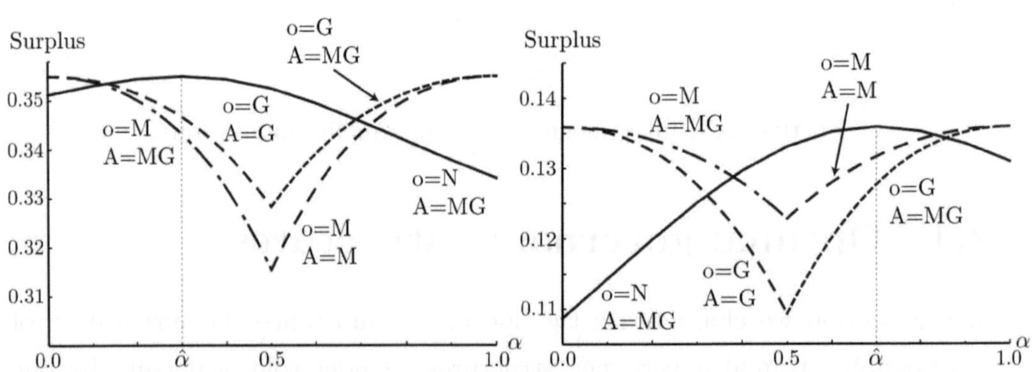

Figure 2.4. The total surplus.

Figure 2.4 illustrates the two preceding propositions. Consider the V-shaped curve which depicts the total surplus under $o = M$. Recall that under $o = M$, the investment e in cost innovation is always at its first-best level, regardless of the manager's bargaining power α. The investment i in quality innovation (and hence the surplus) is decreasing in α when this investment task is assigned to the government (i.e., if $\alpha < 1/2$) and it is increasing in α otherwise. Similarly, the other V-shaped curve shows the total surplus under G-ownership. Under $o = N$, the total surplus (depicted by the solid curve) attains its maximum at $\alpha = \hat{\alpha} \in (0, 1)$, where the first-best outcome is achieved. In contrast, sole ownership by one party is optimal for sufficiently small or sufficiently large values of the manager's bargaining power. The relative importance of cost and quality innovations determines whether $o = M$ or $o = G$ leads to a larger surplus.[15]

In particular, whether M-ownership or G-ownership can be optimal depends on the strength of the side effects of the cost and quality innovations. Specifically, $o = G$ cannot be optimal if the deterioration to quality from cost innovations vanishes, provided the manager's bargaining power is not too small. Recall that under $o = N$ it is always possible to induce first-best quality investments (just as under $o = G$) by specifying the quantity $\tilde{q}$, but in general this may lead to over- or underinvestment in cost innovation. Yet, overinvestment cannot occur when cost innovations have no negative side effects. Moreover, investment in cost innovation is larger under $o = N$ than under $o = G$ provided the manager's bargaining power is sufficiently large.

Similarly, $o = M$ cannot be optimal if the negative side effect of quality innovation disappears, provided that the manager's bargaining power is sufficiently small. In this case, $o = N$ is superior, because it allows to induce first-best cost investment just as $o = M$, but it leads to larger quality invest-

[15]In Figure 2.4, $B_0 = 2$, $C_0 = 1.1$, and $b(e) = 0.5c(e)$. In the left panel, $\gamma(i) = 0.3\beta(i)$ while in the right panel, $\gamma(i) = 0.7\beta(i)$. Note that when the side effect of the quality innovation becomes stronger, then $\hat{\alpha}$ increases (from 0.3 to 0.7) and public ownership becomes less attractive.

ment (where overinvestment is not a problem anymore). As a consequence, when the side effects of both kinds of innovations go to zero, then N-ownership must always be optimal.

Proposition 2.7 *(i) Consider* $\alpha > (1-\tilde{q})/(2-\tilde{q})$. *Suppose that* $b(e) \equiv \theta\breve{b}(e)$, *where* $\theta > 0$. *Then for* θ *sufficiently small,* $o = N$ *is better than* $o = G$.

(ii) Consider $\alpha < 1/(2-\bar{q})$. *Suppose that* $\gamma(i) \equiv \psi\breve{\gamma}(i)$, *where* $\psi > 0$. *Then for* ψ *sufficiently small,* $o = N$ *is better than* $o = M$.

(iii) Suppose that $b(e) \equiv \theta\breve{b}(e)$ *and* $\gamma(i) \equiv \psi\breve{\gamma}(i)$, *where* $\theta > 0$ *and* $\psi > 0$. *Then for* θ *and* ψ *sufficiently small,* $o = N$ *is better than both* $o = M$ *and* $o = G$.

Proof. See the appendix. ■

Finally, let us investigate what happens if the negative side effect of an innovation becomes as large as its desired effect. If the reduction of the government's benefit associated with a cost innovation approaches the extent of the cost reduction, then the first-best investment in cost innovation becomes negligibly small. Recall that under $o = G$ the investment in cost innovation is always below its first-best level, while the quality investment is at its first-best level if the parties specify the quantity $\tilde{q}$ in their date-0 contract. Hence, under $o = G$ the first-best outcome is approached when the side effect of the cost innovation tends to offset its desired effect. In contrast, under $o = M$ the investment in quality innovation is always below its first-best level. Moreover, $o = G$ is also better than $o = N$. Under $o = N$, the first-best investment in quality innovation could be achieved by specifying the quantity $\tilde{q} > 0$. But this would create incentives for the manager to invest in cost reduction, which is undesirable when the total return of the cost investment vanishes.

Similar arguments explain why $o = M$ is always optimal if the cost increase that is caused by a quality innovation becomes as large as the additional benefit of the government generated by the quality innovation.

Proposition 2.8 *(i) Suppose that* $b(e) \equiv \theta c(e) + (1-\theta)\breve{b}(e)$, *where* $\theta \in (0,1)$. *Then for* $\theta \to 1$, $o = G$ *is better than both* $o = M$ *and* $o = N$.

(ii) Suppose that $\gamma(i) \equiv \psi\beta(i) + (1-\psi)\breve{\gamma}(i)$, *where* $\psi \in (0,1)$. *Then for* $\psi \to 1$, $o = M$ *is better than both* $o = G$ *and* $o = N$.

Proof. See the appendix. ■

As an illustration, suppose that the side effects of the innovations are given by fractions of their desired effects, $b(e) = \theta c(e)$ and $\gamma(i) = \psi\beta(i)$.[16] Consider Figure 2.5, which shows (for given values of α) how the optimal governance structures depend on the strengths θ and ψ of the side effects caused by the cost and quality innovations, respectively.

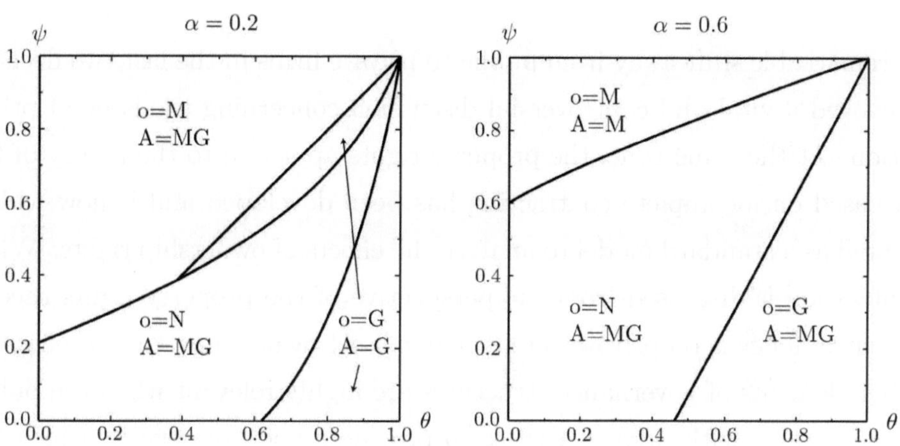

Figure 2.5. Optimal governance structures.

Observe that if θ goes to 1, so that the side effect of the cost innovation offsets its benefit, then $o = G$ (which leads to first-best quality investments) must become optimal. Similarly, for sufficiently large values of ψ, the ownership structure $o = M$ (which leads to first-best cost investments) must be optimal. In contrast, if both side effects become small, then the parties prefer $o = N$, which implies more balanced incentives for both types of investments. Specifically, due to symmetry, in the example displayed in the figure, $o = M$ is better than $o = G$ whenever $\psi > \theta$. As illustrated for the case $\alpha = 0.6$,

[16] Hence, $\breve{b}(e) = c(e)$, $\breve{\gamma}(i) = \beta(i)$ in Proposition 2.7 and $\breve{b}(e) = \breve{\gamma}(i) = 0$ in Proposition 2.8.

the parameter range for which $o = N$ is optimal can be so large that a small change of the side effects will never induce the parties to directly jump from public to private ownership (or vice versa). In contrast, when the parties' bargaining powers become more extreme (cf. the case $\alpha = 0.2$), there must be more parameter constellations for which ownership by a single party is better than $o = N$, so that a small change of θ or ψ can make a direct transition between public and private ownership optimal.

2.5 Concluding remarks

The remarkable shift away from public to private firms in the last two decades has evoked a vital and controversial discussion concerning the issue of privatization. At the same time, the property rights approach to the theory of the firm based on incomplete contracting has been developed and is now widely accepted as a standard model to analyze the effects of ownership rights. When privatization is discussed from the perspective of the property rights theory, the central focus is on private versus public asset ownership. Yet, empirically, further elements of governance structures are highly relevant when the public sector interacts with private entities to provide a good or service, which has motivated us to consider a richer set of contractual arrangements.

As a general lesson, our model implies that in order to avoid the overinvestment problem identified by Hart, Shleifer, and Vishny (1997), the scope of public projects may be extended during the implementation phase, so that the government may end up paying more than what was originally agreed upon. Thus, it seems to be an interesting question for empirical research to test to which extent the often observed cost overruns in public procurement can be attributed to a change in quantity. Further predictions from the model that might be interesting to test empirically include (a) partnerships between the public and the private sector should be observed if the bargaining powers are relatively balanced and if the side effects of cost and quality innovations are relatively unimportant, while (b) public (resp. private) ownership should be observed if the side effects of cost (resp. quality) innovations are strong. Since in the model the optimal quantity, the optimal assignment of investment tasks, and the optimal ownership structure depend on the parties' bargaining powers, in future research it would be very helpful to find a good empirical proxy for the distribution of the bargaining powers, which might be related to the degree of competition.

2.6 Appendix

Proof of Lemma 2.1

(i) By the implicit function theorem,

$$\frac{de_M^M}{dq} = -\frac{(1-\alpha)c'(e_M^M) + \alpha b'(e_M^M)}{qc''(e_M^M) + \alpha(1-q)[c''(e_M^M) - b''(e_M^M)]} > 0.$$

(ii) Inspection of the first-order conditions shows that $e_M^M < e^{FB}$ if $q = 0$. Moreover, if $q = 1$, then $e_M^M > e^{FB}$. As $e_M^M(q)$ is continuous and strictly increasing, an intermediate value argument implies that there exists a unique $\bar{q} \in (0,1)$ such that $e_M^M(\bar{q}) = e^{FB}$. The conjecture follows from the first-order conditions for e_M^M and e^{FB}. ■

Proof of Remark 2.1

(i) Part (i) follows from inspection of the first derivative

$$\frac{d\bar{q}}{d\alpha} = \frac{1 - c'(e^{FB})}{[c'(e^{FB}) - \alpha]^2} < 0,$$

where the inequality holds because $c'(e^{FB}) = 1 + b'(e^{FB}) > 1$.
(ii) Suppose that initially $b'(e) = b_0'(e)$, so that the first-best level of the cost innovation is characterized by $c'(e_0^{FB}) - b_0'(e_0^{FB}) = 1$. Consider now an increase of the marginal side effect, $b'(e) = b_1'(e) > b_0'(e)\ \forall e$. Now $c'(e_1^{FB}) - b_1'(e_1^{FB}) = 1$. By the definition of $\bar{q}$ in Lemma 2.1 (ii), we have to show that $c'(e_1^{FB}) > c'(e_0^{FB})$. The latter inequality follows from $e_1^{FB} < e_0^{FB}$, which is implied by the concavity of $c(e) - b(e)$. ■

Proof of Lemma 2.2

The first derivative of the manager's date-1 payoff $U_M^G(e,i) - e - i$ with respect to i is given by $-q\gamma'(i) + \alpha(1-q)[\beta'(i) - \gamma'(i)] - 1$. Hence, if $q = 0$, then $i_M^G(0) = i_M^M$, which is implicitly defined by $\alpha\left[\beta'(i_M^M) - \gamma'(i_M^M)\right] - 1 = 0$. Now consider $q > 0$. Note that the derivative of the manager's payoff can be rewritten as $-\alpha q\beta'(i) - (1-\alpha)q\gamma'(i) + \alpha[\beta'(i) - \gamma'(i)] - 1$. Since $\beta''(i) - \gamma''(i) \leq 0$ and $-\alpha q\beta'(i) - (1-\alpha)q\gamma'(i) < 0$, the manager's payoff is strictly decreasing for all $i \geq i_M^M$, so that she will invest strictly less than i_M^M. ■

Proof of Proposition 2.1

At date 1 the parties agree on the ownership structure that maximizes the total surplus S^o_M, which is concave in e and in i. The ownership structure $o = M$ is better than $o = G$ since $e^G_M < e^M_M(\bar{q}) = e^{FB}$ and $i^G_M(0) = i^M_M$. Similarly, $o = M$ is better than $o = J$ since $e^J_M < e^M_M(\bar{q}) = e^{FB}$ and $i^J_M = i^M_M$. Finally, to see that $o = M$ is better than $o = N$, recall that $i^N_M(q) < i^M_M$ for $q > 0$ and $i^N_M(0) = i^M_M$. In other words, under N-ownership the quality investment is smaller than under M-ownership except for $q = 0$. But for $q = 0$, the cost investment given $o = N$ is smaller than the cost investment when the manager is the owner, $e^N_M(0) < e^M_M(\bar{q}) = e^{FB}$. ■

Proof of Proposition 2.3

For any ownership structure the task assignment $A = GM$ is dominated by allocating both tasks to the manager and letting her be the owner ($A = M$, $o = M$). In the latter case, the investment levels are $e^M_M(\bar{q}) = e^{FB}$ and i^M_M.

Now consider $A = GM$. If $o = M$, the investment levels are $e^M_G(q) < e^{FB}$ and i^M_M. Similarly, if $o = G$, the investment levels are $e^G_G < e^{FB}$ and $i^G_M(q) \leq i^M_M$. If $o = J$, the investment levels are $e^J_G < e^{FB}$ and $i^J_M = i^M_M$. Finally, if $o = N$, the investments are $e^N_G(q) < e^{FB}$ and $i^N_M(q) \leq i^M_M$. ■

Proof of Lemma 2.5

(i) If $\hat{q} = \bar{q} = \tilde{q}$, then $e^N_{MG}(\hat{q}) = e^M_M(\bar{q}) = e^{FB}$ and $i^N_{MG}(\hat{q}) = i^G_G(\tilde{q}) = i^{FB}$.

(ii) The parties choose q in order to maximize the total surplus. Note that

$$\frac{dS^N_{MG}}{dq} = \left[\beta'(i^G_G(q)) - \gamma'(i^G_G(q)) - 1\right]\frac{di^G_G}{dq} + \left[c'(e^M_M(q)) - b'(e^M_M(q)) - 1\right]\frac{de^M_M}{dq}.$$

Without loss of generality, let $\bar{q} > \tilde{q}$. If $\hat{q} \geq \bar{q}$, then $e \geq e^{FB}$ and $i > i^{FB}$, so that $dS^N_{MG}/dq < 0$; i.e., decreasing $\hat{q}$ increases the total surplus. If $\hat{q} \leq \tilde{q}$, then $e < e^{FB}$ and $i \leq i^{FB}$, so that $dS^N_{MG}/dq > 0$; i.e., increasing $\hat{q}$ increases the total surplus. ■

Proof of Remark 2.3

From the definition of $\bar{q}$ and from Remark 2.1, we know that $\bar{q}$ is continuous, bounded from above, strictly decreasing in α, and it is equal to zero at $\alpha = 1$.

Analogously, $\tilde{q}$ is equal to zero at $\alpha = 0$ and it is continuous, bounded from above, and strictly increasing. Hence, there exists a unique $\hat{\alpha} \in (0,1)$ such that $\bar{q} = \tilde{q}$. The expression for $\hat{\alpha}$ is obtained from solving this equality. The remainder of the Remark follows immediately from Lemma 2.5. ■

Proof of Proposition 2.5

(i) According to Table 2.1, under M-ownership we have to consider the task assignments $A = M$ and $A = MG$ only. The investment in cost reduction is always at its first-best level, $e_M^M(\bar{q}) = e_{MG}^M(\bar{q}) = e^{FB}$. If $\alpha > 1/2$, the first-order conditions for the quality investments immediately show that $i_{MG}^M < i_M^M < i^{FB}$. Hence, $A = M$ is optimal. If $\alpha < 1/2$, then $i_M^M < i_{MG}^M < i^{FB}$, so that $A = MG$ is optimal. (ii) The proof is analogous to part (i). ■

Proof of Proposition 2.6

Consider $o = M$, so that the parties agree on the quantity $\bar{q}$ which implies $e_M^M(\bar{q}) = e^{FB}$. If $\alpha > \frac{1}{2}$, then according to Proposition 2.5 the parties assign both investment tasks to the manager, so that the quality investment is characterized by $\alpha\left[\beta'(i_M^M) - \gamma'(i_M^M)\right] = 1$. Note that $i_M^M \to i^{FB}$ when $\alpha \to 1$. If $\alpha < \frac{1}{2}$, then they assign the cost investment to the manager and the quality investment to the government, so that the latter investment is implicitly given by $(1-\alpha)\left[\beta'(i_G^M) - \gamma'(i_G^M)\right] = 1$. Hence, $i_G^M \to i^{FB}$ when $\alpha \to 0$.

Similarly, if $o = G$, then $i_G^G(\tilde{q}) = i^{FB}$. If $\alpha > \frac{1}{2}$, then the cost investment is assigned to the manager and $e_M^G \to e^{FB}$ when $\alpha \to 1$. If $\alpha < \frac{1}{2}$, then e is assigned to the government and $e_G^G \to e^{FB}$ when $\alpha \to 0$.

Finally, consider $o = N$, so that $A = MG$ is optimal. In this case, if $\alpha \to 1$, in the limit the equilibrium investment levels are characterized by $qc'(e_M^N) + (1-q)[c'(e_M^N) - b'(e_M^N)] = 1$ and $q\beta'(i_G^N) = 1$. Note that q must be close to 0 for e_M^N to be close to e^{FB}, but as q approaches zero, i_G^N becomes arbitrarily small. A similar argument holds for $\alpha \to 0$. ■

Proof of Proposition 2.7

(i) Assume that under $o = N$ the parties would specify the quantity $\tilde{q}$, so that $i_G^N = i_G^G = i^{FB}$. If $\theta \to 0$, then in the limit $\tilde{q}c'(e_M^N) + \alpha(1-\tilde{q})c'(e_M^N) = 1$ when

$o = N$. Under G-ownership, in the limit we have $\alpha c'(e_M^G) = 1$ if $\alpha \geq 1/2$ and $(1-\alpha)c'(e_G^G) = 1$ if $\alpha < 1/2$. Note that the cost investment is in both cases smaller than the first-best, but it is larger under N-ownership than under G-ownership if $\tilde{q}+\alpha(1-\tilde{q}) > \max\{\alpha, 1-\alpha\}$, which holds when $\alpha > (1-\tilde{q})/(2-\tilde{q})$. Note that the surplus under $o = N$ were even larger if instead of $\tilde{q}$ the quantity $\hat{q}$ would be chosen.

(ii) Suppose that under N-ownership the parties would specify $\bar{q}$, so that $e_M^N = e_M^M = e^{FB}$. If $\psi \to 0$, then in the limit $\bar{q}\beta'(i_G^N)+(1-\alpha)(1-\bar{q})\beta'(i_G^N) = 1$ when $o = N$. Under $o = M$, in the limit we have $\alpha\beta'(i_M^M) = 1$ if $\alpha \geq 1/2$ and $(1-\alpha)\beta'(i_G^M) = 1$ if $\alpha < 1/2$. Note that the quality investment is in both cases smaller than the first-best, but it is larger under $o = N$ than under $o = M$ if $\bar{q}+(1-\alpha)(1-\bar{q}) > \max\{\alpha, 1-\alpha\}$, which holds when $\alpha < 1/(2-\bar{q})$.

(iii) When both θ and ψ go to zero, then the first best is approached under $o = N$ with $\hat{q} = 1$. In contrast, if $o = M$ there remains to be underinvestment with regard to i, while under G-ownership there is still underinvestment with regard to e. ■

Proof of Proposition 2.8

(i) If $\theta \to 1$, then $e^{FB} \to 0$, so that under G-ownership (where $i_G^G(\tilde{q}) = i^{FB}$) the first-best outcome is approached. In contrast, under $o = M$ there is still underinvestment with regard to i. Under $o = N$, the parties must set $\hat{q} = \tilde{q} > 0$ if they want to implement i^{FB}. But then $\tilde{q}c'(e_M^N) + \alpha(1-\tilde{q})(1-\theta)[c'(e_M^N) - \breve{b}'(e)] = 1$, so that there is overinvestment with regard to e when $\theta \to 1$.

(ii) If $\psi \to 1$, then $i^{FB} \to 0$, so that under M-ownership (where $e_M^M(\bar{q}) = e^{FB}$) the first best is approached. In contrast, under $o = G$ there is still underinvestment with regard to e. Under $o = N$, the parties must set $\hat{q} = \bar{q}$ if they want to implement e^{FB}. But then there is overinvestment with regard to i when $\psi \to 1$. ■

3

Public-Private Partnerships versus Traditional Procurement: Innovation Incentives and Information Gathering

3.1 Introduction

In the last 15 years, public-private partnerships have become an increasingly popular method to let the private sector provide public infrastructure-based services in various sectors such as health care, education, and transportation. As has been pointed out by Hart (2003), a key property of a public-private partnership is the fact that facility construction and subsequent service provision are bundled and assigned to a single private-sector entity.[1] An often heard argument in favour of public-private partnerships is that bundling encourages innovative design solutions during the construction phase that may

[1]See also Grimsey and Lewis (2004, pp. 129, 222), who point out that a defining characteristic of public-private partnerships is that the tasks of designing and building a facility as well as operating it later on are integrated within a single private-sector party, while under traditional procurement there are separate contractors for construction and management.

E. I. Hoppe-Fischer, *Essays on Contract Design and Incentive Provision*,
Edition KWV, https://doi.org/10.1007/978-3-658-24133-9_3

reduce the subsequent costs of service delivery.[2] Yet, at the same time, it has also been argued that compared to traditional procurement, the long-term relationship inherent in a public-private partnership may create particular scope for information asymmetries to develop between the public sector and the private entity. Specifically, the private-sector entity may become much better informed than the public authority about additional costs that arise in the operation stage when changes in circumstances occur.[3]

In this chapter, we study how incentives to come up with innovative design solutions and incentives to acquire private information relevant for service delivery affect the performance of public-private partnerships compared to traditional procurement. It turns out that a government agency's preferred mode of provision may be different from the one that is optimal from a welfare perspective. In particular, the government agency's preferences for a public-private partnership may be too strong or too weak, depending on the importance of retaining flexibility to adapt the service provision to changing circumstances that were not yet contractible when the public-private partnership was first agreed upon.

Consider a government agency that wants a certain public good or service to be provided. Before provision can take place (stage 2), a suitable infrastructure has to be built (stage 1). For example, in order to provide health care, education, or public transportation, suitable hospitals, schools, or railroad

[2]For example, Yescombe (2007, p. 21) stresses that since the same private-sector entity is responsible for construction and operation of the facility, it will be prepared to spend more during the construction phase in order to reduce the costs to be incurred later on. Similarly, the argument that a public-private partnership encourages the private-sector entity "to plan beyond the bounds of the construction phase and incorporate features that will facilitate operations" has also been brought forward by Grimsey and Lewis (2004, p. 92).

[3]See Yescombe (2007, pp. 24, 273). The fact that in the construction phase, the private-sector entity in a public-private partnership may gain an informational advantage on the costs of future investments in service provision has also been pointed out by Chong, Huet, and Saussier (2006a), Chong et al. (2006b), and De Palma, Leruth, and Prunier (2009). See also Monbiot (2002) and Vickerman (2004), who argue that the informational advantage of the private entity may allow it to exaggerate its costs.

networks have to be built. Initially, only the basic features of the good or service can be described in a contract. But after some time has passed, i.e. when the second stage is reached, it becomes clear how the basic good or service can be improved by adapting it.[4] Hence, at the beginning of the second stage, the government agency can contract for additional features that increase its benefit but also the costs of provision. For instance, advances in the field of medical research may require hospitals to meet growing service standards, e.g. to adapt to new medical equipment or to enlarge the number of operating rooms. Similarly, reforms in the educational system may necessitate that schools are restructured to turn them into all-day schools. When a government agency has contracted for the procurement of public transportation, it may later (e.g., in the light of an increased public interest in safety measures) want trains to be equipped with passenger information and surveillance technology.

At the outset, the government agency can choose between two different modes of provision. In case of a *public-private partnership*, building and service provision are bundled; i.e., the government agency contracts with a single party (a consortium) to build the infrastructure and to operate it. In contrast, under *traditional procurement* the government contracts with one party to build the infrastructure and with another party to provide the public good or service. All parties are risk-neutral and (except for the agency) they are protected by limited liability.

In the first stage, the builder provides the basic version of the infrastructure and he can exert unobservable effort to come up with an innovation, which may reduce the costs of adapting the public good or service to future needs. For example, an innovative layout of a hospital may facilitate a flexible use of rooms that may be required when in-patient treatment is increasingly

[4]The importance of keeping flexibility to adapt the service provision to new developments that were not taken into account in the original public-private partnership arrangement has also been emphasized by Cambridge Economic Policy Associates (2005), HM Treasury (2003), OECD (2008), Public Accounts Select Committee (2000), and Renda and Schrefler (2006).

substituted by ambulatory treatment.[5] Similarly, structuring school grounds in innovative ways can affect future efforts that are needed to supervise children during breaks and in the afternoons. Moreover, carefully designed trains and railway stations may reduce the efforts of security guards that may be required in the future to meet increasing needs for security.

When only a standard design was developed in the first stage, the costs of improving the service provision in the second stage by making suitable adaptations are known to be high. Yet, when the design developed in the first stage is innovative, then these costs may be lower. In this case, the costs of service improvements are initially unknown, but the party in charge of construction in the first stage may spend resources to acquire private information about these costs. For instance, a firm that came up with an innovative layout for a hospital or a school may have the opportunity to find out how much effort would be needed to restructure the building to increase the number of operating rooms or to accommodate more students. Similarly, a firm that has developed innovative designs for trains and railway stations may be in a good position to evaluate which future efforts would be required to meet more ambitious security standards.

If there were no incentive problems, the optimal mode of provision would depend on technological issues only. Specifically, if it is more expensive to let a different party be in charge of the second stage, so that the tasks in the two stages are complements, then a public-private partnership would be preferred by the government agency. This is the case if the builder has lower costs to improve the service provision in the second stage because of his specific knowledge about the characteristics of the infrastructure. In contrast, if the tasks are substitutes, such that a party different from the builder can respond to changing service provision needs at lower costs, then the government agency

[5] For instance, Grimsey and Lewis (2004, p. 121) report about the Berwick Hospital Project, in which strong efforts were made to come up with design solutions that retain the flexibility "to address ongoing changes in medical and health care practices, to accommodate demands for the future development of new services, and to maximise the opportunities for greater integration of in-patient care with ambulance and community-based services."

would prefer traditional procurement. This scenario prevails if the firm in charge of the first stage is specialized in building the infrastructure, while the firm in charge of the second stage has special skills regarding the management of service provision.

However, in the presence of incentive problems, the government agency's choice between a public-private partnership and traditional procurement is no longer determined by technological considerations only. To see this, let us first investigate the case in which no mode of provision is accompanied by technological (dis-)advantages. At first sight, one might guess that the government agency then prefers a public-private partnership. After all, when the same party is in charge of both stages, then it might be motivated to exert effort in the first stage just because of the prospect to earn a rent in the second stage by reducing the adaptation costs that it will then have to incur. In contrast, to induce first-stage effort under traditional procurement, the party in charge of the first stage has to be directly motivated by a suitable bonus payment in case of an innovation, since it does not care about the second-stage adaptation costs. Yet, it turns out that in the absence of technological (dis-)advantages, the government agency prefers traditional procurement.

Given a public-private partnership, the consortium will gather information about future costs of improving the service provision with positive probability, so that it may earn a rent in the second stage when these adaptation costs are low. In contrast, under traditional procurement, there is no scope for acquiring private information, since the party in charge of the first stage does not care about the second-stage costs. Actually, there are two cases. (i) If the government agency's additional benefit from implementing the second-stage improvement is relatively small, then it offers only relatively small payments for the implementation, so that the consortium cannot earn a second-stage rent. Hence, in this case under both modes of provision first-stage effort can be induced only by directly rewarding an innovation with a suitable bonus payment. But since given a public-private partnership, the consortium may be privately informed, the relatively small payments for implementing the second-stage improvement are not always accepted. As a consequence, the government agency's additional benefit from the second-stage improvement is realized less often than under traditional procurement, where the party in charge of the second stage is never privately informed. Hence, if the government agency chooses the same first-stage bonus payment as is optimal in case of a public-private partnership, then the agency is better off under traditional procurement. Moreover, it can do even better if under traditional procurement a larger first-stage effort is induced. (ii) If the government agency's additional benefit from implementing the second-stage improvement is relatively large, then given a public-private partnership, the agency offers relatively large payments for the implementation, so that the consortium can earn a second-stage rent. Yet, the rent left to the consortium is so large that the government agency can no longer benefit from a first-stage innovation. Hence, the government agency offers no direct reward for an innovation in the first stage, while under traditional procurement it benefits from an innovation and thus induces a positive first-stage effort, which means that the government agency must be better off under traditional procurement. Note that nevertheless, the prospect to earn the second-stage rent may lead the consortium to choose a larger first-stage effort level than the one induced by the government agency under traditional procurement. In particular, this may happen when the information acquisition costs are small, such that the second-stage rent that the consortium may earn becomes large.

Given that the government agency opts for traditional procurement when technological issues are not relevant, it will prefer a public-private partnership only if traditional procurement is accompanied by sufficiently large technological disadvantages; i.e., if the complementarities between the tasks in the two stages are sufficiently strong. On the other hand, if technologically the tasks in the two stages are substitutes, then the government agency will always prefer traditional procurement.

A central question motivating our study is whether the government agency's preferred mode of provision coincides with the one that is optimal from a welfare perspective; i.e., would the agency's decision between the two modes be supported or would it be overruled by a welfare-maximizing government? Our results depend on the potential merits of adapting the service provision to future needs. (i) Consider first the case in which the additional benefit from implementing the second-stage improvements is relatively small, such that second-stage rents never occur. If the technological disadvantages of separating the two tasks are sufficiently large (resp., small), a welfare-maximizing government would agree with the agency's choice of a public-private partnership (resp., traditional procurement). However, for intermediate levels of the technological disadvantages, the agency may prefer a public-private partnership, whereas a welfare-maximizing government may opt for traditional procurement (while the opposite can never occur). The fact that the first-stage effort level is larger under traditional procurement implies that, given limited liability, also the first-stage rent is larger. Hence, traditional procurement is more attractive for a welfare-maximizing government, since it takes the rents into account, while the agency does not. (ii) Consider now the case in which the additional benefit from the second-stage adaptations is relatively large. In this case, the results depend on the costs of gathering information. If the information acquisition costs are large, so that given a public-private partnership the second-stage rent and hence also the first-stage effort incentives are small, then there are again situations in which the government agency chooses a public-private partnership while a welfare-maximizing government would opt for traditional procurement. In contrast, if the information gathering costs are small, the second-stage rent and therefore the first-stage effort given a public-private partnership become large. This makes a public-private partnership relatively more attractive for a welfare-maximizing government than for the agency, since the latter does not care about the consortium's rent. In particular, in contrast to the agency, a welfare-maximizing government may prefer a public-private partnership, even if technological issues are irrelevant or if the tasks in the two stages are substitutes. That is, even if separating the tasks has technological advantages, this may be overcompensated by the fact that given a public-private partnership, stronger incentives to exert effort in the first stage may be generated by the prospect to earn an information rent in the second stage.

There is by now a vast literature on the role of private firms in the provision of public goods.[6] Specifically, the theoretical literature on public-private partnerships has various strands. As pointed out above, we follow Hart (2003) who argues that a key property of a public-private partnership is the fact that building the infrastructure and service provision are bundled. Bundling implies that the builder internalizes the second-stage operating costs when he exerts effort in the first stage. While Hart (2003) considers a model with symmetric information, our aim is to highlight the implications of the possibility to gather private information; hence, we study a framework in which under symmetric information the mode of provision would be irrelevant in the absence of technological (dis-)advantages. In order to focus on the key question whether or not the two stages should be separated, we follow Hart (2003) in that we do not complicate the analysis by introducing the choice between public and private ownership.[7] The interaction of the mode of provision and different ownership structures under symmetric information has been studied by Bennett and Iossa (2006a,b) and Chen and Chiu (2010). A common feature of their models and our framework is that second-stage service improvements are non-contractible ex ante but become verifiable ex post. In contrast, Bentz, Grout, and Halonen (2005) study related questions in a complete contracting

[6] For surveys on privatization, see e.g. Vickers and Yarrow (1988), Bös (1991), Shleifer (1998), and Martimort (2006). In this literature, the focus is generally on informational asymmetries and/or contractual incompleteness (e.g., Shapiro and Willig, 1990, Laffont and Tirole, 1991, Schmidt, 1996a,b).

[7] The effects of public and private ownership on investment incentives are studied by Hart, Shleifer, and Vishny (1997), who build on the property rights approach based on incomplete contracting (Grossman and Hart, 1986; Hart and Moore, 1990; Hart, 1995). In Chapter 2 we have extended their model by considering a richer set of contractual arrangements. See also Besley and Ghatak (2001), Francesconi and Muthoo (2006), and Halonen-Akatwijuka and Pafilis (2009) who build on the property rights approach to analyze whether non-governmental organizations should own public goods.

framework. Martimort and Pouyet (2008) develop a model that encompasses both traditional agency problems and property rights and they find that the important issue is not who owns the assets, but instead whether tasks are bundled or not. Iossa and Martimort (2008, 2009) provide extensions and applications of this framework, also highlighting the positive (resp., negative) effects of bundling in the presence of positive (resp., negative) externalities between the stages.[8]

The remainder of the chapter is organized as follows. In the next section, the model is introduced. The two different modes of provision are studied in Section 3.3 (public-private partnership) and Section 3.4 (traditional procurement). In Section 3.5, we analyze which mode of provision is preferred by the government agency and whether or not a welfare-maximizer would overrule this decision. Concluding remarks follow in Section 3.6. All proofs have been relegated to the appendix.

3.2 The model

The principal (a government agency) wants to delegate the provision of a public good or service. There are two stages. In the first stage, a suitable infrastructure has to be designed and built (task 1), while in the second stage it has to be managed and operated (task 2). The principal can choose between two different modes of provision. Either the principal opts for a public-private partnership, i.e. she contracts with one agent (a consortium) in charge of both tasks, or she contracts with two different agents each in charge of one task (traditional procurement). The agents are protected by limited liability, their reservation utilities are zero, and all parties are risk-neutral.

An agent in charge of task 1 can build a basic version of the infrastructure, causing monetary and verifiable costs c_1. Additionally, to come up with an

[8]On the pros and cons of bundling sequential tasks in the absence of information gathering when complete contracts can be written, see also Schmitz (2005) and the literature discussed there.

innovation, the agent can exert unobservable effort $e \in [0,1]$ at non-monetary effort costs $\frac{1}{2}e^2$. The verifiable outcome of his effort is a success ($x = 1$) with probability e and a failure ($x = 0$) otherwise. A success means that an innovation has been developed that reduces the expected costs of undertaking adaptations (not yet describable in stage 1) to improve the service provision in the second stage.

Specifically, in the second stage the agent in charge of task 2 can provide a standard version of the public good or service, which entails monetary and verifiable costs c_2 and yields a benefit B to the principal. We assume that $B > c_1 + c_2$, so that at least, it is always desirable to build the basic infrastructure and to provide the standard service. Moreover, in stage 2 it is possible to contract upon the improvement of the service provision which yields an additional benefit b to the principal. If the same agent is in charge of both tasks, then the effort costs of improving the second-stage service provision are c, while they are $c + \Delta$ if a different agent is in charge of task 2. We assume that these costs are non-monetary. If there was no innovation ($x = 0$), then $c = c_h$, while $c \in \{c_l, c_h\}$ with $\Pr\{c = c_l\} = p$ if an innovation was made ($x = 1$). We normalize $0 < c_l < c_h < 1$ and we assume that $\Delta > -c_l$, which means that the costs of improving the second-stage service provision by undertaking adaptations are always strictly positive. A positive Δ implies that task 1 and implementation of the second-stage improvement are complements, while a negative Δ means that they are substitutes.[9]

If an innovation was made, initially no one knows the realization of c. However, at the end of stage 1, the agent in charge of task 1 can exert unobservable effort in order to gather information about the costs c of improving the second-stage service provision. In particular, if the agent incurs non-monetary effort costs $\gamma > 0$, then he learns the realization of c, while he remains uninformed otherwise.

[9]The relevance of cost complementarities for the desirability to bundle tasks has been discussed by Holmström and Milgrom (1991) and Itoh (1994). See Laffont and Martimort (2002, Section 5.2) for an excellent textbook exposition.

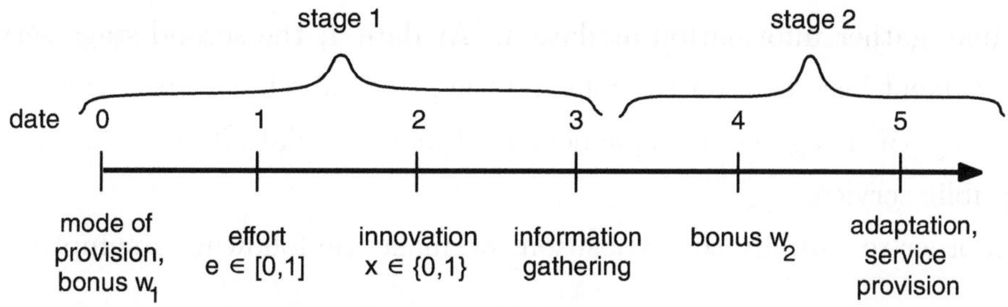

Figure 3.1. The sequence of events.

The sequence of events is illustrated in Figure 3.1. At date 0, the principal chooses the mode of provision. Consider first the case of a public-private partnership, so that the principal makes an offer to one agent (i.e., a consortium) who will be in charge of both tasks. In this case, at date 0 the principal offers the agent to cover his verifiable costs c_1 at date 1 and c_2 at date 5 and she offers to pay him a bonus w_1^{PPP} if an innovation is made at date 2.[10] At date 1, the agent builds the basic version of the infrastructure and decides how much effort e he wants to exert to come up with an innovation. If an innovation was made, the agent can gather information at date 3. At the beginning of the second stage, the adaptations necessary to improve the second-stage service provision become contractible and hence at date 4 the principal offers the agent to pay him a bonus w_2^{PPP} if he agrees to undertake the adaptations. At date 5, the agent provides the public good or service.

Next, consider the case of traditional procurement, so that the principal contracts with two different agents each in charge of one stage. At date 0, the principal offers agent 1 to bear the costs c_1 of building the basic infrastructure at date 1 and to pay him the bonus w_1^{TP} for an innovation at date 2. Moreover, the principal offers agent 2 to cover the costs c_2 of providing the basic version of the public good or service at date 5.[11] Agent 1 exerts effort e at date 1

[10]Note that at date 0, the parties are symmetrically informed, so that an agent will always accept a contract that ensures that his expected payoff is at least equal to his reservation utility zero.

[11]The precise date of the contract offer to agent 2 is irrelevant, as long as it is made until date 4.

and may gather information at date 3. At date 4, the second-stage service improvement becomes contractible and the principal offers to pay agent 2 the bonus w_2^{TP} if he agrees to implement it. Finally, at date 5, agent 2 provides the public service.

In order to simplify the exposition, we make the following assumptions.

Assumption 3.1 *(i)* $\gamma < p(E[c] - c_l)$.

(ii) $b > E[c]$.

The assumptions rule out uninteresting cases. Specifically, Assumption 3.1(i) excludes the case in which information gathering is prohibitively expensive. If this assumption were violated, an agent would never gather information and the optimal mode of provision would depend only on straightforward technological considerations; i.e., a public-private partnership would be preferred whenever Δ is positive. Moreover, if Assumption 3.1(ii) were violated, it turns out that the second-stage service improvement would never be implemented given a public-private partnership.

The first-best benchmark. Consider for a moment a first-best world in which the effort decisions and the information gathered are verifiable. Then the choice between a public-private partnership and traditional procurement is based on their technological (dis-)advantages only. Hence, if $\Delta > 0$ a public-private partnership is chosen, if $\Delta < 0$ traditional procurement is chosen, and if $\Delta = 0$ the mode of provision is irrelevant.

Consider the case in which a public-private partnership is optimal, $\Delta \geq 0$. Suppose first that $b \geq c_h$. Then no information gathering occurs,[12] and at date 1 the first-best effort level is $e^{FB} = \arg\max e(b - E[c]) + (1 - e)(b -$

[12]Note that information gathering can be productive only if $b < c_h$. Otherwise, implementation of the improvement is known to be always ex post efficient, so that information gathering is a rent-seeking activity only. In different contexts, productive information gathering has been studied by Aghion and Tirole (1997), Lewis and Sappington (1997), Crémer, Khalil, and Rochet (1998a), Kessler (1998), and Khalil, Kim, and Shin (2006), while socially undesirable information gathering has been addressed by Crémer and Khalil (1992), Crémer, Khalil, and Rochet (1998b), and Schmitz (2006). See also the discussion in Chap-

$c_h) - \frac{1}{2}e^2 = c_h - E[c]$. Next, suppose that $E[c] < b < c_h$ which implies that the stage-2 improvement will not be implemented if no innovation was made ($x = 0$). If $x = 1$, then information gathering is optimal whenever $p(b - c_l) - \gamma \geq b - E[c]$. Observe that in the case that information is gathered, the second-stage improvement is implemented only if $c = c_l$, so that the first-best date-2 effort level is $e^{FB} = p(b - c_l)$. In the case that, after an innovation, information gathering does not occur, the second-stage improvement is always implemented, such that $e^{FB} = b - E[c]$.

Consider now the case in which traditional procurement is optimal, $\Delta \leq 0$. Suppose that $b \geq c_h + \Delta$. Then no information is gathered, the second-stage service improvement is always implemented, and $e^{FB} = c_h - E[c]$. Next, suppose that $E[c] < b < c_h + \Delta$. If $p(b - c_l - \Delta) - \gamma \geq b - E[c] - \Delta$, then it is optimal to gather information and the stage-2 improvement is implemented whenever $c = c_l$, such that $e^{FB} = p(b - c_l - \Delta)$. Otherwise, information gathering does not take place, the stage-2 improvement is always implemented, and $e^{FB} = b - E[c] - \Delta$.

3.3 Public-private partnership

3.3.1 No innovation at date 2 ($x = 0$)

Suppose first that there was no success at date 2 ($x = 0$), so that the effort costs of implementing a second-stage service improvement are $c = c_h$. Note that then there is no scope for information gathering at date 3. At date 4, if $b \geq c_h$, the principal asks the agent to implement the stage-2 improvement and she offers him to reimburse him for his effort costs, $w_2^{PPP} = c_h$. The agent will always accept the offer. If $b < c_h$, then the improvement will not be implemented. Hence, if $x = 0$, the implementation of the second-stage service improvement occurs whenever it is ex post efficient. At date 2, the principal's

ter 4 where we consider two scenarios in which costly information gathering is a pure rent seeking activity.

continuation payoff is $B - c_2 + [b - c_h]^+$, where $[b - c_h]^+ := \max\{b - c_h, 0\}$, and the agent's continuation payoff is zero.

3.3.2 An innovation at date 2 ($x = 1$)

Next, suppose that at date 2 there was a success ($x = 1$), so that $c = c_l$ with probability p and $c = c_h$ with probability $1 - p$. The agent will agree to implement the second-stage service improvement whenever the principal's offer w_2^{PPP} is weakly larger than his effort costs c (resp., his expected costs $E[c]$) if he is informed (resp., uninformed). Hence, at date 4, the principal will choose among the offers c_l, $E[c]$, and c_h only.

Lemma 3.1 *In equilibrium, at date 4 the principal chooses $w_2^{PPP} \in \{c_l, E[c], c_h\}$. Given that the agent is informed with probability $\pi \in [0, 1]$, the principal's expected date-5-profit is $B - c_2 + \pi p[b - c_l]$ if $w_2^{PPP} = c_l$, it is $B - c_2 + (\pi p + 1 - \pi)[b - E[c]]$ if $w_2^{PPP} = E[c]$, and it is $B - c_2 + b - c_h$ if $w_2^{PPP} = c_h$.*

Proof. See the appendix. ■

At date 3, the agent will mix between gathering and not gathering information and at date 4, the principal will mix between different offers. To see this, note that the agent can gain by gathering information only if he is offered $w_2^{PPP} = E[c]$ with strictly positive probability. Yet, if he always gathered information, the principal would never offer $E[c]$. Moreover, if the agent never gathered information, the principal would always offer $E[c]$, but then the agent's best response would be to gather information (due to Assumption 3.1(i)). Hence, in equilibrium the agent must be indifferent between gathering and not gathering information, and the principal must offer $w_2^{PPP} = E[c]$ with a probability strictly between zero and one.

Lemma 3.2 *In equilibrium, the probability that the agent gathers information at date 3 is $0 < \pi < 1$.*

Proof. See the appendix. ■

Lemma 3.3 *There exists no equilibrium in which the principal plays a pure strategy; i.e., at date 4 she must mix between at least two of the three wage offers* c_l, $E[c]$, *and* c_h.

Proof. See the appendix. ■

Let the probability that the principal offers $w_2^{PPP} = c_l$ be denoted by α_l and let α_h be the probability that she offers $w_2^{PPP} = c_h$ (hence, she offers $w_2^{PPP} = E[c]$ with probability $1 - \alpha_l - \alpha_h$).

If the principal's benefit b from implementing the second-stage service improvement is relatively small, the principal mixes between the offers c_l and $E[c]$. In this case, the expected second-stage rent of the agent is zero. To see this, recall that the agent must be indifferent between gathering and not gathering information. If the agent does not gather information, he will accept the offer $E[c]$ only, so that his expected effort costs will be reimbursed without leaving him a rent. In contrast, if the principal's benefit b is sufficiently large, she mixes between the offers c_h and $E[c]$. If now the agent does not gather information, he enjoys a rent when the offer is c_h and he is of the low type ($c = c_l$). Since the agent must be indifferent between gathering and not gathering information, his expected second-stage rent is hence $\alpha_h (c_h - E[c])$.

Proposition 3.1 *Let* $\tilde{b} > c_h$ *be implicitly defined by* $\frac{(\tilde{b}-E[c])^2}{\tilde{b}-pc_l-(1-p)E[c]} = \frac{c_h-E[c]}{1-p}$.

(i) If $E[c] < b < \tilde{b}$, *then in equilibrium the agent gathers information with probability* $\pi = \frac{b-E[c]}{b-pc_l-(1-p)E[c]}$ *and the principal mixes between the wage offers* $w_2^{PPP} = c_l$ *and* $w_2^{PPP} = E[c]$, *where* $\alpha_l = 1 - \frac{\gamma}{p(E[c]-c_l)}$. *Hence, at date 2 the principal's expected continuation payoff is* $B - c_2 + \Pi$, *where* $\Pi := \frac{b-E[c]}{b-pc_l-(1-p)E[c]}p[b - c_l]$, *and the agent's expected continuation payoff is* 0.

(ii) If $b \geq \tilde{b}$, *then in equilibrium the agent gathers information with probability* $\pi = \frac{c_h-E[c]}{(1-p)(b-E[c])}$ *and the principal mixes between the wage offers* $w_2^{PPP} = c_h$ *and* $w_2^{PPP} = E[c]$, *where* $\alpha_h = 1 - \frac{\gamma}{p(E[c]-c_l)}$. *Thus, at date 2 the principal's expected continuation payoff is* $B - c_2 + b - c_h$ *and the agent's expected continuation payoff is* $\alpha_h (c_h - E[c]) = c_h - E[c] - \frac{\gamma}{1-p}$.

Proof. See the appendix. ■

Observe that the probability with which the agent gathers information is a function of the principal's benefit b, since the agent's behavior must ensure that the principal is indifferent between making different offers. Specifically, consider the case where the benefit b is relatively small ($b < \tilde{b}$), such that the principal mixes between the offers c_l and $E[c]$. Suppose now that b increases, which implies that the offer $E[c]$ would become more attractive for the principal (since the offer c_l is more often rejected than the offer $E[c]$) if the agent did not change his information gathering probability. Hence, the agent must increase the information gathering probability, which in turn increases the attractiveness of the offer c_l, since in case of an informed agent both offers are accepted with probability p. Next, consider the case where the benefit b is relatively large ($b \geq \tilde{b}$), so that the principal mixes between the offers $E[c]$ and c_h. If b increases, the principal would prefer to offer c_h (which is always accepted), unless the agent decreases his information gathering probability (since in case of an uninformed agent, both offers $E[c]$ and c_h are accepted).

Note also that the probability with which the principal mixes between her offers is a function of the agent's information gathering costs γ, because the offers must be such that the agent is indifferent between gathering and not gathering information. In particular, when it becomes more expensive to gather information (γ increases), information gathering must become more useful, which is the case if the probability of an offer $E[c]$ increases.

Finally, consider the principal's expected profit $B - c_2 + \Pi$ in the case that the benefit is relatively small, $b < \tilde{b}$, such that the principal mixes between the offers c_l and $E[c]$. Note that $B - c_2 + \Pi$ must be larger than the profit $B - c_2 + b - c_h$ that she would make if she made the offer c_h. Moreover, $\Pi < b - E[c]$ must hold, because the principal's expected profit is $B - c_2 + \Pi$, regardless of whether she offers c_l or $E[c]$, and an offer of $E[c]$ is not always accepted by the agent.

Remark 3.1 *(i) If $E[c] < b < \tilde{b}$, then the probability π that the agent gathers information is increasing in b.*

(ii) If $b \geq \tilde{b}$, then the probability π that the agent gathers information is decreasing in b.

(iii) The probability with which the principal makes the offer $E[c]$ is increasing in the agent's information gathering costs γ.

(iv) $b - c_h < \Pi < b - E[c]$.

Proof. The proof is straightforward. ■

3.3.3 The effort decision at date 1

Consider now the agent's effort decision at date 1. Observe that the agent can be motivated to exert effort for two different reasons. First, the principal can directly reward the agent by offering to pay him a bonus $w_1^{PPP} > 0$ in case an innovation is made ($x = 1$). Second, investment incentives can arise indirectly when the agent anticipates to enjoy a second-stage rent whenever he comes up with an innovation in the first stage. Recall that if the principal's benefit b from implementing the second-stage service improvement is relatively small ($b < \tilde{b}$), then the agent does not obtain a second-stage rent. Yet, in this case the principal will offer a direct reward, because her expected second-stage profit when an innovation is made is $B - c_2 + \Pi$, which is larger than $B - c_2 + [b - c_h]^+$, her profit when there was no innovation. In contrast, if b is sufficiently large ($b \geq \tilde{b}$), the principal's (expected) second-stage profit is always $B - c_2 + b - c_h$, regardless of whether or not there was an innovation in the first stage. This implies that the principal offers the agent no direct reward ($w_1^{PPP} = 0$). However, the agent exerts effort at date 1 because of the prospect to earn the expected second-stage rent $c_h - E[c] - \frac{\gamma}{1-p}$ when he comes up with an innovation at date 2.

Proposition 3.2 *(i) If $E[c] < b < \tilde{b}$, then the principal offers a bonus $w_1^{PPP} = \frac{1}{2}\left(\Pi - [b - c_h]^+\right)$, so that at date 1 the agent chooses the effort level $e_i^{PPP} = w_1^{PPP}$. The expected payoffs at date 0 are $B - c_1 - c_2 + [b - c_h]^+ + \left(e_i^{PPP}\right)^2$ for the principal and $\frac{1}{2}\left(e_i^{PPP}\right)^2$ for the agent. Thus, the expected welfare is $B - c_1 - c_2 + [b - c_h]^+ + \frac{3}{2}\left(e_i^{PPP}\right)^2$.*

(ii) If $b \geq \tilde{b}$, then the principal offers no direct reward for an innovation ($w_1^{PPP} = 0$). At date 1, the agent chooses $e_{ii}^{PPP} = c_h - E[c] - \frac{\gamma}{1-p}$. The expected payoffs at date 0 are $B - c_1 - c_2 + b - c_h$ for the principal and $\frac{1}{2}(e_{ii}^{PPP})^2$ for the agent. Hence, the expected welfare is $B - c_1 - c_2 + b - c_h + \frac{1}{2}(e_{ii}^{PPP})^2$.

Proof. See the appendix. ■

3.4 Traditional procurement

In the second stage, agent 2 provides a basic version of the good or service. In addition, if there was no innovation in the first stage ($x = 0$), then at date 4, whenever $b \geq c_h + \Delta$, the principal will offer agent 2 the payment $w_2^{TP} = c_h + \Delta$ for implementing the second-stage service improvement. The agent will accept the offer as he is reimbursed for his effort costs. If agent 1 came up with an innovation in the first stage ($x = 1$), then whenever $b \geq E[c] + \Delta$, the principal will offer agent 2 the payment $w_2^{TP} = E[c] + \Delta$ for implementation of the service improvement. Agent 2 will accept the offer since he is uninformed about the realization of c.

Consider next agent 1's incentives to exert effort at date 1. Under traditional procurement, agent 1 knows that he will not be in charge of task 2 in the second stage, and hence he can be incentivized to exert effort only by the bonus payment w_1^{TP}. Moreover, knowing that the information he can gather is not relevant for him, agent 1 does not engage in costly information gathering.

Proposition 3.3 *At date 0, the principal offers the bonus $w_1^{TP} = \frac{1}{2}([b - E[c] - \Delta]^+ - [b - c_h - \Delta]^+)$. At date 1, the agent chooses the effort level $e^{TP} = w_1^{TP}$. The expected payoffs at date 0 are $B - c_1 - c_2 + [b - c_h - \Delta]^+ + (e^{TP})^2$ for the principal, $\frac{1}{2}(e^{TP})^2$ for agent 1, and 0 for agent 2. Thus, the expected welfare is $B - c_1 - c_2 + [b - c_h - \Delta]^+ + \frac{3}{2}(e^{TP})^2$.*

Proof. See the appendix. ■

3.5 Public-private partnership versus traditional procurement

We can now analyze the principal's date-0 decision regarding the mode of provision. Suppose first that traditional procurement has no technological (dis-)advantages compared to a public-private partnership; i.e., $\Delta = 0$. Then due to incentive considerations, the principal will always prefer traditional procurement. To see this, consider first the case where the benefit b is relatively small ($b < \tilde{b}$), so that given a public-private partnership, the agent would not get a second-stage rent. This means that under both modes of provision, the principal extracts the (expected) total surplus generated in stage 2. While for $x = 0$ this surplus is $B - c_2 + [b - c_h]^+$ under both modes, for $x = 1$ it is $B - c_2 + b - E[c]$ under traditional procurement, but it is only $B - c_2 + \Pi$ given a public-private partnership. Hence, if under traditional procurement the principal set the same bonus w_1 as in case of a public-private partnership (thereby inducing the same first-stage effort level), she would be better off under traditional procurement. Moreover, she can increase her expected profit under traditional procurement even further by inducing $e^{TP} > e_i^{PPP}$.

Consider now the case where the benefit b is relatively large ($b \geq \tilde{b}$). Given a public-private partnership, the principal's second-stage payoff is $B - c_2 + b - c_h$ regardless of whether an innovation was made or not. In contrast, under traditional procurement, the principal's second-stage payoff is $B - c_2 + b - c_h$ if no innovation was made, while it is $B - c_2 + b - E[c]$ otherwise. Hence, if the principal set the first-stage bonus w_1^{TP} equal to zero, her expected profit would be the same under both modes of provision. Actually, the principal sets $w_1^{TP} > 0$, such that her expected profit under traditional procurement is strictly larger.

Given that the principal prefers traditional procurement when technological matters are not relevant, she finds this mode of provision even more attractive when it comes along with technological advantages (i.e., when $\Delta < 0$). On the other hand, if traditional procurement is accompanied by sufficiently strong technological disadvantages (i.e., when Δ is larger than a critical value $\tilde{\Delta} > 0$), then the principal prefers a public-private partnership. Note that $\tilde{\Delta} < b - E[c]$, because if $\Delta \geq b - E[c]$, the principal could never benefit from implementation of the second-stage improvement under traditional procurement, while given a public-private partnership, she benefits from the fact that the improvement is implemented with strictly positive probability.

Proposition 3.4 *There exists a unique cut-off value $\tilde{\Delta} \in (0, b - E[c])$ such that the principal prefers a public-private partnership for $\Delta \geq \tilde{\Delta}$ and traditional procurement otherwise.*

Proof. See the appendix. ■

We now investigate which one of the two modes of provision leads to a larger expected welfare (measured by the parties' expected total surplus). Consider first the case in which the benefit b is relatively small, $b < \tilde{b}$. In this case, if neither mode of provision brings about technological (dis-)advantages ($\Delta = 0$), traditional procurement yields a larger welfare. To see this, recall that we already know that in this case the principal's expected profit is larger under traditional procurement. Moreover, regardless of the mode of provision, the agent cannot earn a second-stage rent, while the first-stage rent under traditional procurement is larger than under a public-private partnership, since $e^{TP} > e_i^{PPP}$. Hence, a public-private partnership leads to a larger welfare only if the technological disadvantage of traditional procurement, Δ, is larger than a critical value $\bar{\Delta} > 0$. Note that $\bar{\Delta} < b - E[c]$, because if $\Delta \geq b - E[c]$, the principal could never benefit from implementing the stage-2 improvement under traditional procurement, implying $e^{TP} = 0$ and thus a rent of zero, so that under a public-private partnership the agent is better off and, according to Proposition 3.4, the principal makes a larger profit.

Next, consider the case in which the benefit is relatively large, $b \geq \tilde{b}$. Now a public-private partnership can yield a larger welfare even in the absence of any technological (dis-)advantages. If $\Delta = 0$, the principal is better off under traditional procurement, but this may be overcompensated by the fact that the agent's rent given a public-private partnership can be larger than the agents' rent under traditional procurement. This is because in the case $b \geq \tilde{b}$, the public-private partnership effort level e_{ii}^{PPP} (which is motivated by the prospect to earn the second-stage rent $c_h - E[c] - \frac{\gamma}{1-p}$) is larger than the effort level under traditional procurement e^{TP} (which is induced by the first-stage bonus payment) whenever the information gathering costs are sufficiently small (such that the expected second-stage rent is large).[13]

Observe that given a public-private partnership, the agent's rent is decreasing in γ. Since the principal's profit is independent of γ, the expected welfare given a public-private partnership is decreasing in γ as well. Hence, the larger is γ, the larger has to be the technological disadvantage of traditional procurement, Δ, for a public-private partnership to yield a larger welfare level.

Proposition 3.5 *(i) Consider the case $E[c] < b < \tilde{b}$. There exists a unique cut-off value $\bar{\Delta} \in (0, b - E[c])$ such that a public-private partnership yields a larger expected welfare level than traditional procurement if and only if $\Delta \geq \bar{\Delta}$.*

(ii) Consider the case $b \geq \tilde{b}$. There exists an increasing threshold function $\bar{\Delta}(\gamma)$ such that a public-private partnership leads to a larger expected welfare than traditional procurement if and only if $\Delta \geq \bar{\Delta}(\gamma)$.

Proof. See the appendix. ■

Consider the case where the benefit is relatively small, $b < \tilde{b}$. From Propositions 3.4 and 3.5 we know that traditional procurement (resp., a public-private partnership) is better for the principal and also for the welfare level if $\Delta \leq 0$ (resp., $\Delta \geq b - E[c]$). Hence, consider now $\Delta \in (0, b - E[c])$.

Suppose first that neither mode of provision leads to technological (dis-)advantages ($\Delta = 0$). We have already seen that in this case, the principal's expected profit as well as agent 1's expected rent are larger under traditional procurement, so that compared to a public-private partnership, traditional procurement is even more attractive from a welfare perspective

[13]Specifically, if $\Delta = 0$, then $e_{ii}^{PPP} > e^{TP}$ whenever $\gamma < \frac{1}{2}(1-p)(c_h - E[c])$.

than from the principal's point of view. Now consider traditional procurement and an increase in Δ, which reduces the principal's profit, while with regard to agent 1's rent, two cases have to be distinguished.

If $b \leq c_h$, then the principal implements the second-stage improvement if and only if there was an innovation at date 2 (because otherwise the implementation would cost her $c_h + \Delta > b$). But this implies that Δ will be incurred if and only if $x = 1$, so that the marginal return of the agent's date-1 effort and hence also his rent decrease in Δ. Hence, when $\Delta = 0$, the welfare gap between traditional procurement and a public-private partnership is larger than the profit gap, while the former shrinks faster than the latter when Δ increases. In fact, these two aspects offset each other, such that the critical values of Δ above which traditional procurement becomes inferior from a profit and a welfare perspective coincide.[14]

If $b > c_h$, the agent's rent is independent of Δ as long as $\Delta \leq b - c_h$. To see this, observe that then under traditional procurement, the principal implements the stage-2 improvement regardless of whether or not there was an innovation at date 2. Hence, the additional costs Δ will be incurred in any situation such that the marginal return of the agent 1's effort and thus his rent do not depend on Δ. As a consequence, when Δ increases, the welfare gap and the profit gap between traditional procurement and a public-private partnership shrink by the same amount; but since the former is larger than the latter, there are values of Δ such that the principal already prefers a public-private partnership, while the welfare level is still larger under traditional procurement (see Figure 3.2).

[14] Specifically, if no innovation is made, the principal's second-stage profit under both modes of provision is $B - c_2$. If an innovation is made, the principal's second-stage profit under traditional procurement is $B - c_2 + b - E[c] - \Delta$, while it is $B - c_2 + \Pi$ given a public-private partnership. Hence, whenever $\Delta < b - E[c] - \Pi$, the principal is better off under traditional procurement, and she will induce a larger first-stage effort level by offering a bonus $w_1^{TP} > w_1^{PPP}$, implying first-stage rents $\frac{1}{2}(e^{TP})^2 > \frac{1}{2}(e_i^{PPP})^2$. Thus, in this case, whenever the principal prefers traditional procurement, this mode of provision also yields a larger welfare.

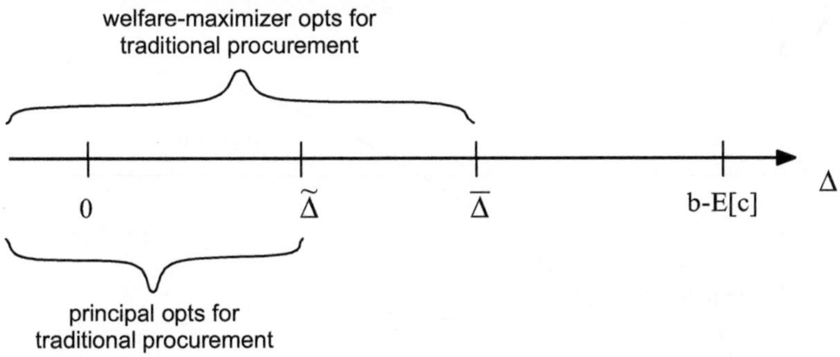

Figure 3.2. In the region $\Delta \in (\tilde{\Delta}, \bar{\Delta})$, the principal's preferred mode of provision deviates from the welfare-maximizer's choice.

Consider now the case where the benefit is relatively large, $b \geq \tilde{b}$. In this case there do not only exist situations in which the principal prefers a public-private partnership while traditional procurement is desirable from a welfare perspective, but there exist also situations in which the principal is better off under traditional procurement, while expected welfare is larger given a public-private partnership. As an illustration, consider Figure 3.3. Recall that the principal prefers a public-private partnership whenever $\Delta > \tilde{\Delta}$, while the welfare level is larger given a public-private partnership whenever $\Delta > \bar{\Delta}(\gamma)$. We already know that for $\Delta = 0$, the principal prefers traditional procurement regardless of the information gathering costs γ. But if γ is small, then given a public-private partnership the effort level and the agent's rent are relatively large, so that even for $\Delta = 0$ a public-private partnership may yield a larger welfare level. Yet, if γ increases, the agent's rent given a public-private partnership and hence its welfare advantage decrease such that region I, in which the principal's preferred decision to choose traditional procurement would be overruled by a welfare-maximizer, shrinks. If the information gathering costs are sufficiently large ($\gamma > \hat{\gamma}$), there exist again values of Δ such that the principal prefers a public-private partnership, while traditional procurement yields a larger welfare level (region II).

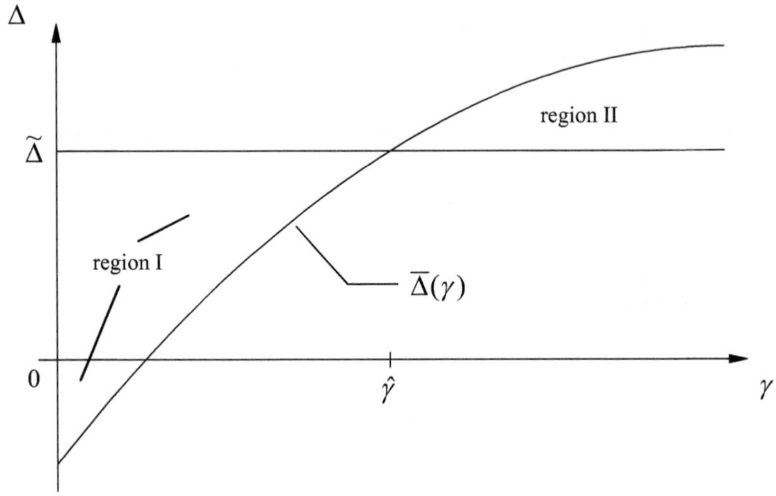

Figure 3.3. The principal opts for a public-private partnership for $\Delta \geq \tilde{\Delta}$, while a welfare-maximizer opts for a public-private partnership for $\Delta \geq \bar{\Delta}(\gamma)$.

Proposition 3.6 *(i) Consider the case $E[c] < b < \tilde{b}$. If $b \leq c_h$, then $\tilde{\Delta} = \bar{\Delta} = b - E[c] - \Pi$, so that the principal prefers a public-private partnership (resp., traditional procurement) whenever the expected welfare is larger given a public-private partnership (resp., traditional procurement). If $b > c_h$, then $\tilde{\Delta} < \bar{\Delta}$, so that for $\Delta \in (\tilde{\Delta}, \bar{\Delta})$ the principal prefers a public-private partnership while expected welfare would be larger given traditional procurement.*

(ii) Consider the case $b \geq \tilde{b}$. There exists a critical value $\hat{\gamma}$ defined by $\bar{\Delta}(\hat{\gamma}) = \tilde{\Delta}$. If $\gamma < \hat{\gamma}$, then $\bar{\Delta}(\gamma) < \tilde{\Delta}$, so that for $\Delta \in (\bar{\Delta}(\gamma), \tilde{\Delta})$ the principal prefers traditional procurement while expected welfare would be larger given a public-private partnership. If $\gamma > \hat{\gamma}$, then $\tilde{\Delta} < \bar{\Delta}(\gamma)$, so that for $\Delta \in (\tilde{\Delta}, \bar{\Delta}(\gamma))$ the principal prefers a public-private partnership while expected welfare would be larger given traditional procurement.

Proof. See the appendix. ■

3.6 Concluding remarks

When it comes to public-private partnerships, it "all revolves around incentives. In a world of 'incomplete' contracts, where it is difficult to foresee and contract about uncertain future events, it is important to get the incentive structure right" (Grimsey and Lewis, 2004, p. 247). It has often been argued that the delegation of the tasks of building, maintaining, and managing a facility to a single private contractor is the central characteristic of a public-private partnership. Indeed, bundling the tasks may provide the private contractor with strong incentives to develop a flexible design that will be particularly cost-effective in the operation stage and that can respond efficiently to changing requirements and new technologies in the future. However, as has been emphasized by Prendergast (1999), the provision of incentives can often give rise to dysfunctional responses. Given a public-private partnership, the private contractor enters into a long-term relationship with the public sector, which may create scope for the private party to engage in rent-seeking behavior. Specifically, to the best of our knowledge, the present study is the first one that formally models the private contractor's incentives to spend resources during the construction phase in order to obtain private information, so that he will be able to extract an information rent in the management stage. While the prospect to earn an information rent in the second stage can be a source of effort incentives in the first stage, private information may also trigger ex post inefficiencies. Moreover, the resources spent to gather information are socially wasteful when it is known from the outset that the benefits of adaptations to changing circumstances outweigh their costs. In our framework, it depends on the relevance of these benefits and on the information gathering costs whether a government agency's decision for or against a public-private partnership would be supported by a welfare-maximizing authority.

To highlight the effects that bundling different tasks in a public-private partnership has on the incentives to innovate and to gather information, we have confined our attention to a very stylized model. Hence, while beyond the scope of the present study, it might be worthwhile to extend our framework to incorporate further aspects that are also relevant when a decision between a public-private partnership and traditional procurement has to be made. For example, modelling the award procedure, explicitly taking into account contracting costs, or investigating the effects of private financing under a public-private partnership might be interesting avenues for future research.

3.7 Appendix

Proof of Lemma 3.1

If $0 \leq w_2^{PPP} < c_l$, then the agent would reject the offer and the principal's profit would be $B - c_2$. If $c_l \leq w_2^{PPP} < E[c]$, only an informed agent with costs $c = c_l$ would accept the offer, so that the best the principal can do is to offer $w_2^{PPP} = c_l$, yielding an expected profit of $B - c_2 + \pi p[b - c_l] \geq B - c_2 + \pi p[b - w_2^{PPP}]$. Since $b > c_l$, the offer $w_2^{PPP} = c_l$ also strictly dominates offers $w_2^{PPP} < c_l$. If $E[c] \leq w_2^{PPP} < c_h$, then both an uninformed agent and an informed agent with costs c_l would accept, so that the principal offers $w_2^{PPP} = E[c]$, which leads to an expected profit of $B - c_2 + (\pi p + 1 - \pi)[b - E[c]] \geq B - c_2 + (\pi p + 1 - \pi)[b - w_2^{PPP}]$. If $c_h \leq w_2^{PPP}$, then the offer would always be accepted and the principal chooses $w_2^{PPP} = c_h$, since $B - c_2 + b - c_h \geq B - c_2 + b - w_2^{PPP}$. ■

Proof of Lemma 3.2

First, suppose that π were equal to 1. Then the principal would never offer $w_2^{PPP} = E[c]$, because $w_2^{PPP} = c_l$ would yield a larger expected profit. But if the agent anticipated that the principal would offer either $w_2^{PPP} = c_l$ or $w_2^{PPP} = c_h$, he would have no incentive to undertake costly information gathering (since he could always reject the offer c_l and accept the offer c_h).

Next, suppose that π were equal to 0. Then the principal would offer $w_2^{PPP} = E[c]$, so that without information gathering the agent's expected date-5-payoff would be 0. Yet, if he deviated and gathered information, he would accept the offer if and only if $c = c_l$, so that his expected payoff would be larger, $p(E[c] - c_l) - \gamma > 0$. ■

Proof of Lemma 3.3

If the principal always offers $w_2^{PPP} = c_l$, then the agent could never earn a rent and would therefore never gather information ($\pi = 0$), which contradicts Lemma 3.2. If the principal always offers $w_2^{PPP} = E[c]$, the agent's payoff is 0 if he does not gather information, while it is $p(E[c] - c_l) - \gamma > 0$ otherwise, so the agent would always gather information ($\pi = 1$), contradicting Lemma 3.2.

If the principal always offers $w_2^{PPP} = c_h$, then the agent would always accept without information gathering ($\pi = 0$), which is in contradiction to Lemma 3.2. ■

Proof of Proposition 3.1

Note that $\frac{d}{db}\frac{(b-E[c])^2}{b-pc_l-(1-p)E[c]} = \frac{(b-E[c])^2+2p(b-E[c])(E[c]-c_l)}{(b-pc_l-(1-p)E[c])^2}$ is strictly positive for $b > E[c]$. Hence, the LHS of $\frac{(b-E[c])^2}{b-pc_l-(1-p)E[c]} = \frac{c_h-E[c]}{1-p}$ is strictly increasing in b for $b > E[c]$. Moreover, the LHS is smaller than the RHS for $b = c_h$ and it goes to infinity for $b \to \infty$, so that given continuity there must exist a unique $\tilde{b} > c_h$.

Recall that the case $\alpha_l + \alpha_h = 1$ cannot occur in equilibrium, since the agent would have no incentives to gather information (see Lemma 3.2). Hence, according to Lemma 3.3, the principal must be indifferent between offering c_l and $E[c]$ or between offering c_h and $E[c]$.

(i) According to Lemma 3.1, the principal's expected profit given the offer $w_2^{PPP} = c_l$ is $B - c_2 + \pi p[b - c_l]$ and her expected profit given the offer $w_2^{PPP} = E[c]$ is $B - c_2 + (\pi p + 1 - \pi)[b - E[c]]$. Hence, she is indifferent between the offers c_l and $E[c]$ if the agent gathers information with probability $\pi = \frac{b-E[c]}{b-pc_l-(1-p)E[c]} \in (0,1)$. Moreover, an offer of $E[c]$ is more profitable than offering $w_2^{PPP} = c_h$ (yielding an expected profit $B - c_2 + b - c_h$) if $\pi \leq \frac{c_h-E[c]}{(1-p)(b-E[c])}$. Given that $\pi = \frac{b-E[c]}{b-pc_l-(1-p)E[c]}$, the latter condition is equivalent to $b \leq \tilde{b}$.

In equilibrium, the principal must mix between the offers c_l and $E[c]$ such that the agent is indifferent between gathering and not gathering information. Suppose the agent does not gather information. Then he will accept the principal's offer only if it is $w_2^{PPP} = E[c]$, so that his expected payoff is 0. Next, suppose the agent gathers information. Then he will accept the principal's offer whenever he is of the low type $c = c_l$, such that his expected payoff is $p(1 - \alpha_l)(E[c] - c_l) - \gamma$. Hence, the agent is indifferent between gathering and not gathering information if $\alpha_l = 1 - \frac{\gamma}{p(E[c]-c_l)}$.

(ii) The principal's expected profit when she offers $w_2^{PPP} = E[c]$ is $B - c_2 + (\pi p + 1 - \pi)[b - E[c]]$, while her expected profit given $w_2^{PPP} = c_h$ is

$B - c_2 + b - c_h$. Thus, she is indifferent between offering $E[c]$ and c_h if the agent gathers information with probability $\pi = \frac{c_h - E[c]}{(1-p)(b-E[c])} > 0$. Note that $\pi < 1$ whenever $b > \frac{c_h - pE[c]}{1-p}$, which is always the case if $b \geq \tilde{b}$. In order to see this, one can check that $\frac{(b-E[c])^2}{b-pc_l-(1-p)E[c]} < \frac{c_h-E[c]}{1-p}$ for $b = \frac{c_h-pE[c]}{1-p}$.

Moreover, an offer of $E[c]$ is more profitable than offering $w_2^{PPP} = c_l$ (which yields an expected profit $B - c_2 + \pi p[b - c_l]$) if $\pi \leq \frac{b-E[c]}{b-pc_l-(1-p)E[c]}$. Given that $\pi = \frac{c_h-E[c]}{(1-p)(b-E[c])}$, the latter condition is equivalent to $b \geq \tilde{b}$.

We now characterize how in equilibrium the principal must mix between c_h and $E[c]$. Suppose the agent does not gather information. Then he will always accept the principal's offer, so that his expected payoff is $\alpha_h (c_h - E[c])$. Next, suppose the agent gathers information. Then he will always accept the principal's offer except when he is of the high type ($c = c_h$) and the offer is $w_2^{PPP} = E[c]$. Hence, his expected payoff is $p[\alpha_h c_h + (1-\alpha_h)E[c] - c_l] - \gamma$. The agent is indifferent between gathering and not gathering information if $\alpha_h = 1 - \frac{\gamma}{p(E[c]-c_l)}$.

Finally, in the special case where $b = \tilde{b}$, the principal is indifferent between offering c_l, $E[c]$, and c_h when the agent gathers information with probability $\pi = \frac{c_h-E[c]}{(1-p)(b-E[c])}$. In this case, there are multiple equilibria. The principal offers $E[c]$ with probability $\frac{\gamma}{p(E[c]-c_l)}$, while the probabilities that she offers c_l or c_h must add up to $1 - \frac{\gamma}{p(E[c]-c_l)}$. Note that in all equilibria the principal makes the same expected profit, while the equilibrium in which $\alpha_h = 1 - \frac{\gamma}{p(E[c]-c_l)}$ is the best one for the agent, so that we assume that they coordinate on the latter one. ■

Proof of Proposition 3.2

(i) In this case, the agent obtains no rent in the second stage. Hence, given that the principal has offered to pay him a bonus $w_1^{PPP} \geq 0$ whenever an innovation is made ($x = 1$), at date 1 the agent chooses $e_i^{PPP} = \arg\max_{e\in[0,1]} ew_1^{PPP} - \frac{1}{2}e^2 = \min\{w_1^{PPP}, 1\}$. Note that the principal will never choose $w_1^{PPP} > 1$, hence $e_i^{PPP} = w_1^{PPP}$. Recall that the principal's continuation payoff if $x = 1$ is $B - c_2 + \Pi$, while it is $B - c_2 + [b - c_h]^+$ if $x = 0$. The principal thus offers the bonus w_1^{PPP} that maximizes her expected profit $B - c_1 - c_2 +$

$w_1^{PPP}\left(\Pi - w_1^{PPP}\right) + (1 - w_1^{PPP})[b - c_h]^+$, so that $w_1^{PPP} = \frac{1}{2}\left(\Pi - [b - c_h]^+\right)$. Note that $w_1^{PPP} < 1$, because $\Pi - [b - c_h]^+ < b - E[c] - [b - c_h]^+ \leq c_h - E[c] < 1$. The payoffs then follow immediately.

(ii) In this case, the principal's expected continuation payoff is $B - c_2 + b - c_h$ regardless of whether or not there was a success. Hence, at date 0 the principal will not offer a bonus to the agent for an innovation ($w_1^{PPP} = 0$). However, the agent still has incentives to exert effort since if $x = 1$ he expects to get the second-stage rent $c_h - E[c] - \frac{\gamma}{1-p}$. Thus, the agent chooses $e_{ii}^{PPP} = \arg\max e\left(c_h - E[c] - \frac{\gamma}{1-p}\right) - \frac{1}{2}e^2 = c_h - E[c] - \frac{\gamma}{1-p}$. The payoffs again follow immediately. ■

Proof of Proposition 3.3

At date 1, agent 1 chooses $e^{TP} = \arg\max_{e\in[0,1]} ew_1^{TP} - \frac{1}{2}e^2 = \min\{w_1^{TP}, 1\}$. The principal will offer a bonus $w_1^{TP} \leq 1$, so that $e^{TP} = w_1^{TP}$. In particular, she sets $w_1^{TP} = \arg\max w_1\left([b - E[c] - \Delta]^+ - w_1\right) + (1 - w_1)\left[b - c_h - \Delta\right]^+$. Hence, $e^{TP} = \frac{1}{2}\left([b - E[c] - \Delta]^+ - [b - c_h - \Delta]^+\right)$. Note that $0 \leq e^{TP} < 1$. The payoffs then follow immediately. ■

Proof of Proposition 3.4

(i) Consider the case $E[c] < b < \tilde{b}$. According to Propositions 3.2 and 3.3, the principal's expected profit is larger in case of a public-private partnership than in case of traditional procurement if $D_i^{pr}(\Delta) := [b - c_h]^+ + \frac{1}{4}\left(\Pi - [b - c_h]^+\right)^2 - [b - c_h - \Delta]^+ - \frac{1}{4}([b - E[c] - \Delta]^+ - [b - c_h - \Delta]^+)^2 \geq 0$. Note that $D_i^{pr}(\Delta) = [b - c_h]^+ + \frac{1}{4}\left(\Pi - [b - c_h]^+\right)^2 - [b - c_h - \Delta] - \frac{1}{4}(c_h - E[c])^2$ for $\Delta \leq b - c_h$, $D_i^{pr}(\Delta) = [b - c_h]^+ + \frac{1}{4}\left(\Pi - [b - c_h]^+\right)^2 - \frac{1}{4}(b - E[c] - \Delta)^2$ for $b - c_h < \Delta \leq b - E[c]$, and $D_i^{pr}(\Delta) = [b - c_h]^+ + \frac{1}{4}\left(\Pi - [b - c_h]^+\right)^2$ for $\Delta > b - E[c]$.

Observe that $D_i^{pr}(0) < 0$. To see this, note that $\Pi < b - E[c]$ and hence $D_i^{pr}(0) = \frac{1}{4}\left(\Pi - [b - c_h]\right)^2 - \frac{1}{4}(c_h - E[c])^2 < 0$ if $b \geq c_h$ and $D_i^{pr}(0) = \frac{1}{4}\Pi^2 - \frac{1}{4}(b - E[c])^2 < 0$ if $b < c_h$. Moreover, observe that $D_i^{pr}(b - E[c]) = [b - c_h]^+ + \frac{1}{4}\left(\Pi - [b - c_h]^+\right)^2 > 0$. Furthermore, $D_i^{pr}(\Delta)$ is continuous and strictly increasing for $\Delta < b - E[c]$. Thus, there exists a unique $\tilde{\Delta}$ such that $D_i^{pr}(\tilde{\Delta}) = 0$, so that the claim follows immediately from a straightforward intermediate value argument.

(ii) Consider the case $b \geq \tilde{b}$. The principal prefers a public-private partnership if $D_{ii}^{pr}(\Delta) := b - c_h - [b - c_h - \Delta]^+ - \frac{1}{4}([b - E[c] - \Delta]^+ - [b - c_h - \Delta]^+)^2 \geq 0$. Observe that $D_{ii}^{pr}(\Delta) = \Delta - \frac{1}{4}(c_h - E[c])^2$ for $\Delta \leq b - c_h$, $D_{ii}^{pr}(\Delta) = b - c_h - \frac{1}{4}(b - E[c] - \Delta)^2$ for $b - c_h < \Delta \leq b - E[c]$, and $D_{ii}^{pr}(\Delta) = b - c_h$ for $\Delta > b - E[c]$. Note that $D_{ii}^{pr}(0) = -\frac{1}{4}(c_h - E[c])^2 < 0$ and $D_{ii}^{pr}(b - E[c]) = b - c_h > 0$. Moreover, $D_{ii}^{pr}(\Delta)$ is continuous and strictly increasing for $\Delta < b - E[c]$. Hence, there exists a unique $\tilde{\Delta}$ such that $D_{ii}^{pr}(\tilde{\Delta}) = 0$ and the claim follows immediately. ■

Proof of Proposition 3.5

(i) The expected welfare given a public-private partnership is larger than under traditional procurement if $D_i^{wf}(\Delta) := [b - c_h]^+ + \frac{3}{8}\left(\Pi - [b - c_h]^+\right)^2 - [b - c_h - \Delta]^+ - \frac{3}{8}([b - E[c] - \Delta]^+ - [b - c_h - \Delta]^+)^2 \geq 0$. Note that $D_i^{wf}(\Delta) = [b - c_h]^+ + \frac{3}{8}\left(\Pi - [b - c_h]^+\right)^2 - [b - c_h - \Delta] - \frac{3}{8}(c_h - E[c])^2$ for $\Delta \leq b - c_h$, $D_i^{wf}(\Delta) = [b - c_h]^+ + \frac{3}{8}\left(\Pi - [b - c_h]^+\right)^2 - \frac{3}{8}(b - E[c] - \Delta)^2$ for $b - c_h < \Delta \leq b - E[c]$, and $D_i^{wf}(\Delta) = [b - c_h]^+ + \frac{3}{8}\left(\Pi - [b - c_h]^+\right)^2$ for $\Delta > b - E[c]$.

Note that $D_i^{wf}(0) < 0$. To see this, observe that $\Pi < b - E[c]$ and thus $D_i^{wf}(0) = \frac{3}{8}\left(\Pi - [b - c_h]\right)^2 - \frac{3}{8}(c_h - E[c])^2 < 0$ if $b \geq c_h$ and $D_i^{wf}(0) = \frac{3}{8}\Pi^2 - \frac{3}{8}(b - E[c])^2 < 0$ if $b < c_h$. Moreover, notice that $D_i^{wf}(b - E[c]) = [b - c_h]^+ + \frac{3}{8}\left(\Pi - [b - c_h]^+\right)^2 > 0$. Furthermore, $D_i^{wf}(\Delta)$ is continuous and strictly increasing for $\Delta < b - E[c]$. Hence, there exists a unique $\bar{\Delta}$ such that $D_i^{wf}(\bar{\Delta}) = 0$, so that the claim follows immediately.

(ii) Given Propositions 3.2 and 3.3, a public-private partnership leads to a larger expected welfare than traditional procurement if $D_{ii}^{wf}(\Delta, \gamma) := b - c_h + \frac{1}{2}(c_h - E[c] - \frac{\gamma}{1-p})^2 - [b - c_h - \Delta]^+ - \frac{3}{8}([b - E[c] - \Delta]^+ - [b - c_h - \Delta]^+)^2 \geq 0$. Observe that $D_{ii}^{wf}(\Delta, \gamma) = \Delta + \frac{1}{2}(c_h - E[c] - \frac{\gamma}{1-p})^2 - \frac{3}{8}(c_h - E[c])^2$ for $\Delta \leq b - c_h$, $D_{ii}^{wf}(\Delta, \gamma) = b - c_h + \frac{1}{2}(c_h - E[c] - \frac{\gamma}{1-p})^2 - \frac{3}{8}(b - E[c] - \Delta)^2$ for $b - c_h < \Delta \leq b - E[c]$, and $D_{ii}^{wf}(\Delta, \gamma) = b - c_h + \frac{1}{2}(c_h - E[c] - \frac{\gamma}{1-p})^2$ for $\Delta > b - E[c]$.

Consider any given $\gamma \in (0, p(E[c] - c_l))$. Note that $D_{ii}^{wf}(\Delta, \gamma)$ is continuous and strictly increasing in Δ for $\Delta < b - E[c]$. Moreover, $D_{ii}^{wf}(b - E[c], \gamma) > 0$ and $D_{ii}^{wf}(\Delta, \gamma) < 0$ for Δ sufficiently small. Hence, there exists a $\bar{\Delta}(\gamma)$ such that $D_{ii}^{wf}(\bar{\Delta}(\gamma),\gamma)=0$. Observe that if $\bar{\Delta}(\gamma)\leq -c_l$, then a public-private partnership leads to a larger expected welfare than traditional procurement for all admissible values of Δ. On the other hand, if $\bar{\Delta}(\gamma)>-c_l$, then there exist admissible values $\Delta<\bar{\Delta}(\gamma)$ such that traditional procurement leads to a larger expected welfare than a public-private partnership.

Next, we want to show that $\bar{\Delta}(\gamma)$ is strictly increasing for all $\gamma\in(0,p(E[c]-c_l))$. To see this, observe that $D_{ii}^{wf}(\Delta,\gamma)$ is strictly decreasing in γ for all $\gamma\in(0,p(E[c]-c_l))$. Now consider $\gamma_1<\gamma_2$, so that $D_{ii}^{wf}(\bar{\Delta}(\gamma_1),\gamma_1)=0>D_{ii}^{wf}(\bar{\Delta}(\gamma_1),\gamma_2)$. Since $D_{ii}^{wf}(\bar{\Delta}(\gamma_2),\gamma_2)=0$ and $D_{ii}^{wf}(\Delta,\gamma)$ is strictly increasing in Δ, this implies that $\bar{\Delta}(\gamma_1)<\bar{\Delta}(\gamma_2)$. ■

Proof of Proposition 3.6

(i) Consider first the case $b\leq c_h$. Recall that $\tilde{\Delta}>0$ and $\bar{\Delta}>0$. Thus, $D_i^{pr}(\Delta)=\frac{2}{3}D_i^{wf}(\Delta)=\frac{1}{4}\Pi^2-\frac{1}{4}(b-E[c]-\Delta)^2$, so that $\tilde{\Delta}=\bar{\Delta}=b-E[c]-\Pi$.

Consider next the case $b>c_h$. Note that $\tilde{\Delta}\in(0,b-c_h)$ if $D_i^{pr}(b-c_h)=b-c_h+\frac{1}{4}\left(\Pi-[b-c_h]\right)^2-\frac{1}{4}(c_h-E[c])^2>0$, and $\tilde{\Delta}\in[b-c_h,b-E(c))$ otherwise. Moreover, $\bar{\Delta}\in(0,b-c_h)$ if $D_i^{wf}(b-c_h)=b-c_h+\frac{3}{8}\left(\Pi-[b-c_h]\right)^2-\frac{3}{8}(c_h-E[c])^2>0$, and $\bar{\Delta}\in[b-c_h,b-E(c))$ otherwise. Observe that $D_i^{pr}(b-c_h)>D_i^{wf}(b-c_h)$.

Now suppose $D_i^{wf}(b-c_h)>0$, which implies $D_i^{pr}(b-c_h)>0$, so that $\tilde{\Delta}$ and $\bar{\Delta}$ lie in the interval $(0,b-c_h)$. In this case, $\bar{\Delta}-\tilde{\Delta}=\frac{1}{8}(c_h-E[c])^2-\frac{1}{8}(\Pi-(b-c_h))^2>0$. Suppose next that $D_i^{wf}(b-c_h)\leq 0$ and $D_i^{pr}(b-c_h)>0$. Then $\tilde{\Delta}\in(0,b-c_h)$ and $\bar{\Delta}\in[b-c_h,b-E(c))$, so that $\tilde{\Delta}<\bar{\Delta}$. Finally, suppose that $D_i^{wf}(b-c_h)\leq 0$ and $D_i^{pr}(b-c_h)\leq 0$. Consider $\Delta\in(b-c_h,b-E(c))$, where the functions $D_i^{pr}(\Delta)$ and $D_i^{wf}(\Delta)$ are strictly increasing. Recall that $D_i^{pr}(b-c_h)>D_i^{wf}(b-c_h)$ and, moreover, $D_i^{wf}(b-E[c])>D_i^{pr}(b-E[c])$. It is straightforward to show that $D_i^{pr}(\Delta)=D_i^{wf}(\Delta)$ implies $\Delta=\hat{\Delta}:=2b-E[c]-\Pi-c_h$. The fact that $D_i^{pr}(\hat{\Delta})=b-c_h>0$ then implies that $\tilde{\Delta}<\bar{\Delta}$.

(ii) Recall that $\bar{\Delta}(\gamma)$ is strictly increasing; moreover, it is continuous by the implicit function theorem. Observe that $\lim_{\gamma\to 0}D_{ii}^{wf}(0,\gamma)=\frac{1}{8}(c_h-E[c])^2>\lim_{\gamma\to 0}D_{ii}^{wf}(\bar{\Delta}(\gamma),\gamma)=0$. Since $D_{ii}^{wf}(\Delta,\gamma)$ is strictly increasing in Δ, this means that $\lim_{\gamma \to 0} \bar{\Delta}(\gamma) < 0$. We know from Proposition 3.4 that $\tilde{\Delta} > 0$, hence $\lim_{\gamma \to 0} \bar{\Delta}(\gamma) < \tilde{\Delta}$.

Moreover, $\lim_{\gamma \to p(E[c]-c_l)} \bar{\Delta}(\gamma) > \tilde{\Delta}$. In order to see this, notice that $\tilde{\Delta} \in (0, b - c_h)$ if $D_{ii}^{pr}(b - c_h) = b - c_h - \frac{1}{4}(c_h - E[c])^2 > 0$ which is always the case, since $b - c_h - (c_h - E[c])^2 > 0$ holds for $b \geq \tilde{b}$ (indeed, one can check that $\frac{(b-E[c])^2}{b-pc_l-(1-p)E[c]} < \frac{c_h-E[c]}{1-p}$ for $b = c_h + (c_h - E[c])^2$). Furthermore, observe that $\lim_{\gamma \to p(E[c]-c_l)} \bar{\Delta}(\gamma) \in (0, b - c_h)$ if $\lim_{\gamma \to p(E[c]-c_l)} D_{ii}^{wf}(b - c_h) = b - c_h - \frac{3}{8}(c_h - E[c])^2 > 0$, which also is always satisfied. Hence, $\lim_{\gamma \to p(E[c]-c_l)} D_{ii}^{wf}(\bar{\Delta}(\gamma), \gamma) = \lim_{\gamma \to p(E[c]-c_l)} \bar{\Delta}(\gamma) - \frac{3}{8}(c_h - E[c])^2 = 0$, so that $\lim_{\gamma \to p(E[c]-c_l)} \bar{\Delta}(\gamma) = \frac{3}{8}(c_h - E[c])^2 > \tilde{\Delta} = \frac{1}{4}(c_h - E[c])^2$. The result then follows immediately. ■

4

The Costs and Benefits of Additional Information in Agency Models with Endogenous Information Structures

4.1 Introduction

Agency models with precontractual private information play a central role in modern contract theory.[1] While in the vast majority of models the information structure is exogenously given, more recently a relatively small literature has emerged in which the agent is not privately informed from the outset, but has the ability to acquire private information; i.e., the information structure is endogenous.

We consider two scenarios, in which costly information gathering at the contracting stage is a pure rent seeking activity, because it is commonly known

[1]See the seminal works of Myerson (1981) and Maskin and Riley (1984). See also Laffont and Martimort (2002) and Bolton and Dewatripont (2005) for comprehensive textbooks.

E. I. Hoppe-Fischer, *Essays on Contract Design and Incentive Provision*,
Edition KWV, https://doi.org/10.1007/978-3-658-24133-9_4

that the ex post efficient trade decision does not depend on the state of nature.

In the first scenario, if the agent does not acquire information before the contract is signed, he will not learn the state of nature before trade can take place. In the second scenario, if the agent has not gathered information before signing the contract, he costlessly learns the state of nature before trade can take place. In other words, in the second scenario information gathering is not only a rent-seeking activity in the above-mentioned sense, but it is also only "strategic" according to the classification of Crémer, Khalil, and Rochet (1998a).

We show that there are circumstances under which the agent's expected rent is *smaller* in scenario II than in scenario I; i.e., the agent is worse off when more information becomes available to him over time. In contrast, the principal's expected profit is always weakly larger in scenario II; i.e., she benefits from the fact that the agent costlessly becomes privately informed before trade takes place. If the costs of gathering information at the contracting stage are small, then scenario II leads to a weakly larger expected total surplus than scenario I. However, for intermediate values of information gathering costs, the expected total surplus is weakly larger in scenario I, while the first best is achieved in both scenarios if the information gathering costs are sufficiently large.

In accordance with Crémer and Khalil (1992), strategic information gathering is always deterred in scenario II. However, we find that a principal may well induce costly information acquisition in scenario I, even though this is a pure rent seeking activity in the above-mentioned sense.[2]

[2] Costly information acquisition at the contracting stage is also induced in Crémer, Khalil, and Rochet (1998a), where information gathering is productive (i.e., the ex post efficient trade level depends on the state of nature and the agent does not learn the state before trade can take place). Strategic information gathering occurs with positive probability in Crémer, Khalil, and Rochet (1998b), where however it takes place before the contract is offered. See also Schmitz (2006), who studies information gathering in an incomplete contracting framework.

4.2 The model

Consider a principal who wants an agent to produce the quantity $x \in [0,1]$ of a specific good. Both parties are risk-neutral. If the agent produces the quantity x for the principal, then the principal obtains a return xR and the agent incurs a disutility of production xc. At the outset, while both parties know that the distribution of $c \in \{c_l, c_h\}$ is given by $p = prob\{c = c_l\}$, no one knows the realization of c.

At date 0, nature selects the agent's disutility of production c. At date 1, the principal offers a contract to the agent. At date 2, the agent decides whether ($\lambda = 1$) or not ($\lambda = 0$) he wants to incur information gathering costs γ to learn the realization of his disutility of production. At date 3, the agent decides whether to reject the contract (in which case the principal's and agent's payoffs are 0 and $-\lambda\gamma$, respectively) or whether to accept it. In the latter case, at date 4, production takes place and the principal pays the agent the contractually specified transfer payment t. Then the principal's payoff is $xR - t$ and the agent's payoff is $t - xc - \lambda\gamma$.

We assume throughout that $c_l < c_h < R$. Hence, it is commonly known that $x = 1$ is the first-best trade level, regardless of the state of nature. In other words, costly information gathering has no productive function and is a rent-seeking activity only.

We will compare two scenarios. In scenario I, if the agent does not gather information at date 2, then he will learn the realization of his disutility c only after production has taken place (i.e., when the final payoffs are realized). In scenario II, the agent will costlessly learn the realization of his disutility c at date 3.5, before production takes place.[3] Thus, in scenario II, costly information gathering at date 2 is not only a rent-seeking activity in the above-mentioned sense, but it is also "strategic" in the sense of Crémer, Khalil, and Rochet (1998a).

---

[3]Hence, if he already gathered information at date 2, then he does not learn anything new at date 3.5.

4.3 Scenario I

In scenario I, costly information acquisition at date 2 is the agent's only possibility to learn his type before production takes place.

Suppose first that the principal decides not to induce information acquisition, so production will be independent of the state of nature and the principal offers the agent a contract $[x_0, t_0]$. The principal will maximize her profit $x_0 R - t_0$ subject to the constraints $x_0 \in [0, 1]$,

$$t_0 - x_0 E[c] \geq 0, \qquad \text{(PC)}$$

$$t_0 - x_0 E[c] \geq p \max\{t_0 - x_0 c_l, 0\} + (1-p)\max\{t_0 - x_0 c_h, 0\} - \gamma, \qquad \text{(NIG)}$$

where the (PC) constraint says that the (uninformed) agent will accept the contract and the (NIG) constraint ensures that the agent prefers not to gather information.

Lemma 4.1 *Suppose the principal wants to deter information gathering. Then she sets $x_0 = 1$. Moreover, she sets $t_0 = c_h - \frac{\gamma}{1-p}$ if $\gamma \leq p(E[c] - c_l)$ and $t_0 = E[c]$ otherwise.*

Proof. First observe that $\max\{t_0 - x_0 c_h, 0\} = 0$, because if t_0 was strictly larger than $x_0 c_h$, the principal could increase her profit by reducing t_0 without violating any constraints. Due to (PC), the (NIG) constraint can thus be rewritten as $t_0 - x_0 E[c] \geq p(t_0 - x_0 c_l) - \gamma$. It is easy to see that $x_0 = 1$.[4] If only the (PC) constraint is binding, so that $t_0 = E[c]$, then the (NIG) constraint is satisfied if $\gamma \geq p(E[c] - c_l)$. If only the (NIG) constraint is binding, such that $t_0 = c_h - \frac{\gamma}{1-p}$, then the (PC) constraint is satisfied if $\gamma \leq p(E[c] - c_l)$. ■

If information acquisition were costless ($\gamma = 0$), the principal would have to offer $t_0 = c_h$ if she wants to ensure that the agent has no incentive to gather

[4] Consider a contract $[x_0, t_0]$, where $x_0 < 1$. This contract cannot be optimal. In order to see this, consider the alternative contract $\tilde{x}_0 = 1$, $\tilde{t}_0 = t_0 + (1 - x_0)c_h$. The alternative contract leads to a larger profit for the principal without violating the constraints.

information (so that the uninformed agent gets an expected rent $c_h - E[c] > 0$). The larger is γ, the smaller is the offer that the principal has to make in order to deter information gathering. However, the offer cannot fall below $E[c]$, because otherwise an uninformed agent would reject it.

Next, suppose that the principal wants the agent to gather information. According to the revelation principle, we can confine our attention to direct revelation mechanisms $[x_l, t_l; x_h, t_h]$; i.e., if the agent reports to have disutility c_i, $i \in \{l, h\}$, then the trade level is x_i and the transfer payment is t_i. The principal maximizes her expected profit $p[x_l R - t_l] + (1-p)[x_h R - t_h]$ subject to $x_i \in [0, 1]$,

$$
\begin{aligned}
t_l - x_l c_l &\geq t_h - x_h c_l, && (\text{IC}_l)\\
t_h - x_h c_h &\geq t_l - x_l c_h, && (\text{IC}_h)\\
t_l - x_l c_l &\geq 0, && (\text{PC}_l)\\
t_h - x_h c_h &\geq 0, && (\text{PC}_h)\\
p[t_l - x_l c_l] + (1-p)[t_h - x_h c_h] - \gamma &\geq t_l - x_l E[c], && (\text{IG}_l)\\
p[t_l - x_l c_l] + (1-p)[t_h - x_h c_h] - \gamma &\geq t_h - x_h E[c], && (\text{IG}_h)
\end{aligned}
$$

where the (IC) constraints ensure truthful reporting, the (PC) constraints ensure that the contract is accepted, and the (IG) constraints say that the agent has an incentive to gather information.

Lemma 4.2 *Suppose the principal wants to induce information gathering. Consider the case* $\gamma \leq p(E[c] - c_l)$. *If* $R - c_h < p(R - c_l)$, *then* $x_l = 1$, $x_h = 0$, $t_l = c_l + \frac{\gamma}{p}$, $t_h = 0$. *If* $R - c_h \geq p(R - c_l)$, *then* $x_l = 1$, $x_h = 1 - \frac{\gamma}{p(E[c]-c_l)}$, $t_l = c_h - \frac{\gamma}{1-p}$, $t_h = c_h x_h$. *In the case* $\gamma > p(E[c] - c_l)$, *it is impossible to induce information gathering.*

Proof. Observe first that the (PC_l) constraint is redundant, as it is implied by (IC_l) and (PC_h). We ignore the (IC_h) constraint (which will turn out to be satisfied by the solution). Note that the (PC_h) constraint must be binding (otherwise, we could decrease t_h and t_l by the same small amount), hence

$t_h = x_h c_h$. Thus, the reduced problem is to maximize $p[x_l R - t_l] + (1 - p)x_h[R - c_h]$ subject to $x_i \in [0,1]$,

$$t_l - x_l c_l \geq x_h(c_h - c_l), \quad \text{(IC}_l\text{)}$$

$$(1-p)(x_l c_h - t_l) \geq \gamma, \quad \text{(IG}_l\text{)}$$

$$t_l - x_l c_l \geq x_h(c_h - c_l) + \frac{\gamma}{p}. \quad \text{(IG}_h\text{)}$$

Obviously, (IC$_l$) is redundant, as it is implied by (IG$_h$). It is easy to see that $x_l = 1$.[5] Hence, the principal's problem is to maximize $p[R - t_l] + (1 - p)x_h[R - c_h]$ subject to $x_h \in [0,1]$,

$$t_l \leq c_h - \frac{\gamma}{1-p}, \quad \text{(IG}_l\text{)}$$

$$t_l \geq x_h(c_h - c_l) + c_l + \frac{\gamma}{p}. \quad \text{(IG}_h\text{)}$$

Note that information gathering can be induced only if $\gamma \leq p(E[c] - c_l)(1 - x_h)$. Hence, if $\gamma > p(E[c] - c_l)$, then it is impossible to induce information gathering. Consider the case $\gamma \leq p(E[c] - c_l)$. Observe that (IG$_h$) will always be binding, because otherwise the principal would reduce t_l. The principal thus maximizes $x_h[R - c_h - p(R - c_l)] + p(R - c_l) - \gamma$ subject to $0 \leq x_h \leq 1 - \frac{\gamma}{p(E[c]-c_l)}$. Hence, she sets $x_h = 0$ if $R - c_h < p(R - c_l)$ and $x_h = 1 - \frac{\gamma}{p(E[c]-c_l)}$ otherwise. ■

Consider the case $R - c_h < p(R - c_l)$. In a standard adverse selection model in which the agent is privately informed at the outset (or if $\gamma = 0$), the principal would offer a contract such that trade would occur at price c_l in the good state of nature only (so that the agent gets no rent). If the principal wants to induce costly information acquisition, she has to increase the price in order to compensate the agent for his information gathering costs.

Next, consider the case $R - c_h \geq p(R - c_l)$. In a standard adverse selection model, trade would occur at price c_h regardless of the state of nature (so that

[5] Consider a contract where $x_l < 1$. This contract cannot be optimal, since it could be replaced by a contract where $\tilde{x}_l = 1$ and $\tilde{t}_l = t_l + (1 - x_l)c_l$, which would lead to a larger profit without violating any constraints.

the agent's expected rent is $c_h - E[c]$). If the principal wants to induce costly information gathering, $x_l = x_h = 1$ can no longer be the solution, because then the agent would prefer to stay uninformed and claim to be of the type that obtains the larger transfer payment. Hence, the principal must induce a downward distortion in the bad state of nature.

Lemma 4.1 and Lemma 4.2 imply the following result.

Proposition 4.1 *If $\gamma \leq \frac{1-p}{2-p}[p(R-c_l) - R + c_h]$, then the principal induces information gathering by offering the contract $x_l = 1$, $x_h = 0$, $t_l = c_l + \frac{\gamma}{p}$, $t_h = 0$. Otherwise, the principal does not induce information gathering. In this case, she sets $x_0 = 1$. Moreover, she sets $t_0 = c_h - \frac{\gamma}{1-p}$ if $\gamma \leq p(E[c] - c_l)$ and $t_0 = E[c]$ if $\gamma > p(E[c] - c_l)$.*

Proof. If $\gamma > p(E[c] - c_l)$, it is impossible to induce information gathering. Consider $\gamma \leq p(E[c] - c_l)$. When the principal induces information gathering, her expected profit is $p(R - c_l) - \gamma$ if $R - c_h < p(R - c_l)$ and it is $(R - c_h)(1 - \frac{\gamma}{p(c_h - c_l)}) + \frac{p}{1-p}\gamma$ if $R - c_h \geq p(R - c_l)$. When she does not induce information gathering, her expected profit is $R - c_h + \frac{\gamma}{1-p}$. The proposition follows immediately. ■

Consider the case $R - c_h < p(R - c_l)$. In a standard adverse selection problem, the trade level would depend on the state of nature ($x_l = 1$, $x_h = 0$); i.e., the parties make use of the agent's private information. Accordingly, in our setting where private information does not exist at the outset but has to be acquired at some cost, the principal will induce the agent to gather information if the costs γ of doing so are sufficiently small.

Next, consider the case $R - c_h \geq p(R - c_l)$. In this case the principal does not induce costly information acquisition,[6] since even in a standard adverse selection setting where the information were freely available, the trade level would not depend on the state of nature ($x_l = x_h = 1$).

[6] To see this formally, note that in the present case $\gamma \leq \frac{1-p}{2-p}[p(R - c_l) - R + c_h]$ cannot be satisfied.

4.4 Scenario II

In scenario II, the agent costlessly learns his type at date 3.5. Due to Lemma 1 in Crémer and Khalil (1992), we can confine attention to contracts that avoid costly information gathering at date 2. Intuitively, a contract that induces information gathering can always be replaced by one that does not do so and that allows the agent to opt out after he has learned his type at date 3.5.

We consider again direct revelation mechanisms $[x_l, t_l; x_h, t_h]$. The principal chooses the contract that maximizes her expected profit $p[x_l R - t_l] + (1 - p)[x_h R - t_h]$ subject to $x_i \in [0, 1]$,

$$\begin{aligned} t_l - x_l c_l &\geq t_h - x_h c_l, && (\text{IC}_l) \\ t_h - x_h c_h &\geq t_l - x_l c_h, && (\text{IC}_h) \\ p[t_l - x_l c_l] + (1-p)[t_h - x_h c_h] &\geq 0, && (\text{PC}) \\ p[t_l - x_l c_l] + (1-p)[t_h - x_h c_h] &\geq p \max\{t_l - x_l c_l, 0\} + (1-p) \\ &\quad \cdot \max\{t_h - x_h c_h, 0\} - \gamma, && (\text{NIG}) \end{aligned}$$

where the (IC) constraints ensure that the agent truthfully reports his type at date 4, the (PC) constraint ensures that the (uninformed) agent accepts the contract at date 3, and the (NIG) constraint deters information gathering.

Proposition 4.2 *Consider the case $\gamma \leq p(E[c] - c_l)$. If $R - c_h \geq p(R - c_l)$, then $x_l = x_h = 1$, $t_l = t_h = c_h - \frac{\gamma}{1-p}$. If $R - c_h < p(R - c_l)$, then $x_l = 1$, $x_h = \frac{\gamma}{p(E[c]-c_l)}$, $t_l = c_l + \frac{\gamma}{p}$, $t_h = x_h c_h - \frac{\gamma}{1-p}$. Next, consider the case $\gamma > p(E[c] - c_l)$. Then $x_l = x_h = 1$, $t_l = t_h = E[c]$.*

Proof. It follows from (IC$_l$) and (PC), that $t_l - x_l c_l$ cannot be negative. Hence, the (NIG) constraint can be rewritten as $(1 - p)[t_h - x_h c_h] \geq (1 - p) \max\{t_h - x_h c_h, 0\} - \gamma$. Since $\gamma \geq 0$, the (NIG) constraint can thus be replaced by the constraint $\gamma \geq (1 - p)[x_h c_h - t_h]$. We ignore (IC$_h$), which will be satisfied by the solution of the reduced problem. W.l.o.g., we can assume that (IC_l) is binding, so that $t_l = t_h - (x_h - x_l)c_l$.[7] Hence, the reduced problem is to maximize $x_l p[R - c_l] + x_h[pc_l + (1-p)R] - t_h$ subject to $x_i \in [0,1]$,

$$p[t_h - x_h c_l] + (1-p)[t_h - x_h c_h] \geq 0, \quad \text{(PC)}$$

$$\gamma \geq (1-p)[x_h c_h - t_h]. \quad \text{(NIG)}$$

Obviously, the principal sets $x_l = 1$. If only (PC) is binding, such that $t_h = x_h E[c]$, then the principal's profit is $p(R - c_l) + x_h(1-p)(R - c_h)$, so that she will set $x_h = 1$. This is the solution if (NIG) is satisfied, which is the case when $\gamma > p(E[c] - c_l)$. Next, consider the case $\gamma \leq p(E[c] - c_l)$, so that (NIG) must be binding. Hence, $t_h = x_h c_h - \frac{\gamma}{1-p}$. The principal's problem is then to maximize $p[R - c_l] + x_h[R - c_h - p(R - c_l)] + \frac{\gamma}{1-p}$ subject to $x_h \in [0,1]$ and $x_h \geq \frac{\gamma}{p(E[c]-c_l)}$. Thus, if $R - c_h \geq p(R - c_l)$, then $x_h = 1$. If $R - c_h < p(R - c_l)$, the principal sets $x_h = \frac{\gamma}{p(E[c]-c_l)}$. ■

Consider the case $R - c_h < p(R - c_l)$, so that in a standard adverse selection problem where the agent knows his type at the outset (or if $\gamma = 0$), the principal would introduce a downward distortion of the trade level in the bad state of nature ($x_l = 1$, $x_h = 0$), leaving no rent to the agent. If γ is prohibitively large, the situation turns into a standard hidden information problem, where the principal can extract the first-best total surplus ($x_l = x_h = 1$). Accordingly, in our setting the quantity x_h that maximizes the principal's profit is increasing in γ and the agent obtains no rent.

Next, consider the case $R - c_h \geq p(R - c_l)$, so that in a standard adverse selection model, the trade level would not depend on the state of nature and the principal would pay c_h to the agent (who would thus enjoy a rent in the good state). If information gathering is costly, the principal will still implement $x_l = x_h = 1$, but the larger is γ, the more she can reduce the pay-

[7] To see this, consider a feasible contract where $t_l > t_h - (x_h - x_l)c_l$. This contract can be replaced by an alternative contract where $\tilde{t}_l = pt_l + (1-p)[t_h - (x_h - x_l)c_l]$ and $\tilde{t}_h = pt_l + (1-p)t_h + p(x_h - x_l)c_l$. This contract leads to the same expected profit for the principal and does not violate any side constraints.

ment to the agent (as long as it does not fall below $E[c]$), since the agent would have to incur costs γ in order to be able to reject the offer in the bad state.

4.5 Comparison of the scenarios

Propositions 4.1 and 4.2 immediately imply the following result, which is illustrated in Figure 4.1.

Proposition 4.3 *(i) If* $R - c_h < p(R - c_l)$ *and* $\frac{1-p}{2-p}[p(R - c_l) - R + c_h] < \gamma \leq p(E[c] - c_l)$*, then scenario II (where the agent costlessly learns his type at date 3.5) leads to a decrease of the agent's expected rent, to an increase of the principal's expected profit, and to a smaller expected total surplus compared to scenario I.*

(ii) If $R - c_h < p(R - c_l)$ *and* $\gamma \leq \frac{1-p}{2-p}[p(R - c_l) - R + c_h]$*, then scenario II leads to an increase of the principal's expected profit and to a larger expected total surplus compared to scenario I. The agent's expected rent is always zero.*

(iii) Otherwise, scenarios I and II do not differ and lead to the first-best total surplus.

Consider the case $R - c_h < p(R - c_l)$. For sufficiently small information gathering costs ($\gamma \leq \underline{\gamma}$), in scenario I the principal induces the agent to gather information and implements $x_l = 1$, $x_h = 0$ as in a standard adverse selection problem. Yet, the larger is γ, the more the principal has to pay to the agent as a compensation for his information gathering expenses, and the smaller is the expected total surplus. For larger information gathering costs ($\gamma > \underline{\gamma}$), the principal deters information gathering in order to implement $x_l = x_h = 1$. Hence, the first-best surplus is realized. When γ increases it becomes easier to deter information gathering and hence the principal can extract a larger fraction of the total surplus. For very large information gathering costs ($\gamma > \overline{\gamma}$), the principal can fully extract the first-best surplus.

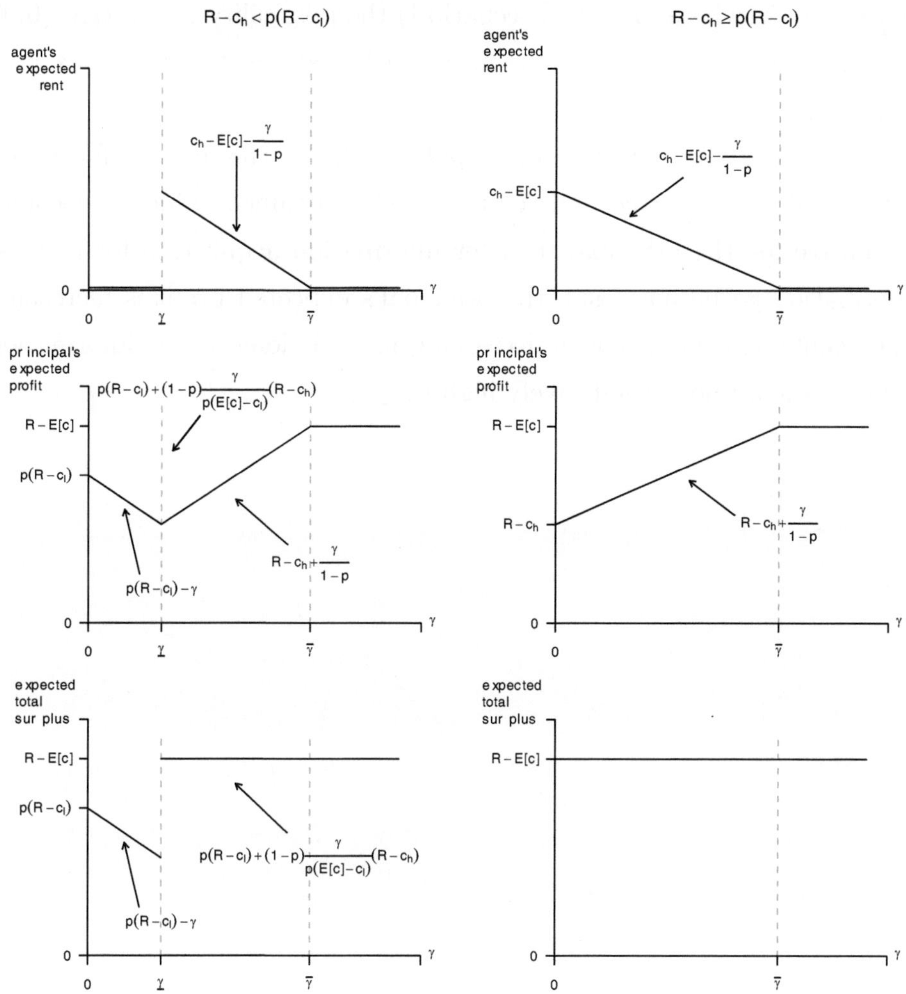

Figure 4.1. The parties' expected payoffs and the expected total surplus as functions of the information gathering costs γ, where $\underline{\gamma} = \frac{1-p}{2-p}[p(R-c_l)-R+c_h]$ and $\overline{\gamma} = p(E[c]-c_l)$. The solid curves correspond to scenario I, while the dotted curves depict scenario II.

In scenario II, the agent costlessly learns the state of nature at date 3.5. Hence, the trade level can now be state-dependent, $x_l = 1, x_h \in (0,1)$, even though the principal always deters costly information gathering. If $\gamma \leq \underline{\gamma}$, so that $x_h = 0$ in scenario I, the principal can use the new possibility to set $x_h \in (0,1)$ in order to increase the total surplus, whereas in the intermediate range $\underline{\gamma} < \gamma \leq \overline{\gamma}$ (where $x_h = 1$ in scenario I) the possibility to set $x_h \in (0, 1)$ enables the principal to extract the agent's rent, at the expense of ex post efficiency.

Next, consider the case $R - c_h \geq p(R - c_l)$. In this case, information gathering is always deterred and the first best is attained. Since it becomes less expensive for the principal to deter information acquisition for increasing information gathering costs, the principal's expected profit is increasing and the agent's expected rent is decreasing in γ, as long as the information gathering costs are not prohibitively high ($\gamma \leq \overline{\gamma}$).

Part II

Contract Design and Incentive Provision: Experimental Evidence

5

Can Contracts Solve the Hold-Up Problem? Experimental Evidence

5.1 Introduction

How to induce trading partners to make relationship-specific investments is a central theme in the contract-theoretic literature. A party may have insufficient incentives to make non-contractible investments if it fears that it will be held up by its partner in the future. This hold-up problem is an important ingredient of the incomplete contracting approach, which has become a leading paradigm in institutional and organizational economics.[1] The possibility to solve the hold-up problem contractually has attracted broad interest and has been studied extensively in a vast theoretical literature initiated by Hart and Moore (1988). However, up to now there is scarce empirical evidence about the effectiveness of different contracts in inducing investment incentives. In this chapter, we report about a large-scale laboratory experiment designed to

[1] See the seminal contributions by Grossman and Hart (1986) and Hart and Moore (1990), which build on the pioneering work by Coase (1937) and Williamson (1975, 1985). Cf. Hart (1995) for a comprehensive textbook exposition.

E. I. Hoppe-Fischer, *Essays on Contract Design and Incentive Provision*, Edition KWV, https://doi.org/10.1007/978-3-658-24133-9_5

explore the role of contracts in mitigating the hold-up problem.

We consider a buyer and a seller who can trade one unit of an indivisible good at some future date 2. It is always ex post efficient to trade. At date 1, the seller can make an observable but unverifiable investment that directly improves the buyer's value of the good; i.e., the investment is "cooperative" in the sense of Che and Hausch (1999). We investigate a cooperative investment, because in the theoretical literature it turned out that the difficulty to find a contractual solution to the hold-up problem is particularly severe in this case.[2]

Suppose first that the parties have not written any contract before the investment stage. Then they will negotiate at date 2 in order to realize the ex post gains from trade. According to contract-theoretic reasoning, in this case the seller may have insufficient incentives to invest because he fears that in the negotiation process he will lose a part of the returns created by his investment. Alternatively, the parties might consider to write a fixed-price contract at an initial date 0. But since this contract specifies that the buyer has to purchase the good from the seller for a fixed price at date 2, the seller has no investment incentives at all, because his revenue is independent of his investment. In contrast, the underinvestment problem can be solved if the parties write a simple option contract at date 0, provided that they can commit not to renegotiate the contract. The idea is that the option contract specifies a strike price such that the buyer will exercise the option only if the seller has chosen the first-best investment level. Anticipating the buyer's behavior, the seller will actually choose the first-best investment level, provided that the strike price at least covers his investment costs. However, if renegotiation cannot be ruled out, the buyer might prefer not to exercise the option, because

[2] Specifically, Maskin and Moore (1999) and Che and Hausch (1999) have shown that in the case of cooperative investments there exists no contractual solution at all to mitigate the hold-up problem if the parties cannot commit not to renegotiate. In contrast, Edlin and Reichelstein (1996) have shown that in the case of "selfish" investments (i.e., when the investment directly benefits the investor), the first-best investment can be induced by a suitable contract even if renegotiation cannot be ruled out.

he anticipates that the ex post inefficient no-trade decision will be reversed and that through renegotiations he will obtain a larger share of the gains from trade. The seller in turn anticipates the buyer's behavior and hence he has the same investment incentives as if there were no contract at all.

Our experimental study consists of two parts. In the first part, we study the investment behavior in the four scenarios just described (no contract, fixed-price contract, option contract, option contract with renegotiation) in four different treatments. For simplicity, in the experiment the seller can choose between only two investment levels, where high investment is first-best. To make the hold-up problem most severe, ex post negotiations are such that the buyer makes a take-it-or-leave-it price offer to the seller. Standard contract-theoretic arguments as outlined above imply that (5.1) the fixed-price contract cannot ameliorate the hold-up problem, (5.2) the non-renegotiable option contract solves the hold-up problem, and (5.3) the renegotiable option contract is less effective in mitigating the hold-up problem than the non-renegotiable option contract; in particular, (5.4) investment behavior given a renegotiable option contract is as in the no-contract benchmark. Our central goal is to find out whether these four predictions are borne out by the data.

We find support for predictions (5.1) to (5.3). Yet, we have to reject prediction (5.4): Compared to the no-contract benchmark, the fraction of high investments turns out to be significantly larger given a renegotiable option contract. This result can be explained neither by standard theory nor by common social preference models in which subjects' utilities depend only on their own and other subjects' final payoffs. This is because in the no-contract treatment and in the option contract with renegotiation treatment the attainable payoff allocations are the same.

We will then investigate whether Hart and Moore's (2008) novel idea that contracts can serve as reference points for trading relationships may shed light on the observed differences regarding the investment behavior in the option contract with renegotiation treatment and in the no-contract benchmark. Hart and Moore (2008) argue that an ex ante contract may shape the parties' feelings of entitlement with regard to ex post outcomes. A party that ex post does not get what it feels entitled to will be aggrieved and may be willing to punish its trading partner, even if this is costly and yields no material gain. For our option contract with renegotiation treatment, this may imply that a buyer might exercise the option (or make a renegotiation offer not too much below the strike price), because he fears that a seller who has chosen high investment feels entitled to the strike price, so that if the option was not exercised, the seller would be aggrieved and hence inclined to reject small offers.

In the second part of our experimental study, we report about additional treatments that we have designed in order to explore whether the observed differences between the option contract with renegotiation treatment and the no-contract treatment may be attributed to Hart and Moore's (2008) idea that contracts can serve as reference points. Specifically, we have conducted variants of the no-contract and the option contract with renegotiation treatments in which instead of making a take-it-or-leave-it offer, the buyer can dictate the trade price. In other words, the seller cannot engage in costly punishment by rejecting offers. Moreover, we have conducted further variants of the original no-contract and the option contract with renegotiation treatments in which the strategy method is used to elicitate the sellers' rejection behavior. The above-outlined arguments in the spirit of Hart and Moore's (2008) reference point theory imply that (5) compared to the no-contract benchmark, an option contract has an effect only if the seller has a punishment opportunity and (6) sellers are more likely to reject small price offers when a renegotiable option contract has been signed than in the absence of a contract. We find strong support for prediction (5.5) and weak support for prediction (5.6).

Our study brings together two different strands of literature. First, our prime motivation stems from the ongoing and extensive debate in contract theory whether clever contractual arrangements such as option contracts can mitigate or even solve the hold-up problem. In particular, does contracting have any value if renegotiation cannot be prevented? Building on Maskin and Moore (1999), several authors have argued that renegotiation undermines the ability of any conceivable contract to create investment incentives (see e.g. Hart and Moore, 1999, Segal, 1999, Che and Hausch, 1999, and Segal and Whinston, 2002). In contrast, other authors such as Nöldeke and Schmidt (1995, 1998) and Lyon and Rasmusen (2004) are more optimistic about the possibility to solve the hold-up problem with suitable option contracts.[3] While the debate in the theoretical literature is focused on details of the renegotiation game (e.g., whether or not the option can still be exercised after a renegotiation offer has been turned down), our experiment suggests that writing option contracts can have a value even in a setting where the renegotiation process is such that according to standard theory option contracts would be useless.

Second, our study provides further evidence in line with Hart and Moore's (2008) recent behavioral idea that contracts may serve as reference points.[4] They focus on the trade-off between rigid and flexible contracts in a setting with ex ante uncertainty about the state of nature. A rigid contract specifies a price at which trade will occur. While trade takes place in the good state only, the parties get what they expect, so there is no reason for aggrievement. A flexible contract determines a price range only, so that trade may take place also in the bad state of the world, but aggrievement and costly punishment may occur if a party gets less than it felt entitled to.[5] Fehr, Hart, and Zehnder

[3]See also Hart and Moore (1988), Chung (1991), Rogerson (1992), Hermalin and Katz (1993), Aghion, Dewatripont, and Rey (1994), Edlin and Reichelstein (1996), Bernheim and Whinston (1998), Maskin and Tirole (1999), Tirole (1999), Edlin and Hermalin (2000), MacLeod (2002), Schmitz (2002), Guriev (2003), Wickelgren (2006), Watson (2007), Evans (2008), Ohlendorf (2009), and Aghion et al. (2009) for further contributions to this vital debate.

[4]See also Hart and Moore (2007), Hart (2008, 2009), and Hart and Holmström (2010).

[5]Given a flexible contract, Hart and Moore (2008) assume that a party feels entitled to the best outcome allowed by the contract. Another plausible assumption (cf. Hart and Moore, 2008, p. 33) would be that a party's entitlement is based on his rational expectation of what he receives in equilibrium, along the lines of Koszegi and Rabin (2006). In a recent experiment, Abeler et al. (2009) find support for theories of expectation-based reference-dependent preferences.

(2010) find experimental evidence that largely confirms the novel theory. However, they consider neither non-contractible investments nor renegotiation, on which we focus in our experiment. In particular, to the best of our knowledge, there is not yet any experimental evidence that option contracts may serve as reference points and thereby help to mitigate the hold-up problem.

The remainder of the chapter is organized as follows. Section 5.2 presents the first part of our experimental study, in which we investigate whether suitable contractual arrangements can mitigate the hold-up problem. In the second part of our study (Section 5.3), we explore whether our finding that option contracts can improve investment incentives even if renegotiation cannot be prevented might be attributed to Hart and Moore's (2008) notion that contracts can serve as reference points. Concluding remarks follow in Section 5.4.

5.2 Can contracts solve the hold-up problem?

5.2.1 Experimental design

Motivated by the ongoing debate in contract theory, the main goal of our study is to experimentally investigate the question whether contracts can mitigate or even solve the hold-up problem. To shed light on this question, we have conducted four main treatments.[6] In each treatment, a seller and a buyer can trade one unit of an indivisible good. Before trade, the seller can make a relationship-specific investment $e \in \{e_l, e_h\}$, which is measured by its costs. In particular, the seller can invest either $e_l = 0$€ or $e_h = 8$€. Thereby, the seller influences the buyer's value from consumption of the good. Depending on the seller's investment decision, the buyer's value is either $v(e_l) = 10$€ or $v(e_h) = 22$€. Note that by assumption $v(e_h) - e_h > v(e_l) - e_l > 0$. Hence, the first-best outcome is achieved if high investment ($e = e_h$) is chosen and trade takes place.

[6]The four treatments are variants of the four scenarios studied in the illustrative example in Section I of Che and Hausch (1999).

No contract (NC) treatment. As a benchmark, suppose first that no contract can be written. There are up to four stages. In the first stage, the parties decide simultaneously whether or not to participate in the subsequent trade-relationship. If one or both parties do not participate, the experiment is over and each party makes zero profit. If both parties choose to participate, then in the second stage the seller makes the investment decision $e \in \{0€, 8€\}$. In the third stage, the buyer learns how much the seller has invested; i.e., the buyer learns his valuation $v(e)$. Then the buyer can make a take-it-or-leave-it offer to the seller; i.e., he offers a price p at which he is willing to buy the good (where p can be any integer between zero and the buyer's valuation).[7] In the fourth stage, the seller decides whether he wants to sell the good to the buyer at price p. If the seller accepts the offer, the seller's profit is $p - e$ and the buyer's profit is $v(e) - p$. If the seller rejects the offer, the seller's profit is $-e$ and the buyer makes zero profit.

Fixed-price contract (FP) treatment. There are up to two stages. In the first stage, the seller and the buyer can decide whether or not to accept the following contract: "Seller and buyer agree contractually, that the buyer will purchase the good at price $p = 15€$ in stage 2." If one or both parties do not accept the contract, the experiment is over and each party makes zero profit, while stage 2 follows if both parties accept the contract. In the second stage, the seller makes the investment decision $e \in \{0€, 8€\}$. The parties' profits then follow immediately from the contract and the seller's investment decision. Specifically, the seller's profit is $15€-e$ and the buyer's profit is $v(e) - 15€$.

Option contract (OC) treatment. There are up to three stages. In the first stage, the seller and the buyer can decide whether or not to accept the fol-

[7]In the contract-theoretic literature studying the hold-up problem, some authors have considered the more general case in which the seller (resp., buyer) can make a take-it-or-leave-it offer with some probability α (resp., $1-\alpha$), see e.g. the appendix of Hart and Moore (1999). We have decided to let the seller's bargaining power α be equal to zero, since this makes the hold-up problem most severe (this assumption is also made in the main part of Hart and Moore, 1999).

lowing contract: "The buyer has the option to buy the good at price $p = 15€$ in stage 3." If one or both parties do not accept the contract, the experiment is over and each party makes zero profit, while stage 2 follows if both parties accept the contract. In stage 2, the seller makes the investment decision $e \in \{0€, 8€\}$. In stage 3, the buyer learns how much the seller has invested and then he can decide whether or not to exercise the option. If the option is exercised, the seller's profit is $15€ - e$ and the buyer's profit is $v(e) - 15€$. If the option is not exercised, the seller's profit is $-e$ and the buyer makes zero profit.

Option contract with renegotiation (OCR) treatment. There are up to five stages. The first three stages are as in the OC treatment, except that the consequences of not exercising the option in stage 3 are different now. If the buyer has not exercised the option, then stage 4 follows. In stage 4, the buyer can make a take-it-or-leave-it offer to the seller; i.e., he offers a price p at which he is willing to buy the good (where p can be any integer between zero and the buyer's valuation). In stage 5, the seller decides whether he agrees to trade the good at price p. If the seller accepts the offer, the seller's profit is $p - e$ and the buyer's profit is $v(e) - p$. If the seller rejects the offer, the seller's profit is $-e$ and the buyer makes zero profit.

Figure 5.1 shows the four game trees corresponding to the main treatments.

Subjects, payments, and procedures. In total, 472 subjects participated in these four treatments. Moreover, 488 subjects participated in four additional treatments which were motivated by the results of the main treatments and which will be described in Section 5.3.1. All 960 subjects were students of the University of Cologne from a wide variety of fields of study. The computerized experiment was programmed and conducted with z-Tree (Fischbacher, 2007) and subjects were recruited using ORSEE (Greiner, 2004). A session lasted between 20 and 30 minutes. Subjects were paid on average 13.12€.[8] In each session, half of the participants were randomly assigned to the role of

[8] To ensure non-negative payoffs, in addition to the profit made in the experiment, all subjects were paid a participation fee of 8€.

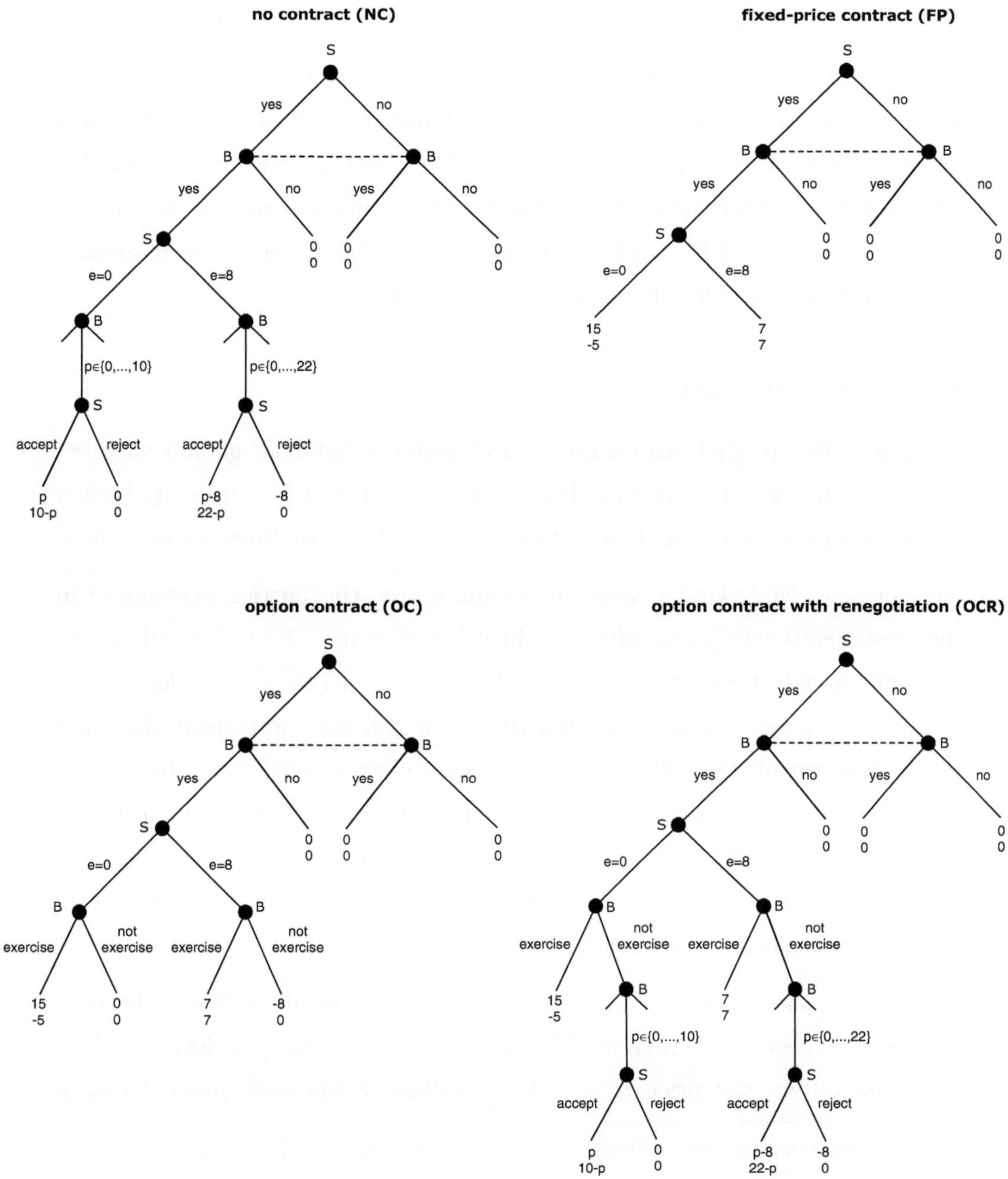

Figure 5.1. The game trees. In the payoff pairs at the end of each branch, the top (resp., bottom) payoff is the seller's (resp., buyer's).

sellers and the others to the role of buyers. Each seller was randomly matched with one buyer. No subject was allowed to participate in more than one session. In order to give subjects a monetary incentive to take their decisions seriously and to ensure a large number of independent observations, each session consisted of only one round; i.e., there were no repetitions and this was known to the subjects. All interactions were anonymous; i.e., no subject knew the identity of its trading partner. At the beginning of each session, written instructions were handed out to each subject.[9]

5.2.2 Predictions

We now derive predictions on how the investment behavior should vary between the different treatments. If it is assumed that it is commonly known that all subjects are rational money-maximizers, the predictions are very clear.

No contract (NC). Under standard assumptions, the parties participate in the trade-relationship and after the investment stage, the seller will accept any offer weakly larger than zero, so that the buyer offers the seller a price $p = 0$€.[10] Anticipating the fact that the buyer will not compensate the seller for his investment, the seller chooses the low investment level $e_l = 0$€.

This means that in the absence of contractual safeguards, no high investments are made. In other words, a hold-up problem occurs, which raises the question whether the following contractual arrangements may be suitable to improve the sellers' investment incentives.

Fixed-price contract (FP). Under standard assumptions, if the fixed-price contract were signed, the seller would choose the low investment level e_l, since he would obtain the price $p = 15$€ regardless of his investment decision.

[9]The instructions of the four main treatments can be found in the appendix.

[10]We make the usual contract-theoretic assumption that a party participates in case of indifference; otherwise the relationship might not be formed. Moreover, since in the experiment 1€ is the smallest monetary unit and the seller is indifferent between accepting and rejecting $p = 0$€, the buyer might also offer $p = 1$€. But still, the seller would never choose the high investment.

But this implies that a buyer will never agree to such a contract, because $p = 15€ > v(e_l) = 10€$. Thus, compared to the no-contract setting, the fixed-price contract cannot enhance the seller's incentives to invest.[11]

Prediction 5.1 *The fixed-price contract cannot mitigate the hold-up problem; i.e., in the FP treatment we will not observe more high investments than in the NC treatment.*

Option contract (OC). If the option contract with the strike price $p = 15€$ is signed, then the buyer will exercise the option if and only if $e = e_h$, because $v(e_l) < p < v(e_h)$. Anticipating the buyer's behavior, the seller invests e_h, because then his payoff is $15€ - 8€$, while it would be only $0€$ if he chose low investment (implying that the option would not be exercised). Since each party then gets a payoff of 7€, both parties sign the contract. Hence, the first-best outcome can be achieved with an option contract.[12] However, this conclusion crucially relies on the assumption that the opportunity to trade is irretrievably forgone once the buyer has not exercised the option; i.e., the parties can commit not to renegotiate.

Prediction 5.2 *The option contract is an effective remedy for the hold-up problem; i.e., in the OC treatment we will observe more high investments than in the NC and in the FP treatments.*

Option contract with renegotiation (OCR). If the buyer decides not to exercise the option, then an ex post inefficiency would occur. When renegotiation cannot be ruled out, the parties will renegotiate to overcome the ex post

[11]More generally, observe that if a fixed-price contract with price p was signed, the seller's profit is $p - e$. Hence, there exists no price p such that the seller has an incentive to invest. In the experiment, we have set $p = 15€$, since this price equalizes the parties' net payoffs given high investment, so it seems to be the price that gives the fixed-price contract the best chance to mitigate the hold-up problem when fairness concerns matter.

[12]More generally, any strike price p such that $\max\{e_h, v(e_l)\} \leq p \leq v(e_h)$ leads to the first-best outcome, because the buyer will exercise the option whenever the seller has chosen high investment and the seller is at least reimbursed for his investment costs e_h. In order to compare the effectiveness of the option contract with the fixed-price contract, we have again chosen $p = 15€$.

inefficiency; i.e., they will agree on trade by bargaining and thus split the surplus $v(e)$ as in the no-contract case. This implies that the buyer will never exercise the option, because in the renegotiations he can make a take-it-or-leave-it offer and thus extract the total surplus.[13] Hence, the seller has the same investment incentives as in the no-contract case. Moreover, the decision whether to sign the contract is strategically equivalent to the participation decision in the NC treatment.

Prediction 5.3 *Contract renegotiation is harmful; i.e., in the OCR treatment we will observe fewer high investments than in the OC treatment.*

Prediction 5.4 *Renegotiation makes contracting redundant; i.e., in the OCR treatment we will observe the same fraction of high investments as in the NC treatment.*

A central goal of our experimental study is to test whether these four predictions based on contract-theoretic reasoning are borne out by the data. In particular, will only a non-renegotiable option contract be able to effectively mitigate the hold-up problem?

In the light of previous experiments on hold-up problems (Hackett, 1993; Ellingsen and Johannesson, 2004a,b), we did not expect all subjects to choose low investment in the NC benchmark treatment, in contrast to standard theory. The occurrence of high investments may be explained by fairness concerns.[14] Since it is not the goal of the present study to test a particular theory

[13] More generally, if the seller's bargaining power α (see footnote 7 above) is sufficiently small, then the buyer will not exercise the option. Specifically, this is the case if $v(e) - p < (1 - \alpha)v(e)$. Hence, the seller's date-1 profit is $\min\{p, \alpha v(e)\} - e$. Note that the best the parties can do is to agree on a price $p \geq \alpha v(e_h)$, so that the seller has the same investment incentives as in the no-contract case. See also Maskin and Moore (1999) and Che and Hausch (1999), who have proven even more general versions of the result that contracting may be useless when renegotiation cannot be ruled out.

[14] See e.g. Fehr and Schmidt (1999), Bolton and Ockenfels (2000), and Charness and Rabin (2002) for prominent models of social preferences. However, Ellingsen and Johannesson (2004a) have shown that the fraction of subjects exhibiting inequity aversion as modelled by Fehr and Schmidt (1999) must be rather large in order to explain high investments

of social preferences, we did not make a specific prediction regarding the fraction of high investments in the NC treatment. The main purpose of the NC treatment is to serve as a benchmark; i.e., we want to find out for our subject pool how large the fraction of high investments is in the absence of a contract, in order to then empirically assess whether suitable contractual arrangements can improve investment incentives over and above this benchmark.

5.2.3 Results

In this section we describe and analyze the results of the four main treatments. Figure 5.2 shows for each treatment how often the trade-relationship was established and how much has been invested. In accordance with previous experimental findings, the observed investment levels in the NC benchmark treatment show that not all sellers choose zero investment, but that there is a relevant share of sellers (41.5%) who prefer to invest high. This finding may not be very surprising, given that there is abundant experimental evidence suggesting that the behavior of a substantial fraction of subjects in the lab can be explained by social preferences. With regard to the FP treatment, we find that the contract was rejected in 28.1% of the cases. It is interesting to note that in all cases in which the contract was not accepted, it was always the buyer who rejected it, as predicted. Given that the fixed-price contract was accepted, 32.6% of the sellers chose the high investment level.[15]

in the absence of contracts. Ewerhart (2006) shows that inequity aversion can solve the hold-up problem if the trade surplus is divided by alternating-offers bargaining with an infinite horizon when agents are sufficiently patient. Von Siemens (2009) investigates a model in which sellers have heterogeneous fairness preferences that are private information. Investments may then affect the buyer's beliefs about the seller's type and hence the buyer's bargaining behavior, which can generate strong incentives to invest.

[15] Note that in the FP treatment, the strategic situation resembles a gift-exchange game. When the buyer decides to accept the contract, he actually pays the seller a fixed wage of 15€, and the seller can (but need not) reward him for doing so by exerting high effort. On gift exchange, see e.g. Akerlof (1982) and Fehr, Kirchsteiger, and Riedl (1993).

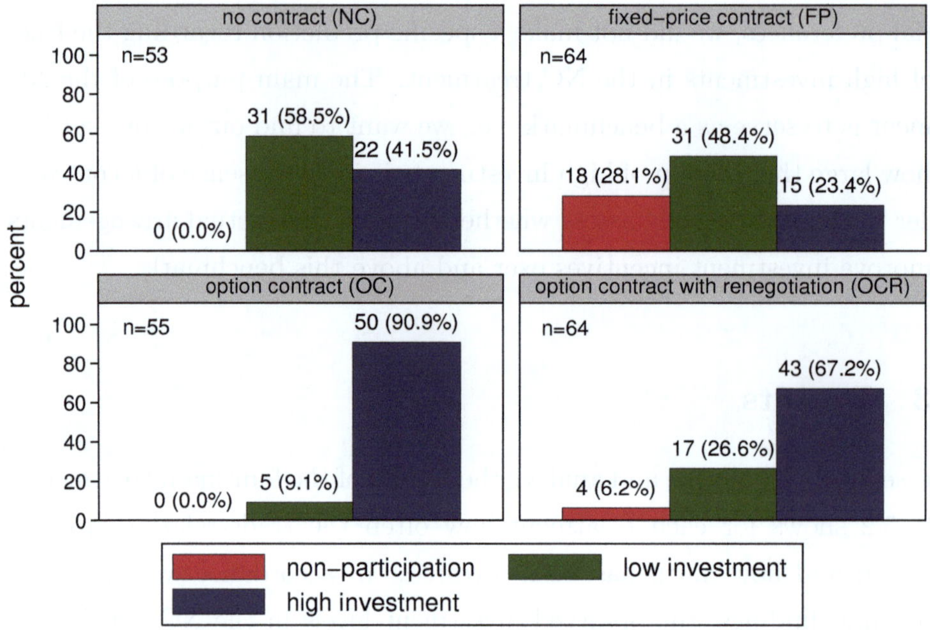

Figure 5.2. Non-participation and investment behavior (n denotes the number of seller-buyer pairs in each treatment).

Furthermore, it is immediate to see that if renegotiation can be ruled out, an option contract is highly effective in inducing investment incentives. The contract was always accepted and there was high investment in 90.9% of the cases. In the OCR treatment, where renegotiation cannot be ruled out, the option contract was rejected in 6.2% of the cases. Conditional on acceptance of the contract, 71.7% of the sellers chose the high investment level.

Table 5.1 reports significance levels with regard to the differences in investment behavior between the treatments. Given that a fixed-price contract was signed, the investment levels in the NC treatment and the FP treatment do not differ significantly. Yet, taking into consideration also the cases in which the fixed-price contract was rejected, the investment levels in the FP treatment are significantly lower. The fact that a fixed-price contract cannot improve investment incentives compared to the no-contract benchmark is in accordance with Prediction 5.1.

Compared to NC (and hence also compared to FP), if renegotiation can be ruled out, then an option contract leads to an extreme improvement in investment incentives, which is highly significant. This result strongly supports Prediction 5.2. If it is possible to prevent renegotiation, then indeed an option contract is very effective in mitigating the underinvestment problem.

	NC vs. FP	NC vs. OC	FP vs. OC	OC vs. OCR	FP vs. OCR	NC vs. OCR
all observations	0.0463	< 0.0001	< 0.0001	0.0018	< 0.0001	0.0086
cond. on particip.	0.4090	< 0.0001	< 0.0001	0.0097	< 0.0001	0.0021

Table 5.1. Significance levels for pairwise comparisons of investment behavior between the treatments. The table reports the p-values according to two-sided Fisher exact tests. In the first row, all observations are taken into consideration, while in the second row, in the FP and OCR treatments only those seller-buyer pairs that accepted the contract are considered.

In the OCR treatment, the chosen investment levels are significantly lower than in the OC treatment, which is in line with Prediction 5.3. This finding provides empirical evidence for the standard contract-theoretic argument that subjects fear to be held-up when renegotiation is possible; i.e., there is a hold-up problem. On the other hand, even if renegotiation cannot be ruled out, it is highly significant that there is more investment if the parties have agreed on an option contract than if there is no contract at all. Hence, we can clearly reject Prediction 5.4.

Figure 5.3 offers a closer look at the data. In particular, it illustrates how often ex post inefficiencies occurred and how the total surplus was split among buyers and sellers in the different treatments. In the four panels, the upper curve represents different combinations of the parties' profits from trading the good given high investment; i.e., different locations of the circles along this curve mark different splits of the total surplus of 14€. Similarly, the lower curve indicates different combinations of the profits from trade given low investment, such that the total surplus is 10€.

First, consider the NC treatment. Observe that given high investment, one offer was rejected, while given low investment, two offers were rejected. The sellers' average profit was 3.55€ given high investment, while it was 3.84€ given low investment; however, the difference in sellers' profits is not statistically significant (p-value=0.9707, two-sided Mann-Whitney U test).

Next, consider the FP treatment. The circle in the origin represents the 28.1% of the cases in which the contract was rejected by the buyer. It is immediate to see that given the contract was signed, the majority of sellers (67.4%) chose low investment. As a result, the average profit of the buyers who accepted the contract was −1.09€, while they could make zero profit by simply rejecting the contract. Hence, rejecting the contract was the more profitable strategy for buyers.

In the OC treatment, in all of the 90.9% of the cases in which the high investment level was chosen the option was actually exercised. When the investment was low, the option was never exercised.

Finally, consider the OCR treatment. The contract was rejected in 6.2% of the cases, as indicated by the circle in the origin. When the contract was signed, three offers were rejected given high investment, while two offers were rejected given low investment. The sellers' average profit in the OCR treatment was 5.07€ given high investment, but it was only 3.47€ given low investment. The difference in the sellers' profits is highly significant (p-value$<$0.0001, two-sided Mann-Whitney U test).

Comparing the panels that illustrate the NC and OCR treatments, one sees immediately that even if renegotiation cannot be ruled out, the option contract strongly influences the split of the surplus given high investment. In the OCR panel, the by far biggest circle corresponds to the case in which the strike price was paid.

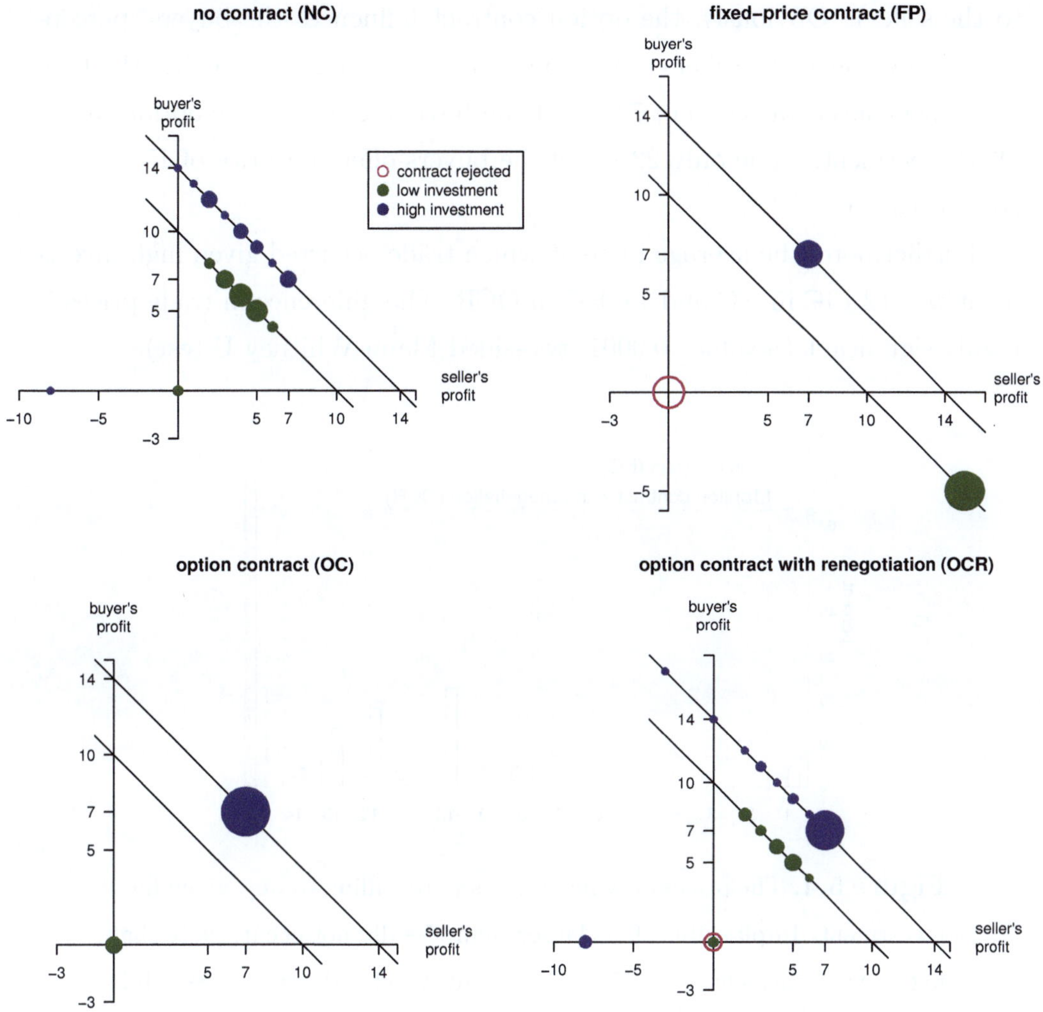

Figure 5.3. Profits of sellers and buyers in the four treatments. The size of the circles represents the number of observations.

Hence, besides that sellers invest more in OCR than in NC, it is also striking that the buyers' behavior differs remarkably between these treatments. Given high investments, Figure 5.4 illustrates for the NC and OCR treatments the distributions of prices at which buyers were willing to buy (i.e., the strike price if the option was exercised in OCR or otherwise the offer made to the seller). Obviously, the option contract influences the buyers' perception of how much the sellers are supposed to get. Indeed, given that the high investment level was chosen, 72.1% of the buyers exercised the option in the OCR treatment, while only 22.7% of the buyers offered a price of 15€ in the NC treatment.

Furthermore, the average price at which trade occurred given high investment was 12.10€ in NC and 14.05€ in OCR. The difference in trade prices is highly significant (p-value=0.0001, two-sided Mann-Whitney U test).

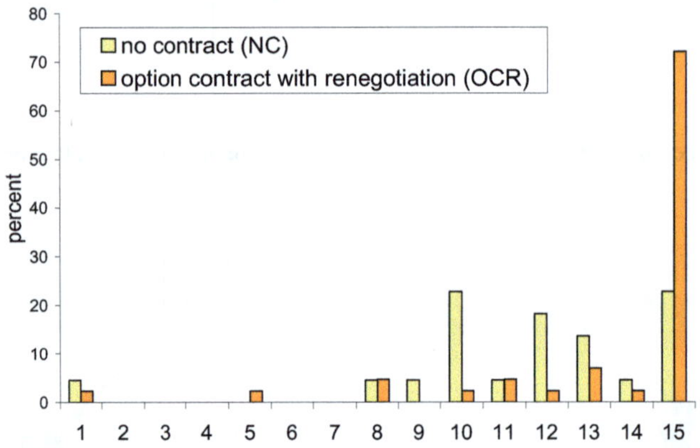

Figure 5.4. The prices at which buyers were willing to buy, given high investment. Implausible offers larger than 15€ did not occur. Note that in the NC treatment, only 27.3% of the buyers offered 14€ or 15€, while in the OCR treatment the option was exercised by 72.1% of the buyers. The average price at which a buyer was willing to buy was 11.73€ in the NC treatment and 13.58€ in the OCR treatment. The difference is statistically significant (p-value=0.0005, two-sided Mann-Whitney U test).

In the next section, we will report about additional treatments that we have carried out in order to investigate whether Hart and Moore's (2008) novel idea that contracts can serve as reference points may shed light on the observed differences between NC and OCR.

5.3 Contracts as reference points

5.3.1 Experimental design and predictions

Let us sum up the results of our four main treatments. The fact that there are high investments already in the no-contract benchmark treatment indicates that social preferences matter for a relevant share of subjects. Yet, the presence of fairness considerations does not invalidate contract-theoretic arguments against fixed-price contracts and in favor of non-renegotiable option contracts as solutions to the hold-up problem. Indeed, we have found strong evidence in support of Predictions 5.1 and 5.2. Moreover, in accordance with Prediction 5.3, the data corroborates the contract-theoretic insight that the impossibility to rule out renegotiation weakens the effectiveness of option contracts to mitigate the hold-up problem. However, we have also found that in the OCR treatment, sellers choose high investment more often than in the NC treatment. This finding is in stark contrast to Prediction 5.4, according to which there should be no difference between OCR and NC.

Observe that in OCR and NC, the buyer has the same possibilities with regard to his price offer, except that in the OCR treatment he first has to decide not to exercise the option. Moreover, the only difference between exercising the option in the OCR treatment and offering a price $p = 15€$ in the NC treatment is that a seller could reject the offer in the latter case; but regardless of the investment level, rejecting an offer of $p = 15€$ is extremely implausible (in fact, an offer of 15€ was never rejected). Hence, neither standard theory nor social preference theories in which subjects' utilities depend only on their own and other subjects' final payoffs can explain why subjects behave differently in the two treatments. In both treatments, a buyer should make the same price offer and, given a seller's expectation about the type of buyer (self-interested or fair-minded) he is going to meet, the seller should choose the same investment level.

However, the observed differences in behavior between OCR and NC might be attributed to Hart and Moore's (2008) recent idea that contracts can serve as reference points. Specifically, if the option contract is perceived as a reference point, then this may lead to more high investments in the OCR treatment. Given that the parties have mutually agreed on the contract, sellers might feel entitled to the strike price when they choose the high investment level. Buyers might then actually exercise the option (or make a price offer not too much below the strike price), because they fear that in case of a (small) renegotiation offer the seller would be aggrieved and hence inclined to reject the offer.[16] This line of reasoning builds on Hart's (2009) argument that if a particular price has been contractually determined (cf. the strike price in OCR) and a lower price is offered in renegotiations, then this triggers a stronger negative response than if the same low price is offered in a setting where no price was made salient from the outset (cf. the NC setting).

Observe, however, that the preceding arguments imply that a renegotiable option contract can improve investment incentives only if the sellers can punish the buyers when they do not exercise the option. In other words, the contract cannot mitigate the hold-up problem when a seller has no opportunity to reject a price dictated by a buyer. Hence, we have conducted the following variants of the NC and OCR treatments in which the buyers can dictate the terms of trade after the investment decision:

Dictatorial no-contract (DNC) treatment. There are up to three stages. The first two stages are as in the NC treatment. In the third stage, the buyer learns his valuation $v(e)$ and then he unilaterally determines the price p at which trade of the good occurs (where p can be any integer between zero and

[16] Note that rejecting the offer is a form of costly punishment and thus related to a "shading" activity in Hart and Moore (2008). They point out (p. 33) that their assumptions regarding shading behavior are not derived from first principles, leaving the microfoundations of the behavioral black box to future research. Note that interdependent preferences (Levine, 1998; Gul and Pesendorfer, 2007) or intention-based reciprocity (Rabin, 1993; Dufwenberg and Kirchsteiger, 2004) might be promising approaches to explore the behavioral black box. In particular, Dufwenberg, Smith, and Van Essen (2010) have recently found experimental support for the role of negative reciprocity in mitigating the hold-up problem, provided that the investor holds the rights of control of his investment proceeds.

the buyer's valuation). The seller's profit is $p - e$ and the buyer's profit is $v(e) - p$.

Option contract with dictatorial renegotiation (OCDR) treatment. There are up to four stages. The first three stages are as in the OCR treatment. If the buyer has not exercised the option, then in stage 4 the buyer unilaterally determines the price p at which trade of the good occurs (where p can be any integer between zero and the buyer's valuation). The seller's profit is $p - e$ and the buyer's profit is $v(e) - p$.

If the option contract serves as reference point in the above-mentioned sense (i.e., buyers are reluctant to make ungenerous renegotiation offers because they fear that sellers might be aggrieved and reject), we can make the following prediction.

Prediction 5.5 *(a) The trade prices and the fractions of high investments do not differ between the OCDR and DNC treatments.*

(b) The prices at which buyers are willing to trade and the fraction of high investments are larger in OCR than in OCDR.

If we find support for Prediction 5.5, then this is in line with a reference point effect in the spirit of Hart and Moore (2008). In a second step, it would then be interesting to investigate whether the buyers' fear that compared to the no-contract treatment, sellers are more likely to reject low price offers in OCR when the option was not exercised, is actually justified. In order to find out whether the sellers' rejection behavior changes once an option contract has been signed, we have conducted two further variants of NC and OCR in which we apply the strategy method to elicitate the sellers' rejection behavior:

No-contract strategy method (NCS) treatment. There are up to three stages. The first stage is as in the NC treatment. If both parties choose to participate, then in the second stage the seller makes the investment decision $e \in \{0€, 8€\}$ and hereafter he decides for any possible price offer p (where p can be any integer between zero and the buyer's valuation) whether or not trade takes place if in stage 3 the buyer offers p. In the third stage, the buyer learns his valuation $v(e)$ and he chooses the price p. If in the second stage the seller had decided to trade at this price, the seller's profit is $p - e$ and the buyer's profit is $v(e) - p$. Otherwise, the seller's profit is $-e$ and the buyer makes zero profit.

Option contract with renegotiation strategy method (OCRS) treatment. There are up to four stages. The first stage is as in the OC treatment. If both parties agree to the contract, then in the second stage the seller makes the investment decision $e \in \{0€, 8€\}$ and hereafter he decides for any possible price offer p (where p can be any integer between zero and the buyer's valuation) whether or not trade takes place if the buyer does not exercise the option and offers p in stage 4. In stage 3, the buyer learns his valuation $v(e)$ and then he can decide whether or not to exercise the option. If the option is exercised, the seller's profit is $15€ - e$ and the buyer's profit is $v(e) - 15€$. If the option is not exercised, then stage 4 follows. In stage 4, the buyer chooses the price p. If in the second stage the seller had decided to trade at this price, the seller's profit is $p - e$ and the buyer's profit is $v(e) - p$. Otherwise, the seller's profit is $-e$ and the buyer makes zero profit.

A reference-point effect in the above-mentioned sense implies that if a particular price has been contractually specified (i.e., the strike price) and a lower price is offered in renegotiations, then this triggers a stronger negative response than if the same low price is offered in a setting without a contract specifying a certain price (cf. Hart, 2009). This leads us to make the following prediction.

Prediction 5.6 *Small price offers are more often rejected in OCRS than in NCS.*

5.3.2 Results

We now report and analyze the results of the four additional treatments that were designed to explore whether the different behavior in NC and OCR may be attributed to the notion that contracts can serve as reference points.

Figure 5.5 shows for the two treatments in which the buyer can dictate a trade price how often the trade-relationship was formed and how much has been invested.

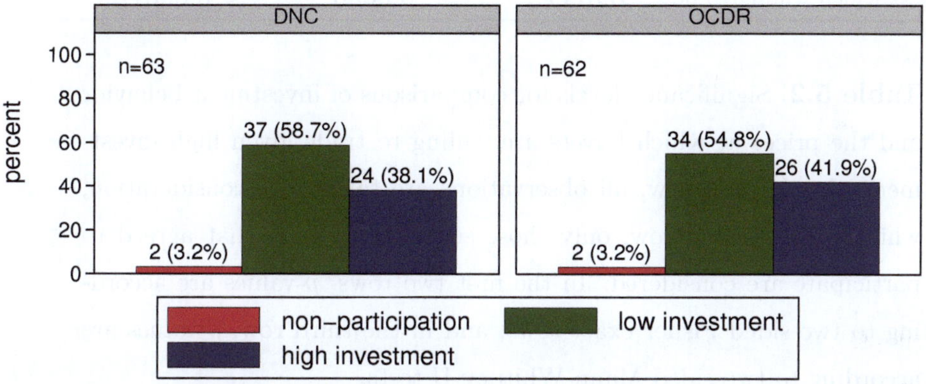

Figure 5.5. Non-participation and investment behavior (n denotes the number of seller-buyer pairs in each treatment).

In the first two rows of Table 5.2 we report the significance levels regarding the differences in investment behavior between treatments. Observe that the investment behavior does not differ significantly between our new benchmark treatment DNC and our previous benchmark NC.[17] However, Figure 5.5 illustrates that if the buyer can dictate the trade price, then a renegotiable option contract can no longer improve investment incentives. Indeed, Table 5.2 shows that the investment behavior does not differ significantly between DNC and OCDR, which is in accordance with Prediction 5.5a. Moreover, in line with Prediction 5.5b, it turns out that the fraction of high investments is significantly larger in OCR, where the seller can reject the buyer's offer, than in OCDR, where costly punishment is not possible.

[17] In future research, it would be interesting to explore a setting with recurrent play, in order to find out whether investments in the dictatorial treatments would decline over time, so that there would then be a more pronounced difference in investment behavior between DNC and NC.

	DNC vs. OCDR	DNC vs. NC	OCDR vs. OCR
investm. (all observations)	0.7168	0.8490	0.0070
investm. (cond. on particip.)	0.7137	0.8499	0.0030
price at which willing to buy	0.3777	0.0030	< 0.0001

Table 5.2. Significance levels for comparisons of investment behavior and the prices at which buyers are willing to trade given high investment. In the first row, all observations are taken into consideration, while in the second row, only those seller-buyer pairs that agreed to participate are considered. In the first two rows, p-values are according to two-sided Fisher exact tests, and in the third row, p-values are according to two-sided Mann-Whitney U tests.

When the buyers have the possibility to dictate the trade price, then given high investment, the average price paid is 7.25€ in DNC and 8.62€ in OCDR. As shown in Table 5.2, the difference between the trade prices in these two treatments is not significant, which is in line with Prediction 5.5a. Hence, mutually agreeing to the option contract which makes the price of 15€ salient does not directly affect the prices at which buyers want to trade. However, given that an option contract has been signed and high investment has been made, the prices at which buyers are willing to trade are significantly larger in OCR than in OCDR; i.e., they are larger when sellers can reject renegotiation offers, which is in accordance with Prediction 5.5b. In particular, in the OCDR treatment, the option was exercised by only 19.2% of the buyers, while in the OCR treatment, the option was exercised by 72.1% of the buyers. The difference is highly significant (p-value<0.0001, two-sided Fisher exact test).

Taken together, the fact that given high investment the buyers are willing to trade at larger prices in OCR than in NC seems to be due to an indirect effect: The buyers fear that the renegotiable option contract changes the sellers' rejection behavior. Hence, we find support for the idea that buyers believe that sellers' feelings of entitlement are influenced by the contract.

Having established that the buyers fear that sellers are more prone to reject small offers in OCR than in NC, the question arises whether this fear is actually justified. To shed some light on this question, we have to resort to the strategy method, since in our main treatments small offers are rare so that we observe only a few rejections. Table 5.3 shows that the sellers' investment behavior as well as the buyers' behavior in NCS and OCRS are qualitatively similar to the corresponding main treatments. However, the differences between NCS and OCRS are less pronounced than the differences between NC and OCR.

	NCS	OCRS
high investment	$\frac{24}{56} = 42.9\%$	$\frac{39}{63} = 61.9\%$
low investment	$\frac{32}{56} = 57.1\%$	$\frac{24}{63} = 38.1\%$
non-participation	0	$\frac{1}{63} = 1.6\%$
price at which willing to buy	12.79€	13.54€

Table 5.3. Investment behavior and non-participation in the strategy method treatments. Pairwise comparisons between the treatments yield p-values 0.0443 for high investments and 0.0418 for high investments conditional on participation (two-sided Fisher exact tests), and 0.2470 for the prices at which buyers were willing to buy (two-sided Mann-Whitney U test).

All sellers except for two in each of the treatments NCS and OCRS had increasing acceptance strategies; i.e., they indicated a minimum acceptable offer such that all smaller (resp., larger) offers were rejected (resp., accepted). When we analyze the sellers' rejection behavior, we take into account only the sellers with increasing acceptance strategies, since presumably the other sellers simply made mistakes.[18]

[18]One omitted seller decided to accept only offers weakly *smaller* than 15 (presumably, he confused rejection with acceptance), while the other three omitted sellers seem to have

Figure 5.6 shows for each possible price offer given high investment the fraction of sellers who were willing to accept the offer. It is striking that the acceptance frequencies in the OCRS treatment are smaller than in the NCS treatment for any given price offer except for the offer $p = 12€$ (in which case the acceptance frequency is 72.97% in OCRS and 72.73% in NCS).[19]

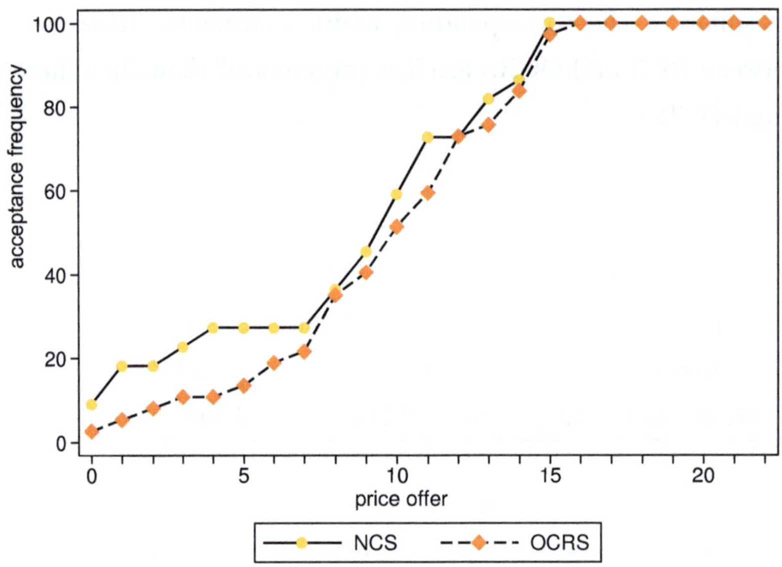

Figure 5.6. Acceptance frequencies per offer given high investment.

In particular, the difference in the acceptance frequencies becomes apparent for price offers smaller than $p = 8€$. While the fact that small offers were more often rejected in OCRS than in NCS is in line with the reference point hypothesis, it should be noted that the difference is only marginally

forgotten to check one or two accept buttons for prices above their minimum acceptable offers. The results do not change qualitatively if we include these four sellers into the analysis.

[19]The average minimum acceptable price offer is 8.68€ in NCS and 9.92€ in OCRS. However, the difference in acceptance rates is not statistically significant when looking at the entire distributions (p-value=0.2203 according to a one-sided Mann-Whitney U test).

significant.[20] However, as already mentioned, when the strategy method is used, the treatment effects that we want to explain (i.e., the differences in the sellers' investment behavior and the buyers' behavior) are less pronounced.[21] Hence, we might expect that when using the strategy method, also the treatment effect with regard to the sellers' rejection behavior might not be as strong as in a setting where subjects have to accept or reject actual offers.[22]

To summarize, exploring the reasons for the differences between OCR and NC, we have found strong evidence for the conjecture that in OCR buyers exercise the option (or make relatively large offers otherwise), because they fear that sellers are more likely to engage in costly punishment by rejecting small offers in OCR than in NC. While a huge number of participants would be required to find out whether this fear is justified in the original setting, the strategy method provides some weak evidence that points in this direction.

5.4 Concluding remarks

The question whether or not suitable contracts can solve or at least mitigate the hold-up problem has been at the center of a long-lasting and controversial debate in the contract-theoretic literature. In this study, we make a first step to address this important question in the laboratory. We consider a setting

[20]If we truncate the distributions and look at acceptances for offers strictly smaller than 8€ only, then the difference in the minimum acceptable offers is marginally significant (p-value=0.0586 according to a one-sided Mann-Whitney U test).

[21]In particular, recall that with regard to the prices at which buyers are willing to buy given high investment, the difference between NC and OCR is highly significant (p-value=0.0005, two-sided Mann-Whitney U test), while it is not significant between NCS and OCRS (p-value=0.2470, two-sided Mann-Whitney U test).

[22]Güth, Huck, and Müller (2001, p. 165) report that the strategy method, which economizes on subjects, may fail to find significant differences in behavioral patterns that are found in the natural design. See also Brandts and Charness (2009), who survey the literature that investigates whether the strategy method and the more natural direct response method lead to different behavior. They conclude that if some treatment effect is found using the strategy method, then it will also manifest using the direct method.

in which the seller's investment influences the buyer's valuation of the good. We find support for the contract-theoretic predictions that, compared to the no-contract benchmark, a fixed-price contract does not improve investment incentives, while a non-renegotiable option contract is very effective in inducing investments. Moreover, also as predicted, the impossibility to prevent renegotiation reduces the effectiveness of the option contract.

However, it turns out that a renegotiable option contract still significantly improves investment incentives compared to the no-contract benchmark. This finding is in contrast to standard contract theory and also cannot be explained by social preference theories in which subjects' utilities depend on their own and other subjects' final payoffs only. Yet, we find support in favor of an explanation along the general lines of Hart and Moore's (2008) idea the contracts can serve as reference points.

Note that in Hart and Moore (2008) for a contract to serve as a reference point it is important that the contract has been concluded in a competitive market. The importance of competition has been confirmed experimentally by Fehr, Hart, and Zehnder (2009). The explanation is that competition insulates a party from blame for the terms of the contract. Yet, in our experiment, the option contract is perceived as a reference point even though its terms have not been negotiated in a competitive market. The difference in findings may not be surprising, given the fact that as a simplification, in our experiment the initial contract is exogenous. The exogeneity of contracts may play the blame-insulation role that competition plays when contracts are endogenous.[23]

Moreover, the fact that given high investment the strike price allowed the parties to share the total surplus evenly, might have had a positive effect on the parties' willingness to accept the price as a reference point. It might be interesting to investigate whether ex ante competition may (further) increase

[23]Note also that in contrast to Fehr, Hart, and Zehnder's (2009) no-competition setting, in our experiment the parties were explicitly asked whether or not they wanted to sign the contract. The fact that they deliberately agreed to the option contract might have strengthened their perception of the strike price as the salient reference point.

the parties' readiness to accept the strike price as a reference point, in particular if the (exogenously given or endogenously determined) strike price were such that exercising the option would lead to an unequal split of the surplus. In future research, we plan to conduct experiments designed to address these questions and to explore the role of additionally allowing for lump-sum payments.[24] Furthermore, in future experimental research we plan to (i) endogenize the choice between different contracts, (ii) assess whether communication may further enhance the effectiveness of contracts,[25] (iii) investigate different renegotiation games, (iv) study the impact of repeated interactions, and (v) explore settings where investments directly affect the investing party.[26]

[24] Note that if a suitable lump-sum payment is chosen, then also a strike price different from 15€ allows the parties to split the total surplus evenly when the seller chooses high investment and the buyer exercises the option.

[25] Note that Ellingsen and Johannesson (2004a,b) and Charness and Dufwenberg (2006, 2010) experimentally confirmed that free-form, personalized statements-of-intent can enhance cooperative behavior.

[26] Segal (1999) and Hart and Moore (1999) have shown that in settings in which investments directly affect the investing party only, the impossibility to rule out renegotiation makes contracting useless if the environment is sufficiently complex. We plan to assess experimentally whether also in this setting contracts can become useful by serving as reference points.

5.5 Appendix

The following instructions were handed out to the participants in the NC treatment:

Experimental instructions

In this experiment there is always one seller who interacts with one buyer. You are randomly assigned either to the role of the seller or to the role of the buyer.

The experiment consists of only one single period.
The period consists of up to four stages.

Stage 1:
On the screen you can see whether you have been assigned to the role of the seller or to the role of the buyer.

Both the seller and the buyer can decide whether or not they want to participate in the trade relationship described in stages 2 to 4.

If one or both parties do not agree to participate, the experiment is over. Then each party makes a profit of 0 €.
If both parties agree to participate in the trade relationship, then stage 2 follows.

Stage 2:
The seller can make an investment decision. He can invest either 0 € or 8 € and thereby he can influence the buyer's valuation for a particular good which can be traded later.
If the seller has invested 0 €, then the buyer's valuation for the good is 10 €.
If the seller has invested 8 €, then the buyer's valuation for the good is 22 €.

Stage 3:
The buyer learns the seller's investment decision and so now he knows his valuation. Then the buyer can make an ultimate price offer p to the seller at which the buyer is willing to buy the good. (The price has to be an integer between zero and the buyer's valuation for the good.)

Stage 4:
The seller can decide whether he wants to sell the good to the buyer at the offered price p. At the end of stage 4, the profits are as follows.

If the seller has invested 0 €:

- If the seller has accepted the offer:
  Seller's profit: p € - 0 € = p €
  Buyer's profit: 10 € - p €
- If the seller has not accepted the offer:
  Seller's profit: 0 €
  Buyer's profit: 0 €

If the seller has invested 8 €:

- If the seller has accepted the offer:
  Seller's profit: p € - 8 €
  Buyer's profit: 22 € - p €
- If the seller has not accepted the offer:
  Seller's profit: -8 €
  Buyer's profit: 0 €

Furthermore, at the end of each of the different experimental instructions, the following information was provided:

Your payoff:
In addition to the (possibly negative) profit realized in the experiment you get 8 € and the resulting amount is paid out to you in cash.

Please note:
During the whole experiment communication is not allowed. If you have a question, please raise your hand out of the cabin. All decisions are anonymous; i.e., no participant ever learns the identity of a person who has made a particular decision. The payment is conducted anonymously, too; i.e., no participant learns what the payoff of another participant is.

The following instructions were handed out to the participants in the FP treatment:

Experimental instructions

In this experiment there is always one seller who interacts with one buyer. You are randomly assigned either to the role of the seller or to the role of the buyer.

The experiment consists of only one single period.
The period consists of up to two stages.

Stage 1:
On the screen you can see whether you have been assigned to the role of the seller or to the role of the buyer.

Both the seller and the buyer can decide whether or not they agree to the following contract: "Seller and buyer agree contractually, that the buyer purchases a particular good at the price of 15 € at the end of stage 2."

If one or both parties do not agree to the contract, the experiment is over. Then each party makes a profit of 0 €.
If both parties agree to the contract, then stage 2 follows.

Stage 2:
The seller can make an investment decision. He can invest either 0 € or 8 € and thereby he can influence the buyer's valuation for the good.
If the seller has invested 0 €, then the buyer's valuation for the good is 10 €.
If the seller has invested 8 €, then the buyer's valuation for the good is 22 €.

At the end of stage 2, the profits result from the signed contract and the investment decision.

If the seller has invested 0 €:
Seller's profit: 15 € - 0 € = 15 €
Buyer's profit: 10 € - 15 € = -5 €

If the seller has invested 8 €:
Seller's profit: 15 € - 8 € = 7 €
Buyer's profit: 22 € - 15 € = 7 €

The following instructions were handed out to the participants in the OC treatment:

Experimental instructions

In this experiment there is always one seller who interacts with one buyer. You are randomly assigned either to the role of the seller or to the role of the buyer.

The experiment consists of only one single period.
The period consists of up to three stages.

Stage 1:
On the screen you can see whether you have been assigned to the role of the seller or to the role of the buyer.

Both the seller and the buyer can decide whether or not they agree to the following contract:
"The buyer has the option to purchase a particular good at the price of 15 € in stage 3."

If one or both parties do not agree to the contract, the experiment is over. Then each party makes a profit of 0 €.

If both parties agree to the contract, then stage 2 follows.

Stage 2:
The seller can make an investment decision. He can invest either 0 € or 8 € and thereby he can influence the buyer's valuation for the good.

If the seller has invested 0 €, then the buyer's valuation for the good is 10 €.
If the seller has invested 8 €, then the buyer's valuation for the good is 22 €.

Stage 3:
The buyer learns the seller's investment decision and so now he knows his valuation. Then the buyer can exercise the option.

At the end of stage 3, the profits are as follows.

If the seller has invested 0 €:

- If the buyer has exercised the option:

Seller's profit: 15 € - 0 € = 15 €

Buyer's profit: 10 € - 15 € = -5 €

- If the buyer has not exercised the option:

Seller's profit: 0 €

Buyer's profit: 0 €

If the seller has invested 8 €:

- If the buyer has exercised the option:

Seller's profit: 15 € - 8 € = 7 €

Buyer's profit: 22 € - 15 € = 7 €

- If the buyer has not exercised the option:

Seller's profit: -8 €

Buyer's profit: 0 €

The following instructions were handed out to the participants in the OCR treatment:

Experimental instructions

In this experiment there is always one seller who interacts with one buyer. You are randomly assigned either to the role of the seller or to the role of the buyer.

The experiment consists of only one single period.
The period consists of up to five stages.

Stage 1:
On the screen you can see whether you have been assigned to the role of the seller or to the role of the buyer.

Both the seller and the buyer can decide whether or not they agree to the following contract:

"The buyer has the option to purchase a particular good at the price of 15 € in stage 3."

If one or both parties do not agree to the contract, the experiment is over. Then each party makes a profit of 0 €.

If both parties agree to the contract, then stage 2 follows.

Stage 2:
The seller can make an investment decision. He can invest either 0 € or 8 € and thereby he can influence the buyer's valuation for the good.

If the seller has invested 0 €, then the buyer's valuation for the good is 10 €.
If the seller has invested 8 €, then the buyer's valuation for the good is 22 €.

Stage 3:
The buyer learns the seller's investment decision and so now he knows his valuation. Then the buyer can exercise the option.

- If the buyer has exercised the option, the experiment is over and the profits are as follows:

If the seller has invested 0 €:

Seller's profit: 15 € - 0 € = 15 €

Buyer's profit: 10 € - 15 € = -5 €

If the seller has invested 8 €:

Seller's profit: 15 € - 8 € = 7 €

Buyer's profit: 22 € - 15 € = 7 €

- If the buyer has not exercised the option, then stage 4 follows.

Stage 4:

Now the buyer can make an ultimate price offer p to the seller at which the buyer is willing to buy the good. (The price has to be an integer between zero and the buyer's valuation for the good.)

Stage 5:

The seller can decide whether he wants to sell the good to the buyer at the offered price p. At the end of stage 5, the profits are as follows.

If the seller has invested 0 €:

o If the seller has accepted the offer:

Seller's profit: p € - 0 € = p €

Buyer's profit: 10 € - p €

o If the seller has not accepted the offer:

Seller's profit: 0 €

Buyer's profit: 0 €

If the seller has invested 8 €:

o If the seller has accepted the offer:

Seller's profit: p € - 8 €

Buyer's profit: 22 € - p €

o If the seller has not accepted the offer:

Seller's profit: -8 €

Buyer's profit: 0 €

6

Conflicting Tasks and Moral Hazard: Theory and Experimental Evidence

6.1 Introduction

In real-world agency problems, it is often the case that principals have to delegate not just one but several tasks. In this chapter we focus on situations in which two different tasks to be delegated may be in direct conflict with each other; i.e., providing effort in one task may have a negative side effect on the success probability of the other task.[1] In such situations, job design becomes a major issue. In particular, it might be the case that implementing effort in both tasks may be facilitated by hiring two different agents each in charge of one task instead of letting one agent be responsible for both tasks. In the

[1] Examples of conflicting tasks abound in the real world. For instance, franchise companies that decide to open a new branch store in close proximity to their existing stores have to investigate carefully to which extent the opening of the new store will affect sales in the existing stores and whether overall company sales will increase. Moreover, when producers of consumer goods have related and competing products in their portfolio, they always have to consider that an advertising campaign for one product may cannibalize the sales levels of their related products.

E. I. Hoppe-Fischer, *Essays on Contract Design and Incentive Provision*,
Edition KWV, https://doi.org/10.1007/978-3-658-24133-9_6

present study we investigate these incentive problems in a theoretical model and provide first experimental evidence that also in the laboratory, where fairness and reciprocity considerations matter, agents are indeed reluctant to perform different tasks when they are in conflict with each other.

To fix ideas, consider a merchant (principal) who wants to sell two products which may be imperfect substitutes. The merchant may hire either one or two sales representatives (agents) who can exert effort to promote the products. The effort decisions are assumed to be non-contractible, but the wages can depend on which products are sold. The agents are risk-neutral and have no wealth, so that the wages must be non-negative. There are no technological (dis-)economies of scope, so that in the absence of incentive problems, the principal would be indifferent between hiring one or two agents.

Suppose first that the merchant has only one sales representative in charge of both products. If the products are imperfect substitutes, then promotion effort in one task increases the probability of sale of the promoted product, but at the same time it lowers the probability of sale of the other product (i.e., there is conflict between the tasks). In contrast, if there is no relation between the products, promotion of one product has no effect on the probability of sale of the other product. We consider a symmetric situation such that in theory, when the products are unrelated (so that there is no conflict), the principal induces either effort in both tasks or no effort at all. However, when there is conflict between the tasks, then it may be optimal for the principal to induce the agent to invest effort in only one task. Intuitively, if there is conflict between the two tasks, a single sales representative is very reluctant to exert effort in both tasks, because he knows that promotion effort does not only increase the probability of sale of the promoted product, but at the same time it also lowers the probability of sale of the other product he is supposed to sell. This makes it very expensive for the principal to induce two efforts.

Suppose next that there are two (identical) sales representatives, each of them responsible for promoting one product. Due to symmetry, in theory the principal induces either effort in both tasks or no effort at all, regardless of whether or not there is conflict.

In general, if there is conflict, it depends on the parameter constellation whether the principal's expected profit is larger with one or with two agents. Yet, if there is no conflict, then the principal's expected profit is unambiguously larger when only one agent is in charge of both tasks. Intuitively, when the tasks are not in conflict with each other, the rent that the principal leaves to the agent to motivate him to work on one task can also be used to motivate him to work on the other task.

In order to find an answer to our research question whether the theoretical incentive problem of inducing a single agent to simultaneously exert efforts in conflicting tasks is empirically relevant, we conducted a laboratory experiment with 474 subjects. There are two treatments with conflict; one where the principal has only a single agent and another one where she has two agents. We have chosen a parameter constellation such that according to standard theory, a merchant who has only one sales representative would induce him to invest effort in only one task, while a merchant with two sales representatives would induce each one to promote his respective product. Moreover, there are two treatments without conflict, one with a single agent and another one with two agents. The theoretical prediction for our parameter constellation is that in the absence of conflict, a merchant would always induce two efforts, regardless of whether she has only one or two sales representatives to perform these tasks.

One central finding of our experiment is that in the one-agent treatment with conflict, two efforts are chosen significantly less often than in the other three treatments. Hence, our experimental data provides strong support for the empirical relevance of the theoretically predicted incentive problem to motivate a single agent to provide efforts in conflicting tasks. However, even in the presence of conflict, a relevant fraction of agents still exerts two efforts. This happens mostly when a principal's wage offer is very generous. Thus, fairness and reciprocity may mitigate the incentive problem. Moreover, in contrast to the theoretical prediction, in the presence of conflict, the principals' average profit is slightly larger in the one-agent treatment than in the two-agent treatment. Two facts contribute to this result. First, the fraction of two efforts in the one-agent treatment with conflict is larger than theoretically predicted, and second, in the two-agent treatment, in sum the principal offers the agents more than in the one-agent treatment. Yet, with regard to the no-conflict treatments, we find significant support for the theoretical prediction that the principals' profits are larger in the case of one agent than in the case of two agents.

Since the seminal work of Holmström and Milgrom (1991), multi-task principal-agent problems have played a prominent role in the contract theoretic literature.[2] However, most of these papers have focused on effort substitution and the trade-off between insurance and incentives when agents are risk-averse. More recently, many authors have studied moral hazard models with risk-neutral but wealth-constrained agents.[3] In the latter framework, several authors have shown that a principal can save agency costs if she lets one agent be in charge of several tasks (see e.g. Hirao, 1993, Che and Yoo, 2001, Laux, 2001, and Mylovanov and Schmitz, 2008).[4] The potential benefits of separating tasks in sequential agency problems have been discussed by Hirao (1993), Schmitz (2005), and Khalil, Kim, and Shin (2006). The fact that conflicts between different tasks may explain why they are delegated to different agents ("advocates") has first been studied by Dewatripont and Tirole (1999). They analyze the optimality of organizing the judicial system in an incomplete contracting framework. The present study is most closely related to a complete contracting variant of their model which is discussed in Bolton and Dewatripont (2005, Section 6.2.2). To the best of our knowledge, only a few experiments on multi-task principal-agent problems have been conducted so far. In particular, Fehr and Schmidt (2004) study a problem where one

[2]For surveys, see e.g. Dewatripont, Jewitt, and Tirole (2000), Laffont and Martimort (2002, ch. 5), and Bolton and Dewatripont (2005, ch. 6).

[3]See e.g. Innes (1990), Pitchford (1998), and Tirole (2001).

[4]See also Dana (1993) and Gilbert and Riordan (1995) who have found related results in other frameworks.

task is contractible and they focus on the pros and cons of piece-rate versus bonus contracts. Brüggen and Moers (2007) investigate the role of financial and social incentives in multi-task settings where agents choose an effort level and an effort allocation.

The remainder of the chapter is organized as follows. The theoretical model which is based on Bolton and Dewatripont (2005) is analyzed in Section 6.2 and serves as a motivation for our experimental study. The experimental design is introduced in Section 6.3 and qualitative hypotheses are derived in Section 6.4. The experimental results are presented and discussed in Sections 6.5 and 6.6. Finally, concluding remarks follow in Section 6.7. All proofs are relegated to Appendix A.

6.2 The model

Consider a principal who wants to sell a single unit of a product 1 and a single unit of a product 2. The sales level for a given product $i \in \{1, 2\}$ is denoted by $q_i \in \{0, 1\}$. If product i is sold, the principal obtains revenue $R > 0$. We consider two different scenarios. In the first scenario the principal employs a single agent to sell products 1 and 2, while she employs two agents in the other scenario. All parties are risk-neutral. An agent has no wealth and his reservation utility is zero. If there is only a single agent, he can exert effort $a_i \in \{0, 1\}$ to promote product $i \in \{1, 2\}$. In case that there are two agents, agent A can promote product 1 and agent B can promote product 2; i.e., A chooses $a_1 \in \{0, 1\}$ and B chooses $a_2 \in \{0, 1\}$. The effort levels are non-contractible.

Effort to promote product i *increases* the probability of sale of product i but (weakly) *lowers* the probability of sale of product $j \neq i$. In other words, there may be a direct conflict between the effort tasks when the products are imperfect substitutes. Formally, let the probability of sale of product i be given by $\Pr(q_i = 1) = \alpha + \rho a_i - \gamma a_j$. The base rate of sale of product i is $\alpha > 0$. If product i is promoted (i.e., $a_i = 1$), the probability of sale of product i increases by $\rho > 0$. If the other product $j \neq i$ is promoted (i.e., $a_j = 1$) and the products are imperfect substitutes, the probability of sale of product i decreases by $\gamma > 0$. When the products are unrelated ($\gamma = 0$), effort to promote one product has no effect on the probability of sale of the other product.

Throughout we assume that $\gamma \leq \alpha \leq 1 - \rho$ to ensure that $0 \leq \alpha + \rho a_i - \gamma a_j \leq 1$ for any combinations of effort decisions a_1 and a_2. An agent has to incur effort costs ψ if he promotes a product i. Hence, product i generates an expected net surplus of $(\alpha + \rho a_i - \gamma a_j)R - a_i\psi$. Due to the symmetry of the model it is either efficient to promote both or no products. We assume $(\rho - \gamma) > \psi/R$ such that $(\alpha + \rho - \gamma)R - \psi > \alpha R$ which implies that the expected total surplus is maximized when both products are promoted (i.e., $a_1 = a_2 = 1$). Hence, if effort were verifiable, the principal would always implement two efforts. Yet, since in our setup effort is not contractible, to induce an agent to exert effort the principal can offer a wage scheme $w_{q_1q_2} := w(q_1, q_2)$ that is contingent only on which products have been sold.

One-agent scenario

Given that the principal has only one agent, she has to decide whether to induce promotion effort in both tasks, in only one task, or in no task.

Let us first consider the case where the principal wishes to induce effort in both tasks. The principal's problem is to minimize the expected compensation $E\left[w_{q_1q_2} \mid a_1 = a_2 = 1\right]$ she has to pay to her agent subject to the constraints $w_{q_1q_2} \geq 0$,

$$E\left[w_{q_1q_2} \mid a_1 = a_2 = 1\right] - 2\psi \geq E\left[w_{q_1q_2} \mid a_1 = 1, a_2 = 0\right] - \psi, \tag{IC 1}$$

$$E\left[w_{q_1q_2} \mid a_1 = a_2 = 1\right] - 2\psi \geq E\left[w_{q_1q_2} \mid a_1 = 0, a_2 = 1\right] - \psi, \tag{IC 2}$$

$$E\left[w_{q_1q_2} \mid a_1 = a_2 = 1\right] - 2\psi \geq E\left[w_{q_1q_2} \mid a_1 = a_2 = 0\right], \tag{IC 3}$$

$$E\left[w_{q_1q_2} \mid a_1 = a_2 = 1\right] - 2\psi \geq 0. \tag{PC}$$

The first two incentive compatibility constraints ensure that the agent prefers exerting two efforts to exerting only one effort and the third one ensures that the agent prefers exerting two efforts to exerting no effort. The last constraint ensures that the agent participates.

Lemma 6.1 *Suppose the principal wants to induce* $a_1 = a_2 = 1$. *Then she sets* $w_{11} = \frac{2\psi}{(\alpha+\rho-\gamma)^2-\alpha^2}$ *and* $w_{10} = w_{01} = w_{00} = 0$. *Given this wage scheme, the principal's expected profit is* $\Pi_{hh} = (\alpha+\rho-\gamma)^2(2R - w_{11}) + 2(\alpha+\rho-\gamma)(1-\alpha-\rho+\gamma)R$.

Suppose next the principal wants to induce effort in only one task. Let us assume w.l.o.g. that the principal wants to induce effort with regard to product 1; i.e., the principal wishes to implement $a_1 = 1, a_2 = 0$. In this case the principal's problem is to minimize $E\left[w_{q_1q_2} \mid a_1 = 1, a_2 = 0\right]$ subject to the constraints $w_{q_1q_2} \geq 0$,

$$E\left[w_{q_1q_2} \mid a_1 = 1, a_2 = 0\right] - \psi \geq E\left[w_{q_1q_2} \mid a_1 = a_2 = 1\right] - 2\psi, \quad \text{(IC 1)}$$

$$E\left[w_{q_1q_2} \mid a_1 = 1, a_2 = 0\right] - \psi \geq E\left[w_{q_1q_2} \mid a_1 = 0, a_2 = 1\right] - \psi, \quad \text{(IC 2)}$$

$$E\left[w_{q_1q_2} \mid a_1 = 1, a_2 = 0\right] - \psi \geq E\left[w_{q_1q_2} \mid a_1 = a_2 = 0\right], \quad \text{(IC 3)}$$

$$E\left[w_{q_1q_2} \mid a_1 = 1, a_2 = 0\right] - \psi \geq 0. \quad \text{(PC)}$$

Lemma 6.2 *Suppose the principal wants to induce* $a_1 = 1$ *and* $a_2 = 0$.[5] *Then it is optimal for her to set* $w_{10} = \frac{\psi}{\alpha\gamma+\rho(1-\alpha+\gamma)}$ *and* $w_{11} = w_{01} = w_{00} = 0$. *Given this wage scheme, the principal's expected profit is* $\Pi_{hl} = (\alpha+\rho)(\alpha-\gamma)2R + (\alpha+\rho)(1-\alpha+\gamma)(R-w_{10}) + (1-\alpha-\rho)(\alpha-\gamma)R$.

Observe that if there is conflict and the principal wants the agent to promote product 1 only, then it is strictly optimal to pay the agent no wage in case that also product 2 is sold. The reason is that effort in task 1 reduces the probability of sale of product 2 and hence the sale of this product can be seen as a signal that the agent may not have promoted product 1. In contrast, if there is no conflict, a wage scheme with $w_{11} = 0$ is not the only solution. This is

---

[5] Note that due to the symmetry of the problem the principal's expected profit is the same if she implements $a_1 = 0$ and $a_2 = 1$.

because then the sale of product 2 provides no signal for the effort level in task 1. Therefore, a positive wage w_{11} can be optimal as long as it does not induce the agent to promote product 2 as well. Specifically, it is easy to show that if $\gamma = 0$, then any wage scheme $0 \leq w_{11} \leq \frac{1+\rho}{\rho(\alpha+\rho)}\psi, w_{10} \geq 0, w_{01} = w_{00} = 0$ which satisfies $\alpha w_{11} + (1-\alpha)w_{10} = \frac{\psi}{\rho}$ is optimal.

Finally the principal could induce no effort at all. It is immediate to see that for this case the optimal wage scheme is simply given by $w_{11} = w_{10} = w_{01} = w_{00} = 0$. Then the principal's expected profit is $\Pi_{ll} = 2\alpha R$.

The preceding discussion immediately implies the following result.

Proposition 6.1 *(i) If* $R > \frac{\psi(\alpha+\rho-\gamma)^2}{[(\alpha+\rho-\gamma)^2-\alpha^2](\rho-\gamma)}$ *and* $R > \frac{2\psi(\alpha+\rho-\gamma)^2}{[(\alpha+\rho-\gamma)^2-\alpha^2](\rho-\gamma)} - \frac{(\alpha+\rho)(1-\alpha+\gamma)\psi}{[\alpha\gamma+\rho(1-\alpha+\gamma)](\rho-\gamma)}$, *then the principal induces effort in both tasks.*

(ii) If $\frac{(\alpha+\rho)(1-\alpha+\gamma)\psi}{[\alpha\gamma+\rho(1-\alpha+\gamma)](\rho-\gamma)} < R < \frac{2\psi(\alpha+\rho-\gamma)^2}{[(\alpha+\rho-\gamma)^2-\alpha^2](\rho-\gamma)} - \frac{(\alpha+\rho)(1-\alpha+\gamma)\psi}{[\alpha\gamma+\rho(1-\alpha+\gamma)](\rho-\gamma)}$, *then the principal induces effort in only one task.*

(iii) Otherwise the principal induces no effort.

It is obvious that the principal will induce promotion for both products if the return is sufficiently large. However for intermediate values of R, if there is conflict, the principal may prefer to induce effort in only one task. The reason is as follows. If the adverse effects of promotion efforts increase, the sale of two products provides weaker evidence that the agent has chosen to exert effort in both tasks, while the sale of only one product provides stronger evidence that the agent has exerted effort to promote this product. As a consequence, if the conflict between tasks increases, it becomes more expensive for the principal to induce the agent to promote both products, while it becomes less expensive to implement effort in only one task.

In contrast, if γ is sufficiently small (in particular, if there is no conflict), the principal will never implement effort in only one task; i.e., the condition in part (ii) cannot be satisfied.

Two-agent scenario

Given that the principal can employ two agents, she has to decide whether to induce both agents to exert effort, whether to provide only one agent with incentives or whether she prefers to induce no efforts at all. The principal will now offer a wage schedule $w^k_{q_1 q_2} := w^k(q_1, q_2)$ with $k \in \{A, B\}$ to the agents. This means she will offer each agent one wage for each possible combination of q_1 and q_2.

Let us first assume the principal wishes to induce agent A to exert effort to promote product 1 and agent B to exert effort to promote product 2. The principal's problem is to minimize the sum of the expected compensation $E\left[w^A_{q_1 q_2} + w^B_{q_1 q_2} \mid a_1 = a_2 = 1\right]$ she has to pay to the agents subject to the constraints $w^k_{q_1 q_2} \geq 0$,

$$E\left[w^A_{q_1 q_2} \mid a_1 = a_2 = 1\right] - \psi \geq E\left[w^A_{q_1 q_2} \mid a_1 = 0, a_2 = 1\right], \tag{IC A}$$

$$E\left[w^B_{q_1 q_2} \mid a_1 = a_2 = 1\right] - \psi \geq E\left[w^B_{q_1 q_2} \mid a_1 = 1, a_2 = 0\right], \tag{IC B}$$

$$E\left[w^A_{q_1 q_2} \mid a_1 = a_2 = 1\right] - \psi \geq 0, \tag{PC A}$$

$$E\left[w^B_{q_1 q_2} \mid a_1 = a_2 = 1\right] - \psi \geq 0. \tag{PC B}$$

The two incentive compatibility constraints ensure that each agent prefers to exert effort to promote his product and the participation constraints ensure that both agents will accept the offered wage scheme.

Lemma 6.3 *Suppose the principal wants to induce* $a_1 = a_2 = 1$. *Then she sets* $w^A_{10} = w^B_{01} = \frac{\psi}{(\alpha+\rho-\gamma)(1-\alpha-\rho+\gamma)-(\alpha-\gamma)(1-\alpha-\rho)}$ *and* $w^k_{11} = w^k_{00} = w^A_{01} = w^B_{10} = 0$. *Given this wage scheme, the principal's expected profit is* $\Pi^{AB}_{hh} = (\alpha + \rho - \gamma)^2 2R + 2(\alpha + \rho - \gamma)(1 - \alpha - \rho + \gamma)(R - w^A_{10})$.

Observe that if there is conflict, then the principal pays an agent a positive wage if and only if the agent was successful in selling his product while the other agent failed. The reason is that in the case of conflict, the failure of an agent to sell his product can be seen as an indication that the other agent has promoted his product, since promotion decreases the probability of sale of the competing agent's product. In contrast, if there is no conflict, a wage scheme with $w^k_{11} = 0$ is not the only one that can be optimal. This is because in the case of no conflict, the success or failure of one agent indicates nothing about the other agent's effort decision. In particular, if $\gamma = 0$, then any wage scheme with $w_{00}^k = w_{01}^A = w_{10}^B = 0$ such that $(1-\alpha-\rho)w_{10}^A + (\alpha+\rho)w_{11}^A = \frac{\psi}{\rho}$ and $(1-\alpha-\rho)w_{01}^B + (\alpha+\rho)w_{11}^B = \frac{\psi}{\rho}$ is optimal.

Suppose next the principal wants to induce effort in only one task. Let us assume w.l.o.g. that the principal wants to induce effort with regard to product 1; i.e., the principal wishes to implement $a_1 = 1, a_2 = 0$. It is obvious that in this case the principal will set $w_{q_1 q_2}^B = 0$ for all possible combinations of q_1 and q_2 such that agent B will not exert effort. Hence, the principal's problem is to minimize $E\left[w_{q_1 q_2}^A \mid a_1 = 1, a_2 = 0\right]$ subject to the constraints $w_{q_1 q_2}^A \geq 0$,

$$E\left[w_{q_1 q_2}^A \mid a_1 = 1, a_2 = 0\right] - \psi \geq E\left[w_{q_1 q_2}^A \mid a_1 = a_2 = 0\right], \qquad \text{(IC A)}$$

$$E\left[w_{q_1 q_2}^A \mid a_1 = 1, a_2 = 0\right] - \psi \geq 0. \qquad \text{(PC A)}$$

Lemma 6.4 *Suppose the principal wants to induce $a_1 = 1$ and $a_2 = 0$. Then it is optimal for her to set $w_{10}^A = \frac{\psi}{\alpha\gamma+\rho(1-\alpha+\gamma)}$ and $w_{11}^A = w_{01}^A = w_{00}^A = w_{q_1 q_2}^B = 0$. Given this wage scheme, the principal's expected profit is $\Pi_{hl}^{AB} = (\alpha+\rho)(\alpha-\gamma)2R + (\alpha+\rho)(1-\alpha+\gamma)(R-w_{10}^A) + (1-\alpha-\rho)(\alpha-\gamma)R$.*

Also with two agents the principal could induce no efforts at all and as in the one-agent case this yields an expected profit of $\Pi_{ll}^{AB} = 2\alpha R$.

It is now straightforward to show that the following result holds.

Proposition 6.2 *(i) If $R > \frac{\psi(\alpha+\rho-\gamma)(1-\alpha-\rho+\gamma)}{[\rho(1-\alpha-\rho)+\gamma(\alpha+\rho-\gamma)](\rho-\gamma)}$, then the principal induces effort in both tasks.*

(ii) Otherwise the principal induces no effort.

Note that if the principal has two agents, then she will never induce only one agent to exert effort. This is obvious in the absence of conflict, because then there is no interaction between the agents, and hence she induces both agents to choose the effort level that she would implement if there were only one agent in charge of one task. If there is conflict, consider a situation where the principal prefers inducing only one effort to inducing no efforts. In such a situation, the principal can always increase her profit further by inducing two efforts. The reason is that if only one agent is induced to exert effort, then even if he deviates, the probability of sale of his product is still relatively large, which makes it expensive for the principal to induce effort. In contrast, if both agents are induced to exert effort, then if an agent chooses low effort, the probability of sale of his product is small due to the adverse effect of the other agent's promotion effort, which makes it less expensive for the principal to induce effort.

Proposition 6.1 and Proposition 6.2 imply the following result.

Proposition 6.3 *There exists a unique* $\hat{\gamma} \in (0, \min\{\alpha, \rho\})$ *such that* $\Pi_{hh}(\hat{\gamma}) = \Pi_{hh}^{AB}(\hat{\gamma})$.

(i) Consider the case $\gamma \leq \hat{\gamma}$. *If* $R > \frac{\psi(\alpha+\rho-\gamma)^2}{[(\alpha+\rho-\gamma)^2-\alpha^2](\rho-\gamma)}$, *then it is optimal for the principal to have one agent and to induce effort in both tasks.*

(ii) Next consider $\gamma > \hat{\gamma}$. *If* $R > \frac{\psi(\alpha+\rho-\gamma)(1-\alpha-\rho+\gamma)}{[\rho(1-\alpha-\rho)+\gamma(\alpha+\rho-\gamma)](\rho-\gamma)}$, *then it is optimal for the principal to have two agents and to induce effort in both tasks.*

(iii) Otherwise it is optimal to induce no efforts and it makes no difference whether the principal has one or two agents.

Observe that if the conflict between the tasks is weak ($\gamma \leq \hat{\gamma}$), then the principal prefers to employ one agent, provided that the return R is sufficiently large such that she wants to induce effort in both tasks.[6] This observation generalizes the well-known result that in the absence of conflict, a principal who wants to delegate several tasks may prefer to assign them to a single agent, because this gives her the possibility to save rents. Specifically, if there are two agents each in charge of one task, then even when there is only one success, the principal has to leave a rent to the successful agent. In contrast, if there is only one agent in charge of both tasks, the principal has to leave a rent to the agent only if he was successful in both tasks.

[6]Note that it is never optimal to hire only one agent and implement only one effort, since this yields the same expected profit as hiring two agents and implementing only one effort, which cannot be optimal according to Proposition 6.2.

Now consider the case where the conflict is strong ($\gamma > \hat{\gamma}$). In this case, inducing two efforts is less expensive for the principal when she hires two agents. Intuitively, consider the limiting case where γ approaches α, so that if only one product is promoted, the probability of sale of the other product approaches zero. This means that in the two-agent case, an agent will almost never sell his product if he shirks, provided that the other agent exerts effort. Hence, the agents' rents tend to zero. In contrast, in the one-agent case, when the agent exerts no effort at all, both products will still be sold with probability α^2. This implies that the principal has to deter the agent from doing so by leaving him a non-negligible rent.

6.3 Experimental design

Our experiment consists of four different treatments. Each treatment was run in four sessions. Each session had 30 participants, except for one session with 28 subjects and one session with 26 subjects (due to no-shows). No subject was allowed to participate in more than one session. In total, 474 subjects participated in the experiment. All subjects were students of the University of Cologne from a wide variety of fields of study. The computerized experiment was programmed and conducted with z-Tree (Fischbacher, 2007) and subjects were recruited using ORSEE (Greiner, 2004). A session lasted between 30 and 40 minutes. Subjects were paid on average 11.03€.[7]

In order to give subjects a monetary incentive to take their decisions seriously and to ensure a large number of independent observations, each session consisted of only one round; i.e., there were no repetitions and this was known to the subjects. In each session there were subjects in the role of principals (merchants) and other subjects in the role of agents (sales representatives). Each principal could sell one single unit of a product 1 and one single unit of a product 2 via a single agent in the one-agent treatments and via two agents in the two-agent treatments. If a product was sold, the principal obtained a

[7]The average payment includes the show-up fee which was 4€.

revenue of $R = 15$€. All interactions were anonymous; i.e., the participants did not know the identity of the subject(s) they were playing with. At the beginning of each session, written instructions were handed out to the subjects.[8] Then they were given 20 minutes to read the instructions and afterwards all participants had to answer some questions to check that they had understood the instructions.

One-agent treatments

In each session, half of the participants are randomly assigned to the role of principals and the others to the role of agents. Each principal is randomly matched with one agent. There are two stages. In the first stage, each principal offers her agent a wage scheme that can be contingent on which products the agent has sold. In particular, the principal sets w_{11}, w_{10} and w_{01}. For w_{11} the principal could choose any number between 0 and 30, while for w_{10} and w_{01}, any numbers between 0 and 15 could be chosen.[9] Since the principal obtains no revenue in the case that no product is sold, the wage w_{00} is set to zero. In the second stage each agent learns the wage scheme his principal has set. Then the agent can exert promotion effort for each of the two products. In particular, the agent can decide whether to promote no product, only one product, or both products. If the agent promotes a product, he has to incur promotion costs $\psi = 2$€. The principal cannot observe the effort decision of her agent. The effect of promotion effort is as follows. If no product is promoted, then each product is sold with a probability of $\alpha = 0.4$. If only one product is promoted, the probability of sale of this product increases by $\rho = 0.5$, while the probability of sale of the other product decreases by γ. If both products are promoted, then each product is sold with probability $\alpha + \rho - \gamma = 0.9 - \gamma$. There is one treatment with $\gamma = 0.3$, which implies that

[8] The instructions of the four different treatments can be found in Appendix C.

[9] All wages could be specified with up to one decimal place. In the experiment, to avoid unlimited losses, the feasible wage offers had to be bounded from above. The stated upper bounds are the ones that arise naturally if also the principal is subject to limited liability. It is easy to show that given the parameter constellations in the experiment, the principal's limited liability constraint will never affect the equilibrium payoffs obtained in Section 6.2.

there is conflict between the two promotion tasks. In another treatment we have $\gamma = 0$, such that there is no conflict between the two tasks. Once the agent has taken the effort decisions with regard to both tasks, the probabilities of sale of the two products are fixed. According to these probabilities the computer decides randomly, whether no, exactly one, or both products are sold. Depending on the wage scheme and on which products are sold, the principal's profit is $15€(q_1 + q_2) - w_{q_1 q_2}$. The agent's profit is given by $w_{q_1 q_2} - 2€(a_1 + a_2)$ and it depends on the wage scheme, on the number of products sold and on the effort decisions regarding both tasks.

Two-agent treatments

In each session, one third of the participants are randomly assigned to the role of principals, another third of the participants are randomly assigned to the role of agents A, and the others are assigned to the role of agents B. Each principal is randomly matched with one agent A and one agent B. The principal pays both agents according to a wage scheme that can be contingent on which products have been sold.

There are two stages. In the first stage, each principal offers her agents A and B a wage scheme that can be contingent on which products are sold. In particular, each principal sets non-negative wages w_{11}^A, w_{10}^A, and w_{01}^A for agent A and w_{11}^B, w_{10}^B, and w_{01}^B for agent B. For the same reasons as explained above, the wages w_{00}^A and w_{00}^B are set to zero, while $w_{11}^A + w_{11}^B$ (resp., $w_{10}^A + w_{10}^B$ and $w_{01}^A + w_{01}^B$) had to be weakly smaller than 30 (resp., 15). In the second stage, each agent learns the wage scheme which the principal has designed. In particular, each agent does not only learn his wage scheme, but he also learns the other agent's wage scheme. Then agent A can decide whether or not to promote product 1 and agent B can decide whether or not to promote product 2. Each agent has to incur promotion costs $\psi = 2€$ if he decides to promote his product. The effect of promotion effort is exactly as in the one-agent treatments. There are again two treatments, one with conflict (where $\gamma = 0.3$) and another one without conflict ($\gamma = 0$). When both agents have taken their effort decision, the probabilities of sale of the two products are fixed.

According to these probabilities the computer decides randomly, whether no, exactly one, or both products are sold. Depending on the wage scheme and on how many products have been sold, the principal's profit is $15€(q_1 + q_2) - w^A_{q_1q_2} - w^B_{q_1q_2}$. The agents' profits $w^A_{q_1q_2} - 2€a_1$ and $w^B_{q_1q_2} - 2€a_2$ depend on the wage scheme, on the number of products that have been sold, and on their respective effort decision.

6.4 Qualitative hypotheses

One agent - Conflict ($\gamma = 0.3$)

According to Proposition 6.1 and Lemma 6.2, under standard theory assumptions, the agent would be induced to exert only one effort. He would get a wage of 3.51€ if only the product he is supposed to promote is sold, and zero otherwise. As a result, the expected wage payment would be 2.84€ and the principal's expected profit would be $\Pi_{hl} \approx 12.16€$. With regard to their structures, we did not expect the wage schemes observed in the experiment to be very close to the theoretical prediction. Taking into consideration the results from many previous experiments,[10] we anticipated that in the laboratory, principals will leave the agents more of the surplus than what in theory would be necessary to induce effort. Specifically, we expected that in our experiment, the principals would set the wages such that an agent obtains a substantial fraction of the revenue if at least one product is sold.[11] This implies that an agent who has exerted effort would not make a loss if at least one product is sold. Yet, we thought that even these more generous wage offers would not induce the majority of agents to exert two efforts. The reason is that agents may be very reluctant to exert two costly efforts because of the adverse effect that effort in one task has on the success probability of the other task. Hence,

---

[10] For recent surveys on fairness and other-regarding preferences in experiments, see e.g. Camerer (2003) and Fehr and Schmidt (2006).

[11] See also Keser and Willinger (2007) who investigate how principals set wages when confronted with a moral hazard problem.

we hypothesized that many agents would exert only one effort and that there would also be a non-negligible fraction of agents exerting no effort at all.

One agent - No conflict ($\gamma = 0$)

As we can see from Proposition 6.1 and Lemma 6.1, according to theory the agent would be induced to exert two efforts. The theoretically predicted wage scheme is such that he would get a wage of 6.15€ if both products are sold and nothing otherwise, leading to an expected wage payment of 4.98€ and to an expected profit of $\Pi_{hh} \approx 22.02$€ for the principal. For similar reasons as explained above, we expected the wage offers in the experiment to be larger than in theory. In the absence of conflict, exerting effort in one task has no adverse effect on the agent's prospects to be successful in the other task. This means, provided that an offer is generous, the probability to sell both products and thus to obtain a relevant share of the revenue of 30€ becomes very likely if the agent exerts two efforts. Hence, in this treatment we actually hypothesized the wage offers to be very effective in inducing two efforts.

Two agents - Conflict ($\gamma = 0.3$)

According to Proposition 6.2 and Lemma 6.3, the theoretical prediction is that both agents would be induced to exert effort. Moreover, an agent would get a wage of 8.70€ whenever only his product is sold and zero otherwise, such that the expected wage payment is 4.17€ and the principal's expected profit is $\Pi_{hh}^{AB} \approx 13.83$€. While we thought again that the wages in the laboratory would be larger, we hypothesized that in line with theory, the vast majority of agents would indeed exert effort. The reason is that in this treatment, the agents might be very inclined to exert effort, since it increases the probability of sale of their own product, while the adverse side effect has an impact only on the probability of sale of the other agent's product. Moreover, if an agent believes that the other agent will exert effort, then his own probability of success would be very low if he shirked.

Two agents - No conflict ($\gamma = 0$)

As we can see from Proposition 6.2 and Lemma 6.3, according to theory, both agents will exert effort. Any wage scheme with $w_{00}^k = w_{01}^A = w_{10}^B = 0$€ such that $0.1w_{10}^{A}+0.9w_{11}^{A} = 4€$ and $0.1w_{01}^{B}+0.9w_{11}^{B} = 4€$ would be optimal, yielding an expected wage payment of 7.20€. The principal's expected profit would be $\Pi_{hh}^{AB} \approx 19.80€$. We expected again that in the experiment the offered wages would be larger and that most agents would indeed exert effort. If an offer is generous, the agent's prospect to get a relevant fraction of the revenue increases considerably if he exerts effort.

The preceding discussion leads us to the following qualitative hypotheses.

Hypothesis 6.1 In the one-agent treatment with conflict, the relative frequency of two efforts will be much lower than in the other three treatments.

Hypothesis 6.2 (i) In the absence of conflict, the principals' average profit will be larger in the one-agent treatment than in the two-agent treatment. (ii) If there is conflict, the principals' average profit will be larger in the two-agent treatment than in the one-agent treatment.

6.5 Data analysis

6.5.1 Experimental results

Figure 6.1 shows the frequencies of zero, one, and two efforts per treatment.[12] The figure concisely illustrates the central finding of our experiment. It is striking that in the one-agent treatment with conflict, two efforts were chosen considerably less often than in the other three treatments. Note that in the other three treatments, two efforts were chosen in the vast majority of the cases, while zero efforts were hardly ever observed. In contrast, in the one-agent case with conflict, two efforts were chosen less often than one effort, and zero efforts were observed in quite a relevant number of cases.

[12] In the one-agent treatments, the average numbers of efforts are 1.13 (conflict) and 1.81 (no conflict). In the two-agent treatments, the average numbers of efforts are 1.73 (conflict) and 1.65 (no conflict).

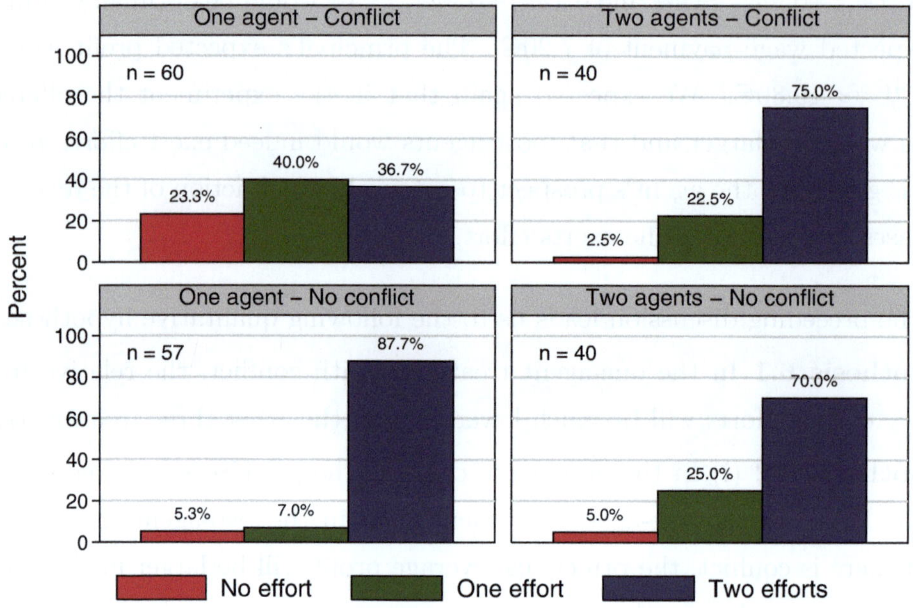

Figure 6.1. Effort levels per treatment (n denotes the number of principal-agent(s) groups per treatment). In the two-agent treatments, 86.3% (resp., 82.5%) of the agents exerted effort if there was conflict (resp., no conflict).

	Percentage of two efforts		p-value
One agent - Conflict vs. Two agents - Conflict	36.7%	75%	0.000
One agent - Conflict vs. One agent - No conflict	36.7%	87.7%	0.000
One agent - Conflict vs. Two agents - No conflict	36.7%	70%	0.002
One agent - No conflict vs. Two agents - Conflict	87.7%	75%	0.174
Two agents - Conflict vs. Two agents - No conflict	75%	70%	0.803
One agent - No conflict vs. Two agents - No conflict	87.7%	70%	0.039

Table 6.1. Significance levels for pairwise comparisons of the shares of two efforts between the treatments. The table reports p-values according to two-sided Fisher exact tests.

As can be seen in Table 6.1, it is highly significant that in the one-agent treatment with conflict, two efforts were chosen less often than in the other treatments, which provides strong support for Hypothesis 6.1.

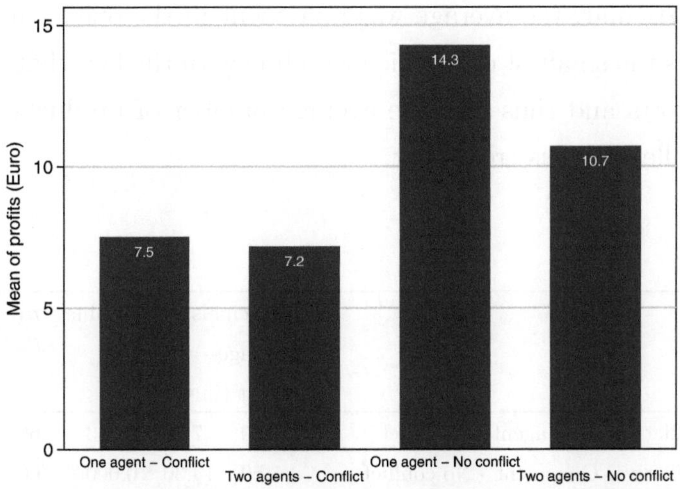

Figure 6.2. The principals' average profits. Recall that the theoretically predicted expected profits are 12.16€, 13.83€, 22.02€, and 19.80€, respectively.

The principals' average profits in the four treatments are shown in Figure 6.2. Observe that in the absence of conflict, the principals' average profit was notably larger if they had only one agent instead of two. The difference is highly significant (see Table 6.2). In line with Hypothesis 6.2(i), this finding provides empirical support for the well-known result that if there is no conflict, then delegation of several tasks to a single agent is profitable, since it gives the principal the possibility to save agency costs. Next observe that, contrary to the theoretical prediction, in the treatments with conflict the principals' average profit was slightly larger if only one agent instead of two was assigned to them. The difference is not statistically significant, though. Note also that the theoretically predicted difference between the expected profits is very small, which made it quite difficult to find support for Hypothesis 6.2(ii).

Finally, the average wage payments that were made to the agents in the four treatments are displayed in Table 6.3. As anticipated, the average payments were larger than the expected wage payments according to standard theory. Yet, the relative order of the magnitudes is exactly as predicted by theory. In particular, the average wage payment in the one-agent treatment with conflict is the smallest one, which is in line with the fact that the average number of efforts and thus also the average number of products a principal sold were smallest in this treatment.

	Principals' average profit (in €)		p-value	n_1	n_2	U
One agent - Conflict vs. Two agents - Conflict	7.50	7.20	0.713	60	40	1147.5
One agent - Conflict vs. One agent - No conflict	7.50	14.30	0.000	60	57	503
One agent - Conflict vs. Two agents - No conflict	7.50	10.70	0.006	60	40	813
One agent - No conflict vs. Two agents - Conflict	14.30	7.20	0.000	57	40	270
Two agents - Conflict vs. Two agents - No conflict	7.20	10.70	0.007	40	40	518.5
One agent - No conflict vs. Two agents - No conflict	14.30	10.70	0.000	57	40	629.5

Table 6.2. Significance levels for pairwise comparisons of the principals' profits between the treatments. The table reports p-values according to two-sided Mann-Whitney U tests.

	One agent - Conflict	Two agents - Conflict	One agent - No conflict	Two agents - No conflict
Average wage payment	7.20	8.60	11.80	12.90
Theoretical prediction	2.84	4.17	4.98	7.20

Table 6.3. Average wage payments in Euro.

6.5.2 Individual wage offers and resulting efforts

One-agent treatments

First of all, it is noteworthy that nearly all wage offers are symmetric.[13] Let us now have a closer look at the symmetric wage offers which for both treatments are illustrated in Figure 6.3. For each offer, the figure also shows the resulting effort choices and the optimal effort choice according to standard theory. The three principles of contract design identified by Keser and Willinger (2000, 2007) are very useful to give an excellent description of the observed wage offers in our experiment. In both treatments, the wage for an agent is always strictly larger when he sells two products than when he sells only one product. This means that principals apply the principle of appropriateness which requires that the payment in case of a high gain is not lower than the payment in case of a low gain. Moreover, most of the principals offer wage schemes that ensure non-negative payoffs to the agent in case that at least one product is sold. For our experiment, this principle of loss avoidance means that principals are reluctant to make wage offers smaller than 4€.[14] In the treatment with (without) conflict, 85.7% (79.2%) of the wage offers are such that w_{10}, w_{01}, and w_{11} are (weakly) larger than 4€. Finally, nearly all wages offers are such that the profit of the principal equals at least 50% of the net surplus. For our experiment, this requires w_{10} and w_{01} to be smaller than 9.50€ and w_{11} to be smaller than 17€.[15] In the treatment with (without) conflict, 94.6% (98.1%)

[13]In the treatment with conflict, only 4 out of 60 offers were asymmetric, and in the treatment without conflict, 4 out of 57 offers were asymmetric. Specifically, the wage offers (w_{10}, w_{01}, w_{11}) were $(8.5, 0, 0)$, $(8.5, 6.5, 18.5)$, $(13, 6, 6)$, and $(4, 2, 9)$ in the treatment with conflict, and $(9, 5, 13)$, $(7, 8, 14)$, $(10, 12, 29)$, and $(4, 7.5, 7.5)$ in the treatment without conflict.

[14]Observe that principals were not able to fully insure agents against losses, since w_{00} was set equal to 0€. However, this design is natural for our experiment, since in case that no product is sold, the principal obtains no revenue which she could share with the agent.

[15]In case one product is sold, the net surplus is minimally 11€ such that the principal does not want to leave more than 5.50€ + 4€ to the agent. Similarly, the principal offers not more than $(30€-4€)/2 + 4€$ when two products are sold.

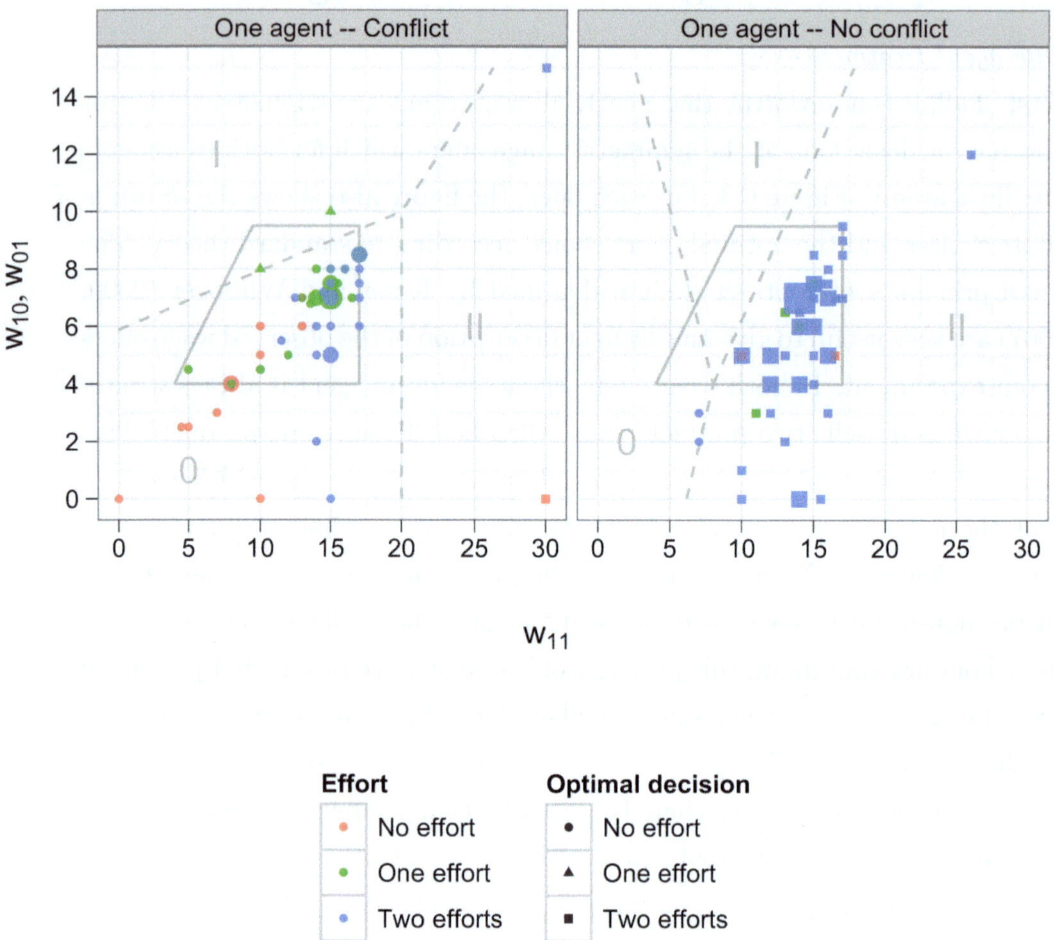

Figure 6.3. Symmetric wage schemes and resulting effort decisions in the one-agent treatments. The actually observed effort decisions are indicated by different colors, while the theoretically optimal effort decisions for given wage offers are indicated by different symbols. The size of the symbols represents the number of observations. The solid line indicates the fair-offers area. The dashed lines divide the panels into three parts where 0, I, or II efforts are optimal given symmetric offers.

of the wage offers are in line with this principle of sharing power. The figure illustrates that the combination of these three principles characterizes a relatively small subset of all possible wage schemes. It is remarkable that in the treatment with (without) conflict, 82.1% (77.4%) of the symmetric wage schemes satisfy all three principles and thus belong to this small subset of possible wage schemes. In the wording of Keser and Willinger (2000), we will refer to this subset of offers as the "fair-offers area."

Now consider the treatment with conflict. Figure 6.3 makes it obvious that if principals intended to make offers in the fair-offers area, then (according to standard contract-theoretic reasoning) it was hardly possible to induce one effort and it was even impossible to induce two efforts. Indeed, taking into account all offers in the fair-offers area, no effort was the best response in 45 out of 46 cases.[16] However, contrary to standard-theoretic reasoning, only six of these 45 agents exerted no effort at all, while 21 agents exerted one effort and 18 agents exerted even two efforts. Hence, we observe that principals make generous wage offers that theoretically do not generate incentives to exert effort, but the vast majority of agents responds to such offers with one or even two efforts. Given offers in the fair-offers area, agents might actually decide to exert effort because they do not risk making a loss and they regard the offer as generous since in case of success, they receive a relevant share of the net surplus. Agents might thus reciprocate the principals' generous offers by effort levels above the theoretical predictions.[17] It is also interesting to compare offers in the fair-offers area that led to one effort with those that led to two efforts. Strikingly, when two efforts were chosen, the difference between w_{11} and $w_{10} = w_{01}$ is 8.74€, while it is only 6.60€ when one effort was chosen ($p = 0.001$, $U = 94$, $n_1 = 20$, $n_2 = 22$, two-sided Mann-Whitney U test). It seems that the stronger principals rewarded the sale of two products

[16] There was only one offer for which it was the agent's best response to exert one effort. Indeed, in this case the agent exerted one effort.

[17] Although the agents did not face fixed wages, note that the situation is related to the gift exchange settings studied by Akerlof (1982) and Fehr, Kirchsteiger, and Riedl (1993).

compared to the sale of one product, the more inclined were agents to choose two efforts. To sum up, in the fair-offers area, agents rewarded the principals for relatively generous offers by exerting one or even two efforts, while the few low wage offers outside of the fair-offers area were reciprocated with no effort.

Next consider the treatment with one agent and no conflict. Figure 6.3 illustrates that all 41 offers in the fair-offers area (77.4% of all 57 offers) were such that it would have been the agent's best response to exert two efforts. Indeed, 36 out of 41 agents that received an offer belonging to the fair-offers area decided to exert two efforts. This result is robust also when we take into account all 57 offers. It was then optimal to exert two efforts in 54 cases, and 48 agents actually decided to do so. In this treatment, it was relatively easy to make offers that belong to the fair-offers area and at the same time create incentives to exert two efforts. The analysis of our data shows that indeed, in the absence of conflict, the majority of principals made such generous and also incentive-compatible offers. The fact that the vast majority of agents exerted two efforts is not very surprising. As can be seen in Table 6.4 in Appendix B, in the absence of conflict, exerting two efforts led to an appreciable profit with a probability of 81% while the probability of making a loss was only 1%. Hence, the majority of agents seemed to perceive this strategy as promising and almost riskless and preferred it to other strategies.

Two-agent treatments

Again we observe that nearly all wage offers are symmetric.[18] Let us first explain Figure 6.4 which shows the symmetric wage offers. Generally, a wage scheme consists of six single wages but since the figure is restricted to symmetric offers, a wage offer is fully characterized by only three wages $w_{11} := w_{11}^A = w_{11}^B$, $w_1 := w_{10}^A = w_{01}^B$, and $w_0 := w_{01}^A = w_{10}^B$. A pair (w_{11}, w_1) appears in a darker shade while each corresponding pair (w_{11}, w_0) is plotted

---

[18] While in the treatment without conflict all wage offers are symmetric, there are four asymmetric wage offers in the treatment with conflict, namely, the asymmetric offers $(w_{10}^A, w_{01}^A, w_{11}^A, w_{01}^B, w_{10}^B, w_{11}^B)$ are $(1, 1.5, 2, 1.5, 1, 2)$, $(5, 4, 10, 6, 4, 10)$, $(4, 2, 7, 4, 0, 7)$, and $(0, 0, 0, 5, 0, 5)$.

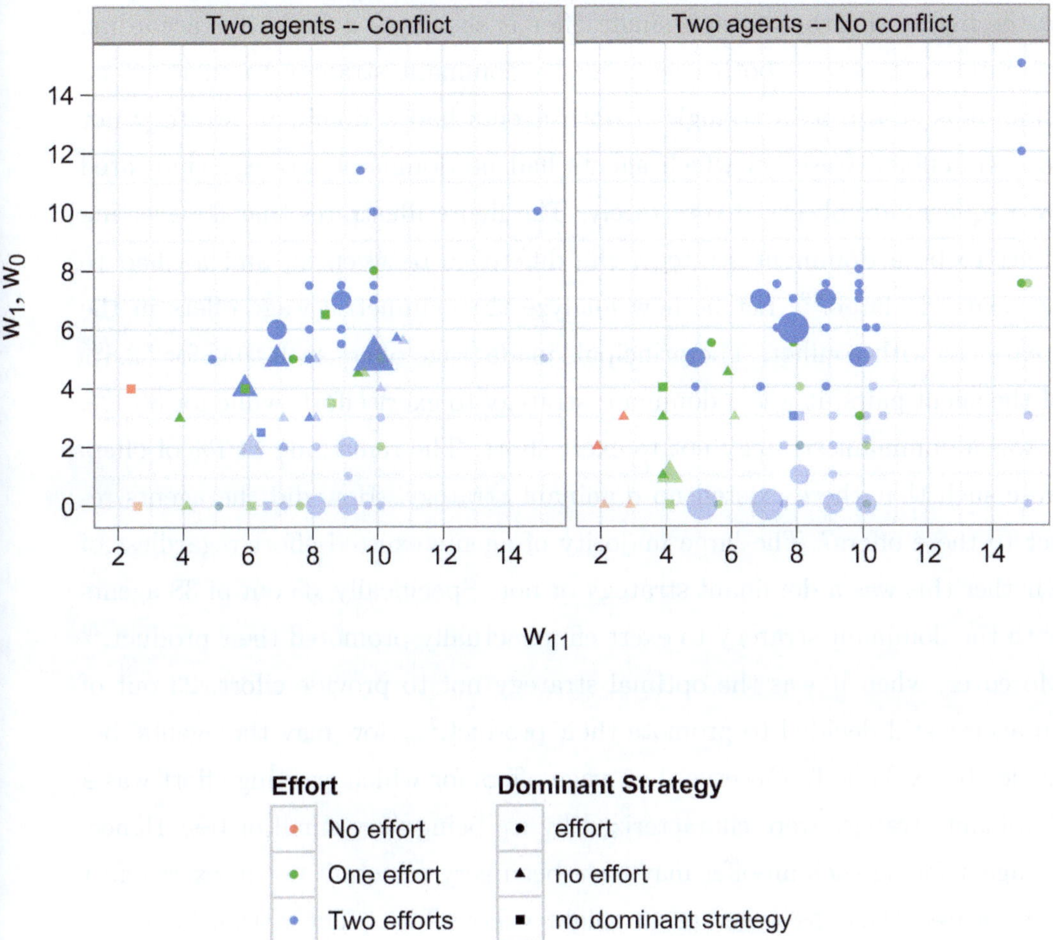

Figure 6.4. Symmetric wage schemes and resulting effort decisions in the two-agent treatments. Symmetric offers are fully characterized by three wages $w_{11} := w_{11}^A = w_{11}^B$, $w_1 := w_{10}^A = w_{01}^B$, and $w_0 := w_{01}^A = w_{10}^B$. A pair (w_{11}, w_1) appears in a darker shade (shifted 0.1 units to the left) while each corresponding pair (w_{11}, w_0) is plotted in a lighter shade (shifted 0.1 units to the right), so each single offer is represented by two points. The actually observed effort decisions are indicated by different colors, while the theoretically optimal effort decisions for given wage offers are indicated by different symbols. The size of the symbols represents the number of observations.

in a lighter shade; so each single wage scheme is represented by two points in the figure. Furthermore, a single offer is shown as a circle if – according to standard theory – both agents had a dominant strategy to exert effort, while it is shown as a triangle if both agents had a dominant strategy not to exert effort. Cases in which agents had no dominant strategy (indicated by a square) are observed very rarely. The figure illustrates that for exerting effort to be a dominant strategy, the difference between w_1 and w_0 had to be relatively large.[19] Let us now analyze the symmetric wage offers in the treatment with conflict. The principals made wage offers such that for 52.8% of the agent pairs, it was a dominant strategy to exert effort, while for 36.1%, it was a dominant strategy not to exert effort. The remaining 11.1% of offers were such that there existed no dominant strategy. How did the agents react to these offers? The large majority of agents exerted effort regardless of whether this was a dominant strategy or not. Specifically, 35 out of 38 agents with the dominant strategy to exert effort actually promoted their product.[20] Moreover, when it was the optimal strategy not to provide effort, 23 out of 26 agents still decided to promote their product.[21] How may the agents' behavior be explained? Observe that wage offers for which exerting effort was a dominant strategy were characterized by w_0 being very small or 0€. Hence, an agent facing such an offer may have been very reluctant not to exert effort if he feared that the other agent might exert effort. The reason is that if an agent exerts no effort, the probability of sale of the own product becomes very small (10%, see Table 6.5 in Appendix B) given that the other agent exerts effort. Hence, with a probability of 90%, the shirking agent's gain would

[19]This becomes apparent by the fact that the vertical distance between the dark and light circles (indicating a dominant strategy to exert effort) is relatively large, while the vertical distance between the dark and light triangles (indicating a dominant strategy not to exert effort) is relatively small.

[20]This led to two efforts in 84.2% and to one effort in 15.8% of the principal-agent triads.

[21]This led to two efforts in 76.9% and to one effort in 23.1% of the principal-agent triads. With regard to the eight agents that had no dominant strategy, we observe four agents that promoted their product.

be 0€ or very small. In contrast, exerting effort might be considered an attractive strategy since the probability of selling the own product and thereby making a reasonable profit increases regardless of the other agent's decision. Next observe that nearly all wage offers for which not exerting effort was a dominant strategy were characterized by w_0 equal to 2€ or even larger. This observation may help to explain why most of the agents exerted effort even if the dominant strategy was not to exert effort. By promoting their product, agents could reciprocate these generous wage offers that insured them against making losses and at the same time, they further increased their chance to obtain a reasonable share of the revenue.

Taking a look at the treatment without conflict, wage offers were such that 82.5% of the agent pairs had the dominant strategy to promote their product, 12.5% had the dominant strategy not to promote their product, and the remaining 5% had no dominant strategy. A telling number of 60 agents (out of 66) with a dominant strategy to provide effort actually promoted their product. There were only ten agents with a dominant strategy not to promote their product, and seven of them decided not to exert effort. Also in this treatment, the decision to exert effort seemed to be an attractive strategy, because it promised a reasonable profit, the probability of a loss was very small, and the agents could again reward the principal for fair wage offers.[22]

6.6 Discussion

In theoretical principal-agent models, inducing a single agent to invest effort in two conflicting tasks is difficult for the principal, because the agent anticipates that exerting effort in one task directly undermines the probability of success regarding the other task. This has led us to formulate Hypothesis 6.1 according to which in the one-agent treatment with conflict, the relative frequency

[22] As can be seen in Figure 6.4, in this treatment w_0 is more often equal to zero than in the treatment with conflict. This might be due to the fact that in the absence of conflict, an agent's probability of not selling his product was very small when he exerted effort.

of two efforts should be much lower than in the other treatments. Indeed, our experimental results provide strong support for this hypothesis: in the one-agent treatment with conflict, only 36.7% of the agents chose two efforts while in all other treatments, two efforts were observed in at least 70% of the cases. This shows that the theoretically predicted incentive problem is of high relevance in the laboratory. Nevertheless, a relevant share of agents decides to exert two efforts even in the presence of conflict. Our analysis in Section 6.5.2 has shown that agents that chose two efforts were those who were offered very generous wage schemes. While offers that led to two efforts were mostly very generous offers in the fair-offers area, they did not satisfy the incentive constraints for choosing two efforts. This means that in the experiment, agents often reciprocated generous offers by exerting two efforts although their best reply according to the incentive constraints would have been different. To sum up, incentive problems due to conflicting tasks are also prevalent in the lab, but the strength of this problem seems to be weaker when principals try to trigger reciprocity by very fair and generous offers.

The observation that in the lab, the incentive problem seems not to be as strong as in theory can help to explain why we cannot find support for Hypothesis 6.2(ii). For our parameter constellation, theory predicts that in the presence of conflict, the principal's expected profit is larger when she employs two agents instead of one. The fact that this result is not supported by our data can be attributed to two reasons. Given the parameter constellation of our experiment and conflicting tasks, in theory the principal will never induce two efforts with one agent, while in the experiment, two efforts are observed in 36.7% of the cases. Moreover, as illustrated in Figure 6.5, when two agents are assigned to the principal, in sum she pays the agents more and thus gives up a larger share of the total surplus.[23] In fact, when there are two agents,

[23]Note that in the two-agent treatments, for any state of nature (one or two products sold), the sum of the wages offered to the agents is on average larger than the respective wage offered to a single agent. The differences are statistically significant on the 5% level according to one-sided Mann-Whitney U tests.

due to fairness considerations the principal tends to give up considerably more than half of the net surplus while if she has only one agent, she tends to keep at least half of the net surplus for herself. These two facts may explain why in contrast to the theoretical prediction, in the treatments with conflict the principal is better off with one agent than with two agents.

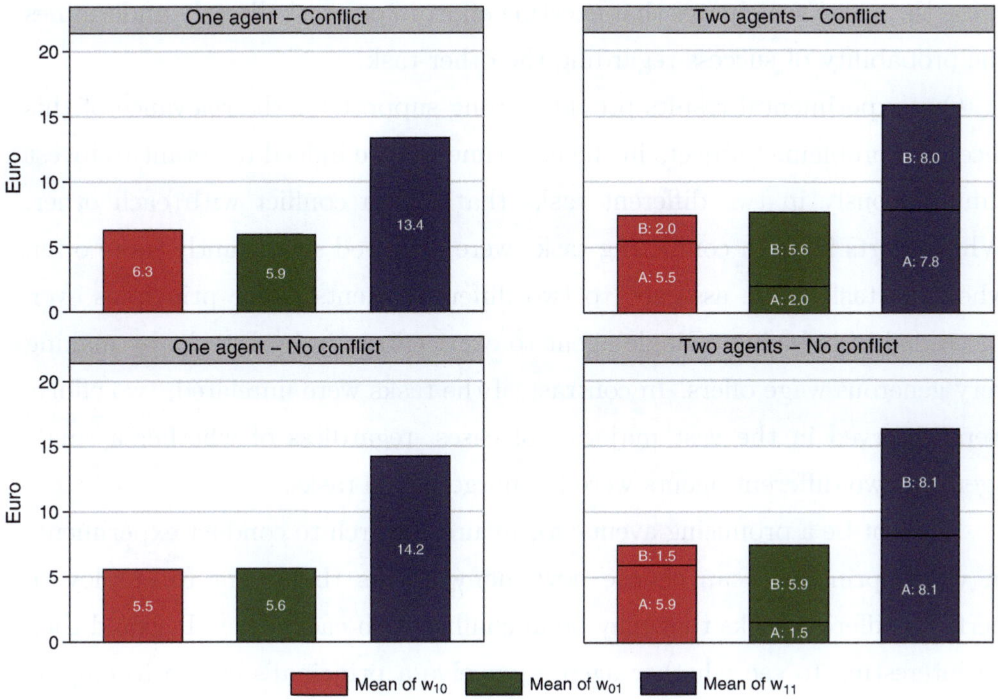

Figure 6.5. Average wage offers. In the two-agent treatments, the mean of w_{10} consists of the sum of the means of w_{10}^A and w_{10}^B, the mean of w_{01} consists of the sum of the means of w_{01}^A and w_{01}^B and the mean of w_{11} consists of the sum of the means of w_{11}^A and w_{11}^B.

6.7 Concluding remarks

While multi-task principal-agent models have attracted considerable attention by contract theorists in recent years, there is scarce experimental evidence on the problems involved. In this study we focus on incentive problems that arise when tasks are in direct conflict with each other. In theory, inducing a single agent to invest effort in two conflicting tasks is difficult for the principal, because the agent anticipates that exerting effort in one task directly undermines the probability of success regarding the other task.

Our experimental results provide strong support for the relevance of this incentive problem. Subjects in the experiment were indeed reluctant to invest simultaneously in two different tasks that are in conflict with each other. While efforts in both conflicting tasks were observed significantly more often when the tasks were assigned to two different agents, some principals even succeeded in inducing a single agent to exert efforts in both tasks by making very generous wage offers. In contrast, if the tasks were unrelated, two efforts were observed in the vast majority of cases, regardless of whether a single agent or two different agents were in charge of the tasks.

It might be a promising avenue for future research to conduct experiments in which principals can choose how many agents they want to employ to perform different tasks that may be in conflict with each other. It would then be interesting to see whether agents perceive a principal's choice to employ two agents when the tasks are conflicting as an unfriendly act. An agent may be demotivated if he knows that the principal intentionally employs another agent whose effort frustrates his own effort. Moreover, it would be interesting to investigate whether our results remain robust when agents face real effort tasks.[24]

---

[24] Note that Brüggen and Strobel (2007) investigate experimentally real effort and chosen effort where participants choose increasingly costly effort levels. They find that the results support equivalence between real and chosen effort.

6.8 Appendix

Appendix A

Proof of Lemma 6.1

First observe that given that the wages cannot be negative, the agent's participation constraint is redundant as it is implied by (IC 3). It is immediate to verify that given the symmetry of the problem, it is optimal for the principal to set $w_{10} = w_{01} = w_1$. Then it is straightforward to show that w_{00} must be equal to zero. Thus, the reduced problem is to minimize $E\left[w_{q_1 q_2} \mid a_1 = a_2 = 1\right] = (\alpha+\rho-\gamma)^2 w_{11} + 2(\alpha+\rho-\gamma)(1-\alpha-\rho+\gamma)w_1$ subject to the constraints $w_{11} \geq 0, w_1 \geq 0$,

$$\begin{aligned}
&(\alpha+\rho-\gamma)^2 w_{11} + 2(\alpha+\rho-\gamma)(1-\alpha-\rho+\gamma)w_1 - 2\psi \geq \qquad \text{(IC 1)}\\
&(\alpha+\rho)(\alpha-\gamma)w_{11} + (\alpha+\rho)(1-\alpha+\gamma)w_1 +\\
&(\alpha-\gamma)(1-\alpha-\rho)w_1 - \psi,
\end{aligned}$$

$$\begin{aligned}
&(\alpha+\rho-\gamma)^2 w_{11} + 2(\alpha+\rho-\gamma)(1-\alpha-\rho+\gamma)w_1 - 2\psi \geq \qquad \text{(IC 3)}\\
&\alpha^2 w_{11} + 2\alpha(1-\alpha)w_1.
\end{aligned}$$

Now it is easy to see that $w_1 = 0$ is optimal. To show this, consider a wage scheme $w_{11}, w_1 > 0$. Then the LHS of the two incentive constraints are unchanged if we change this wage scheme such that $\Delta w_1 = -\Delta w_{11}\frac{\alpha+\rho-\gamma}{2(1-\alpha-\rho+\gamma)} < 0$. But now the RHS of both incentive constraints are relaxed which enables the principal to reduce the expected compensation by reducing w_1. She can do so until $w_1 = 0$. Then it turns out that (IC 3) is binding which implies $w_{11} = \frac{2\psi}{(\alpha+\rho-\gamma)^2-\alpha^2}$. ■

Proof of Lemma 6.2

In analogy to Lemma 6.1, it turns out that the participation constraint is redundant and that $w_{00} = 0$ is optimal. In what follows, we can ignore (IC 2). Let us verify that $w_{01} = 0$ is optimal. Consider a wage scheme with $w_{11}, w_{10}, w_{01} > 0$. If we change this wage scheme such that $\Delta w_{01} = -\Delta w_{10}\frac{(\alpha+\rho)(1-\alpha+\gamma)}{(1-\alpha-\rho)(\alpha-\gamma)} < 0$, the LHS of the two remaining incentive constraints are unchanged, while both RHS are relaxed. So the principal can increase her expected profit by lowering w_{01} until $w_{01} = 0$. In the same way it is straightforward to show that it is optimal to set $w_{11} = 0$. To see this, consider a wage scheme with $w_{11} > 0, w_{10}$. Then the LHS of the two incentive constraints remain unchanged if we change this wage scheme such that $\Delta w_{11} = -\Delta w_{10}\frac{1-\alpha+\gamma}{\alpha-\gamma} < 0$. Given this new wage scheme, the RHS of the two incentive constraints are relaxed which implies that the principal can increase her expected profit by lowering w_{11}. She can do so until $w_{11} = 0$. It is then immediate to see that the claimed solution satisfies all the constraints. ■

Proof of Lemma 6.3

Observe that given the wages cannot be negative, each agent's participation constraint is redundant as it is implied by the agent's incentive compatibility constraint. It is straightforward to show that $w_{00}^A = w_{00}^B = 0$. Moreover it is immediate to verify that given the symmetry of the problem, we can solve the problem for one agent and the other agent will receive the same incentive scheme; i.e., $w_{11}^A = w_{11}^B$, $w_{10}^A = w_{01}^B$, and $w_{01}^A = w_{10}^B$. Let us w.l.o.g. derive the optimal incentive scheme for agent A. The reduced problem is to minimize $(\alpha+\rho-\gamma)^2 w_{11}^A + (\alpha+\rho-\gamma)(1-\alpha-\rho+\gamma)(w_{10}^A + w_{01}^A)$ subject to $w_{q_1q_2}^A \geq 0$ and

$$(\alpha+\rho-\gamma)^2 w_{11}^A + (\alpha+\rho-\gamma)(1-\alpha-\rho+\gamma)(w_{10}^A + w_{01}^A) - \psi \geq \quad \text{(IC A)}$$
$$(\alpha-\gamma)(\alpha+\rho)w_{11}^A + (\alpha-\gamma)(1-\alpha-\rho)w_{10}^A + (\alpha+\rho)(1-\alpha+\gamma)w_{01}^A.$$

It is immediate to verify that in the optimal incentive scheme $w_{01}^A = 0$ must hold. To see this consider a wage scheme $w_{11}^A, w_{10}^A, w_{01}^A > 0$. The LHS of the incentive constraint remains unchanged if we change this wage scheme in the following way: $\Delta w_{01}^A = -\Delta w_{10}^A < 0$. But this relaxes the RHS of the incentive constraint and hence enables us to lower the expected compensation by reducing w_{01}^A until $w_{01}^A = 0$. In the next step we can show that $w_{11}^A = 0$ is optimal. To see this consider a wage scheme $w_{11}^A > 0, w_{10}^A$. The LHS of the incentive constraint remains unchanged if we change this wage scheme such that $\Delta w_{11}^A = -\Delta w_{10}^A \frac{1-\alpha-\rho+\gamma}{\alpha+\rho-\gamma} < 0$. This relaxes the RHS of the incentive constraint and thus makes it possible to lower the expected compensation by reducing w_{11}^A. This can be done until $w_{11}^A = 0$. Then the result follows immediately. ■

Proof of Lemma 6.4

In analogy to Lemma 6.3, the participation constraint is redundant and $w_{00}^A = 0$. To verify that $w_{01}^A = 0$ is optimal, consider a wage scheme with $w_{11}^A, w_{10}^A, w_{01}^A > 0$. If we change this wage scheme such that $\Delta w_{01}^A = -\Delta w_{10}^A \frac{(\alpha+\rho)(1-\alpha+\gamma)}{(1-\alpha-\rho)(\alpha-\gamma)} < 0$, the LHS of the incentive constraint remains unchanged, while the RHS of the incentive constraint is relaxed. So the principal can increase her expected profit by lowering w_{01}^A until $w_{01}^A = 0$. Next, let us show that $w_{11}^A = 0$. To see this, consider a wage scheme with $w_{11}^A > 0, w_{10}^A$. The LHS of the incentive constraint remains unchanged if we change this wage scheme such that $\Delta w_{11}^A = -\Delta w_{10}^A \frac{1-\alpha+\gamma}{\alpha-\gamma} < 0$. Given this new wage scheme, the RHS of the incentive constraint is relaxed which means that the principal can increase her expected profit by lowering w_{11}^A. She can do so until $w_{11}^A = 0$. The lemma follows immediately. ■

Proof of Proposition 6.2

We have to show that it cannot be optimal for the principal to induce only one effort. To show this, assume the contrary. This means the two conditions $\Pi_{hl}^{AB} > \Pi_{hh}^{AB}$ and $\Pi_{hl}^{AB} > \Pi_{ll}^{AB}$ must be satisfied. The former condition can be rewritten as $R < \frac{2\psi(\alpha+\rho-\gamma)(1-\alpha-\rho+\gamma)}{[(\alpha+\rho-\gamma)(1-\alpha-\rho+\gamma)-(\alpha-\gamma)(1-\alpha-\rho)](\rho-\gamma)} - \frac{\psi(\alpha+\rho)(1-\alpha+\gamma)}{[\alpha\gamma+\rho(1-\alpha+\gamma)](\rho-\gamma)}$ and the latter can be rewritten as $R > \frac{\psi(\alpha+\rho)(1-\alpha+\gamma)}{[\alpha\gamma+\rho(1-\alpha+\gamma)](\rho-\gamma)}$. This implies that the RHS of the former condition must be larger than the RHS of the latter, which is equivalent to $(1-\alpha)^2 + \alpha^2 + \alpha(\rho-\gamma) + (1-\alpha-\rho)\gamma < (1-\alpha)\rho$. But this inequality cannot hold under our assumptions. Hence, the two conditions $\Pi_{hl}^{AB} > \Pi_{hh}^{AB}$ and $\Pi_{hl}^{AB} > \Pi_{ll}^{AB}$ cannot be satisfied simultaneously. Then the proposition follows immediately. ■

Proof of Proposition 6.3

If the principal implements $a_i = 1$ and $a_{j \neq i} = 0$ in the one-agent scenario, then she would prefer to have two agents and to implement $a_1 = a_2 = 1$.

To see this, suppose it is optimal for the principal to implement $a_i = 1$ and $a_{j \neq i} = 0$ in the one-agent scenario. Then $\Pi_{hl} > \Pi_{ll}$ holds. But this means that in the two-agent scenario $\Pi_{hl}^{AB} > \Pi_{ll}^{AB}$ must be satisfied, since $\Pi_{hl} = \Pi_{hl}^{AB}$ and $\Pi_{ll} = \Pi_{ll}^{AB}$. But we know from Proposition 6.2 that if $\Pi_{hl}^{AB} > \Pi_{ll}^{AB}$, then $\Pi_{hh}^{AB} > \Pi_{hl}^{AB} = \Pi_{hl}$.

It remains to be shown that there exists a unique $\hat{\gamma} \in (0, \min\{\alpha, \rho\})$ such that $\Pi_{hh}(\hat{\gamma}) = \Pi_{hh}^{AB}(\hat{\gamma})$. Observe that $\Pi_{hh} - \Pi_{hh}^{AB} > 0$ if $\gamma = 0$ and $\Pi_{hh} - \Pi_{hh}^{AB} < 0$ if $\gamma = \min\{\alpha, \rho\}$. Moreover, the condition $\Pi_{hh} - \Pi_{hh}^{AB} > 0$ is equivalent to $f(\cdot) := \gamma(3\alpha\rho + \rho^2 + \alpha^2 - \rho - 2\alpha) + \gamma^2(1 - \alpha - \rho) + \rho\alpha - \rho\alpha^2 - \rho^2\alpha > 0$. The derivative of $f(\cdot)$ with respect to γ is given by $\frac{df(\cdot)}{d\gamma} = (2\gamma - \alpha - \rho)(1 - \alpha - \rho) - (1 - \rho)\alpha < 0$. Hence, a simple intermediate value argument implies that there exists a unique $\hat{\gamma} \in (0, \min\{\alpha, \rho\})$ such that $\Pi_{hh}(\hat{\gamma}) = \Pi_{hh}^{AB}(\hat{\gamma})$. The remainder of the proposition follows immediately from Proposition 6.1 and Proposition 6.2. ■

Appendix B

	No effort	Effort in task 1	Effort in task 2	Efforts in both tasks
No product sold	36%	6%	6%	1%
Only product A sold	24%	54%	4%	9%
Only product B sold	24%	4%	54%	9%
Both products sold	16%	36%	36%	81%

Table 6.4. Probabilities of sale in the no-conflict treatments.

	No effort	Effort in task 1	Effort in task 2	Efforts in both tasks
No product sold	36%	9%	9%	16%
Only product A sold	24%	81%	1%	24%
Only product B sold	24%	1%	81%	24%
Both products sold	16%	9%	9%	36%

Table 6.5. Probabilities of sale in the conflict treatments.

Appendix C

The following instructions were handed out to the participants in the treatment with one agent and conflict ($\gamma = 0.3$):

Experimental instructions

In this experiment, you can earn money. Your payoff depends on your decisions and on other participants' decisions.

During the whole experiment communication is not allowed. If you have a question, please raise your hand out of the cabin. All decisions are anonymous; i.e., no participant ever learns the identity of a person who has made a particular decision. The payment is conducted anonymously, too; i.e., no participant learns what the payoff of another participant is.

In this experiment, you will either be a merchant or a sales representative with equal probability. Each merchant is matched with exactly one sales representative. As soon as the experiment starts, you will learn whether you have been assigned to the role of a merchant or to the role of a sales representative.

The merchant can sell exactly one unit of a product A and exactly one unit of a product B via his sales representative. Product A and product B are similar. The merchant receives a revenue of 15 € for each product sold. He can pay his sales representative a wage depending on the number of products sold.
(Suppose that the costs the merchant had to incur when purchasing the products are not relevant in this experiment. Furthermore, the merchant does not have to bear any stockkeeping costs if product A or product B is not sold.)

The sales representative can promote each product A and B individually. If the sales representative does not promote any product, the probability of sale of each product is 40%. If the sales representative promotes a product, the probability of sale of this product increases by 50 percentage points while the probability of sale of the other product decreases by 30 percentage points.

The sales representative can either *promote no product*, or *promote exactly one product*, or *promote both products.* Depending on the number of products promoted, the probabilities of sale read as follows:

- If the sales representative does not promote any product, then each product will be sold with a probability of 40%.
- If the sales representative promotes *only* product A, then product A will be sold with a probability of 40% + 50% = 90%, and product B will be sold with a probability of 40% - 30% = 10%.
- If the sales representative promotes *only* product B, then product B will be sold with a probability of 40% + 50% = 90%, and product A will be sold with a probability of 40% - 30% = 10%.
- If the sales representative promotes both products, then product A and product B will be sold with a probability of 40% + 50% - 30% = 60% each.

As the products are similar, promotion for one product does not only have a positive effect on the probability of sale of the promoted product, but it has also a negative effect on the probability of sale of the other product.

	No promotion for product B	Promotion for product B
No promotion for product A	40%, 40%	10%, 90%
Promotion for product A	90%, 10%	60%, 60%

In each cell, the first number denotes the probability of sale of product A, while the second number denotes the probability of sale of product B.

If the sales representative promotes a product, he has to incur promotion costs of 2 €; i.e. promoting both products causes promotion costs PC = 2 € + 2 € = 4 €, while promoting one product causes promotion costs PC = 2 €. If he promotes no product, he has to incur no promotion costs (PC = 0 €).

The merchant cannot observe whether his sales representative decides to promote a product or not. Thus, the merchant cannot condition his wage offer on the sales representative's promotion decision but only on the number of products sold.

In detail, the experiment proceeds as follows:

The experiment consists of only a single period.
This period consists of two stages.

Stage 1 – Merchant decides on wage offers

The merchant offers his sales representative wages depending on the number of products sold. There are four possible cases. For each case, the merchant can specify one wage:

1. Neither product A nor product B are sold → wage w_{00}
2. Only product A but not product B is sold → wage w_{10}
3. Only product B but not product A is sold → wage w_{01}
4. Both products A and B are sold → wage w_{11}

As the merchant obtains no revenue in case 1, the wage w_{00} is fixed at 0 €. In the cases 2, 3, and 4, the merchant has to set the wages w_{10}, w_{01}, and w_{11} (see Figure I on the last page).
(All wages can be specified with up to one decimal place. Please use points instead of commas as decimal separators.)

Stage 2 – Sales representative decides on promotion

The sales representative learns his merchant's wage offers $w_{00} = 0$, w_{10}, w_{01}, and w_{11}. He can decide whether to promote no product, only product A, only product B, or whether to promote both products A and B (see Figure II on the last page).
Once the sales representative has decided on his promotion effort, the probabilities of sale of the products are determined (as described above). According to these probabilities, the computer decides randomly whether *no*, *exactly one*, or *both products* are sold.

Diagram of the experiment:

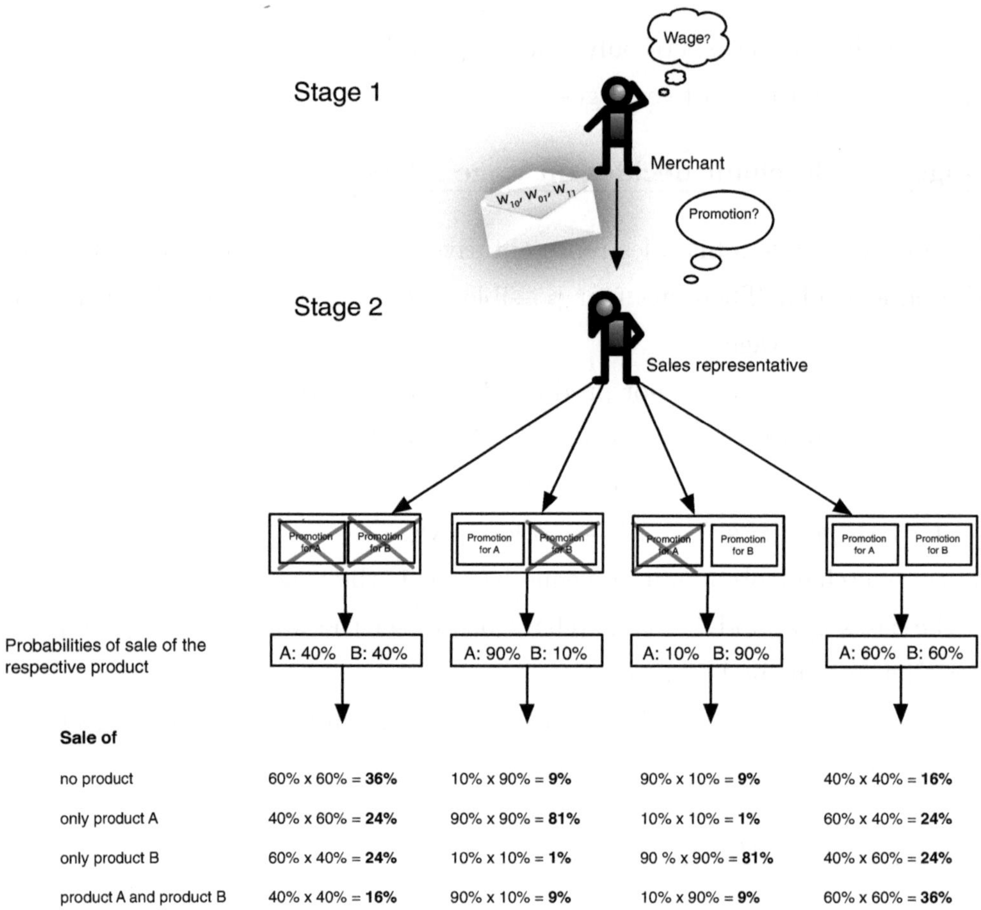

The profits are as follows:

Sale of	Merchant's profit	Sales rep.'s profit
no product	$0 - w_{00} = 0$	$w_{00} - PC = 0 - PC$
only product A	$15 - w_{10}$	$w_{10} - PC$
only product B	$15 - w_{01}$	$w_{01} - PC$
both products	$30 - w_{11}$	$w_{11} - PC$

Your payoff:

In addition to the (possibly negative) profit realized in the experiment you get 4 € and the resulting amount is paid out to you in cash.

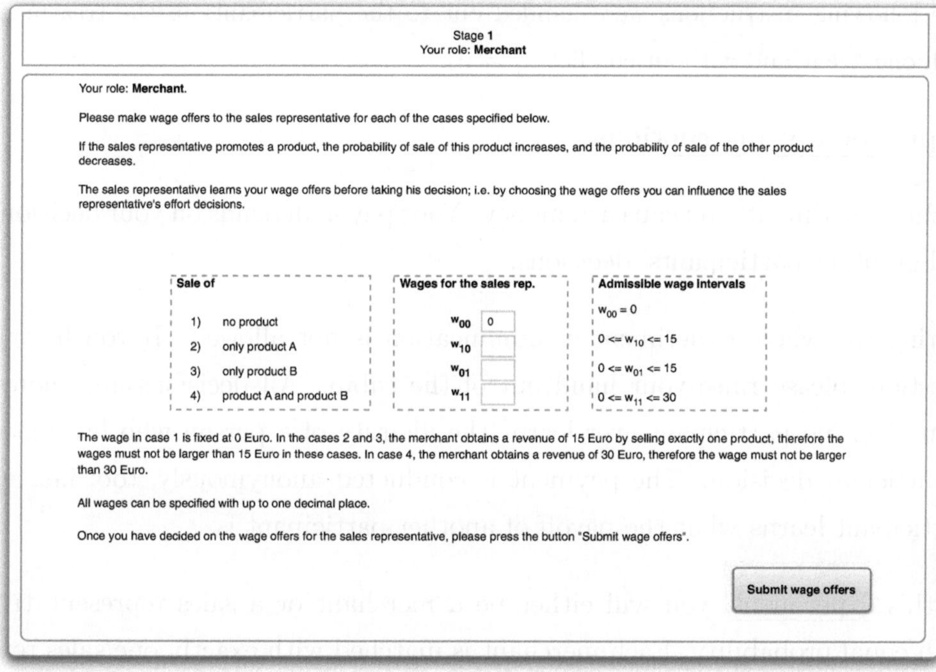

Figure I. Stage 1 – Merchant decides on wage offers.

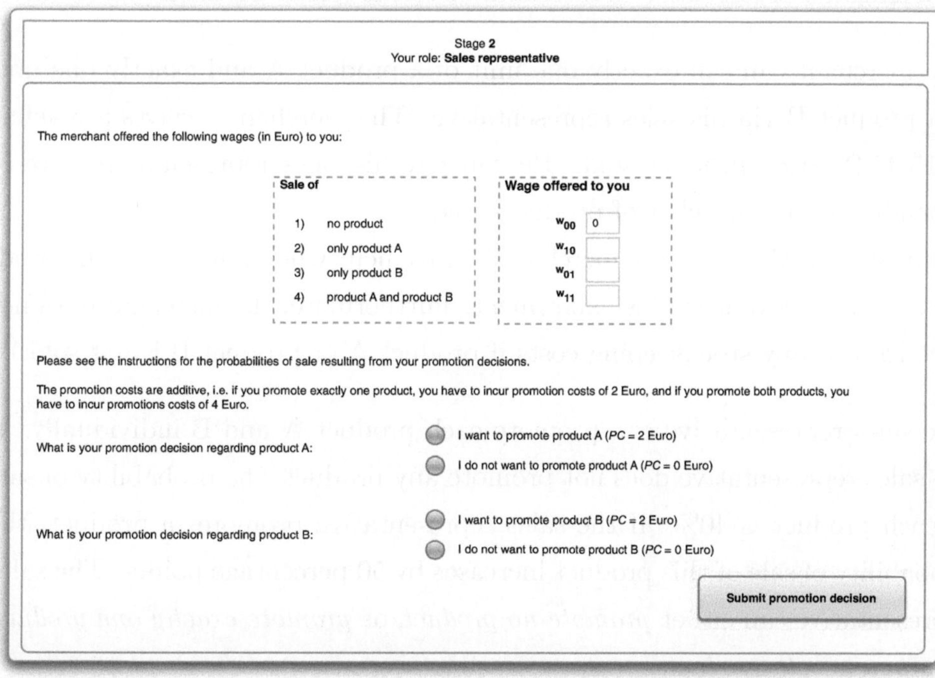

Figure II. Stage 2 – Sales representative decides on promotion.

The following instructions were handed out to the participants in the treatment with one agent and without conflict ($\gamma = 0$):

Experimental instructions

In this experiment, you can earn money. Your payoff depends on your decisions and on other participants' decisions.

During the whole experiment communication is not allowed. If you have a question, please raise your hand out of the cabin. All decisions are anonymous; i.e., no participant ever learns the identity of a person who has made a particular decision. The payment is conducted anonymously, too; i.e., no participant learns what the payoff of another participant is.

In this experiment, you will either be a merchant or a sales representative with equal probability. Each merchant is matched with exactly one sales representative. As soon as the experiment starts, you will learn whether you have been assigned to the role of a merchant or to the role of a sales representative.

The merchant can sell exactly one unit of a product A and exactly one unit of a product B via his sales representative. The merchant receives a revenue of 15 € for each product sold. He can pay his sales representative a wage depending on the number of products sold.
(Suppose that the costs the merchant had to incur when purchasing the products are not relevant in this experiment. Furthermore, the merchant does not have to bear any stockkeeping costs if product A or product B is not sold.)

The sales representative can promote each product A and B individually. If the sales representative does not promote any product, the probability of sale of each product is 40%. If the sales representative promotes a product, the probability of sale of this product increases by 50 percentage points. The sales representative can either *promote no product*, or *promote exactly one product*, or *promote both products*.

Depending on the number of products promoted, the probabilities of sale read as follows:

- If the sales representative does not promote any product, then each product will be sold with a probability of 40%.
- If the sales representative promotes only product A, then product A will be sold with a probability of 40% + 50% = 90%, while product B still will be sold with a probability of 40%.
- If the sales representative promotes only product B, then product B will be sold with a probability of 40% + 50% = 90%, while product A still will be sold with a probability of 40%.
- If the sales representative promotes both products, then product A and product B will be sold with a probability of 40% + 50% = 90% each.

	Probability of sale of the product
No promotion for a product	40%
Promotion for a product	90%

If a sales representative promotes a product, he has to incur promotion costs of 2 €, i.e. promoting both products causes promotion costs PC = 2 € + 2 € = 4 €, while promoting one product causes promotion costs PC = 2 €. If he promotes no product, he has to incur no promotion costs (PC = 0 €).

The merchant cannot observe whether his sales representative decides to promote a product or not. Thus, the merchant cannot condition his wage offer on the sales representative's promotion decision but only on the number of products sold.

In detail, the experiment proceeds as follows:

The experiment consists of only a single period.
This period consists of two stages.

Stage 1 – Merchant decides on wage offers

The merchant offers his sales representative wages depending on the number of products sold. There are four possible cases. For each case, the merchant can specify one wage:

1. Neither product A nor product B are sold → wage w_{00}
2. Only product A but not product B is sold → wage w_{10}
3. Only product B but not product A is sold → wage w_{01}
4. Both products A and B are sold → wage w_{11}

As the merchant obtains no revenue in case 1, the wage w_{00} is fixed at 0 €. In the cases 2, 3, and 4, the merchant has to set the wages w_{10}, w_{01}, and w_{11} (see Figure I on the last page).
(All wages can be specified with up to one decimal place. Please use points instead of commas as decimal separators.)

Stage 2 – Sales representative decides on promotion

The sales representative learns his merchant's wage offers $w_{00} = 0$, w_{10}, w_{01}, and w_{11}. He can decide whether to promote no product, only product A, only product B, or whether to promote both products A and B (see Figure II on the last page).
Once the sales representative has decided on his promotion effort, the probabilities of sale of the products are determined (as described above). According to these probabilities, the computer decides randomly whether *no*, *exactly one*, or *both products* are sold.

Diagram of the experiment:

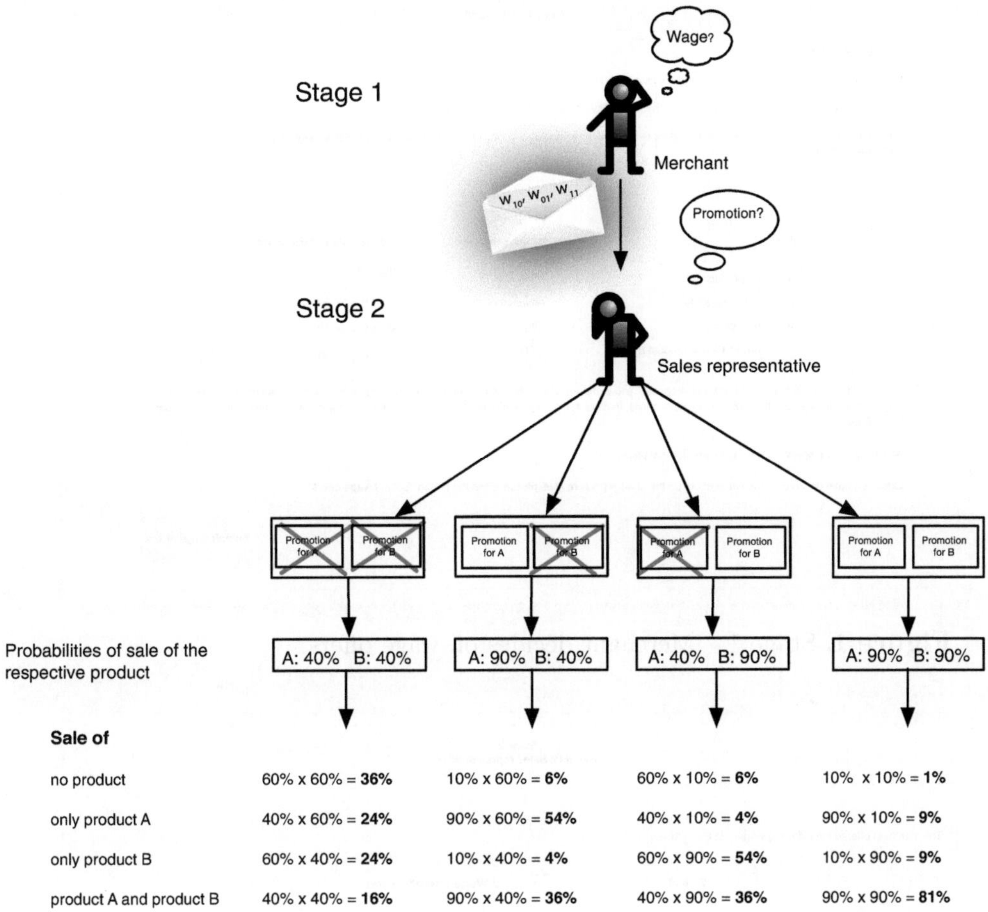

The profits are as follows:

Sale of	Merchant's profit	Sales rep.'s profit
no product	$0 - w_{00} = 0$	$w_{00} - PC = 0 - PC$
only product A	$15 - w_{10}$	$w_{10} - PC$
only product B	$15 - w_{01}$	$w_{01} - PC$
both products	$30 - w_{11}$	$w_{11} - PC$

Your payoff:

In addition to the (possibly negative) profit realized in the experiment you get 4 € and the resulting amount is paid out to you in cash.

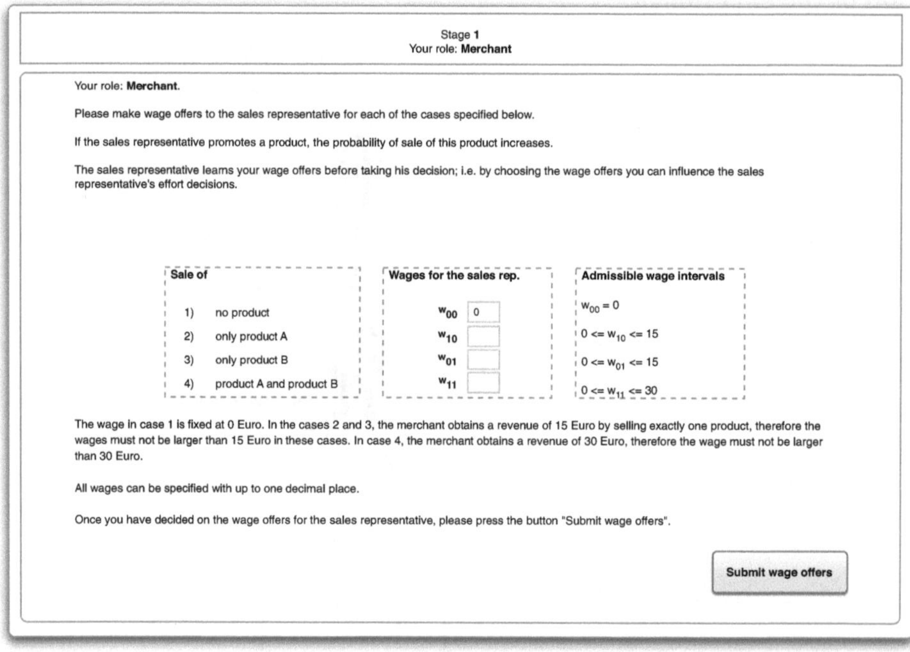

Stage **1**
Your role: **Merchant**

Your role: **Merchant**.

Please make wage offers to the sales representative for each of the cases specified below.

If the sales representative promotes a product, the probability of sale of this product increases.

The sales representative learns your wage offers before taking his decision; i.e. by choosing the wage offers you can influence the sales representative's effort decisions.

Sale of		Wages for the sales rep.	Admissible wage intervals
1)	no product	w_{00} 0	$w_{00} = 0$
2)	only product A	w_{10}	$0 <= w_{10} <= 15$
3)	only product B	w_{01}	$0 <= w_{01} <= 15$
4)	product A and product B	w_{11}	$0 <= w_{11} <= 30$

The wage in case 1 is fixed at 0 Euro. In the cases 2 and 3, the merchant obtains a revenue of 15 Euro by selling exactly one product, therefore the wages must not be larger than 15 Euro in these cases. In case 4, the merchant obtains a revenue of 30 Euro, therefore the wage must not be larger than 30 Euro.

All wages can be specified with up to one decimal place.

Once you have decided on the wage offers for the sales representative, please press the button "Submit wage offers".

Submit wage offers

Figure I. Stage 1 – Merchant decides on wage offers.

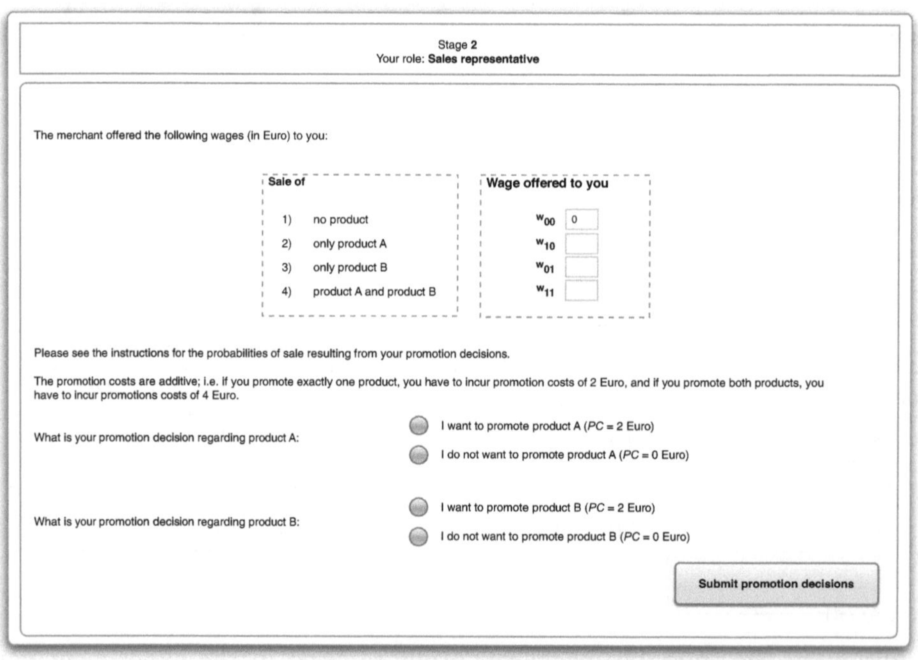

Stage **2**
Your role: **Sales representative**

The merchant offered the following wages (in Euro) to you:

Sale of		Wage offered to you
1)	no product	w_{00} 0
2)	only product A	w_{10}
3)	only product B	w_{01}
4)	product A and product B	w_{11}

Please see the instructions for the probabilities of sale resulting from your promotion decisions.

The promotion costs are additive; i.e. if you promote exactly one product, you have to incur promotion costs of 2 Euro, and if you promote both products, you have to incur promotions costs of 4 Euro.

What is your promotion decision regarding product A:
I want to promote product A (*PC* = 2 Euro)
I do not want to promote product A (*PC* = 0 Euro)

What is your promotion decision regarding product B:
I want to promote product B (*PC* = 2 Euro)
I do not want to promote product B (*PC* = 0 Euro)

Submit promotion decisions

Figure II. Stage 2 – Sales representative decides on promotion.

The following instructions were handed out to the participants in the treatment with two agents and conflict ($\gamma = 0.3$):

Experimental instructions

In this experiment, you can earn money. Your payoff depends on your decisions and on other participants' decisions.

During the whole experiment communication is not allowed. If you have a question, please raise your hand out of the cabin. All decisions are anonymous; i.e., no participant ever learns the identity of a person who has made a particular decision. The payment is conducted anonymously, too; i.e., no participant learns what the payoff of another participant is.

In this experiment, you will either be a merchant with a probability of one-third or a sales representative with a probability of two-thirds. Every merchant is matched with two sales representatives (sales representative A and sales representative B). As soon as the experiment starts, you will learn whether you have been assigned to the role of a merchant or to the role of a sales representative.

The merchant can sell exactly one unit of a product A via sales representative A and exactly one unit of a product B via sales representative B. Product A and product B are similar. The merchant receives a revenue of 15 € for each product sold. He can pay his sales representatives wages depending on the number of products sold.
(Suppose that the costs the merchant had to incur when purchasing the products are not relevant in this experiment. Furthermore, the merchant does not have to bear any stockkeeping costs if product A or product B is not sold.)

Each sales representative (sales representative A and sales representative B, respectively) can decide whether he wants to promote his product (product A and product B, respectively). If no sales representative promotes his product, the probability of sale of each product is 40%. If a sales representative promotes his product, the probability of sale of his product increases by 50 percentage points while the probability of sale of the other sales representative's product decreases by 30 percentage points. Each sales representative can decide whether to promote his product or not. The resulting probabilities of sale depend on whether *no sales representative*, *one sales representative*, or *both sales representatives* promote their respective products:

- If no sales representative promotes his product, then each product will be sold with a probability of 40%.
- If sales representative A promotes his product and sales representative B does not promote his product, then product A will be sold with a probability of 40% + 50% = 90%, and product B will be sold with a probability of 40% - 30% = 10%.
- If sales representative B promotes his product and sales representative A does not promote his product, then product B will be sold with a probability of 40% + 50% = 90%, and product A will be sold with a probability of 40% - 30% = 10%.
- If both sales representatives promote their respective product, then product A and product B will be sold with a probability of 40% + 50% - 30% = 60% each.

As the products are similar, promotion effort for one product does not only have a positive effect on the probability of sale of the promoted product, but it has also a negative effect on the probability of sale of the other product.

		Sales rep. B	
		does not promote product B	promotes product B
Sales rep. A	does not promote product A	40%, 40%	10%, 90%
	promotes product A	90%, 10%	60%, 60%

In each cell, the first number denotes the probability of sale of product A, while the second number denotes the probability of sale of product B.

If a sales representative promotes his product, he has to incur promotion costs PC = 2 €. If a sales representative does not promote his product, he does not have to incur promotion costs (PC = 0 €).

The merchant cannot observe whether his sales representatives decide to promote their products or not. Thus, the merchant cannot condition his wage offers on the sales representatives' promotion decisions but only on the number of products sold. A sales representative also cannot observe the promotion decision of the other sales representative.

In detail, the experiment proceeds as follows:

The experiment consists of only a single period.
This period consists of two stages.

Stage 1 – Merchant decides on wage offers

The merchant offers his sales representatives wages depending on the number of products sold. There are four possible cases. For each case, the merchant can specify one wage:

1. neither product A nor product B are sold
   → wage w_{00}^A for sales representative A and w_{00}^B for sales representative B
2. only product A but not product B is sold
   → wage w_{10}^A for sales representative A and w_{10}^B for sales representative B
3. only product B but not product A is sold
   → wage w_{01}^A for sales representative A and w_{01}^B for sales representative B
4. both products A and B are sold
   → wage w_{11}^A for sales representative A and w_{11}^B for sales representative B

As the merchant obtains no revenue in case 1, the wages w_{00}^A and w_{00}^B are fixed at 0 €. In the cases 2, 3, and 4, the merchant has to set the wages w_{10}^A and w_{10}^B, w_{01}^A and w_{01}^B, w_{11}^A and w_{11}^B for his sales representatives A and B (see Figure I on the last page).
(All wages can be specified with up to one decimal place. Please use points instead of commas as decimal separators.)

Stage 2 – Sales representatives A and B decide on promotion

The sales representatives A and B learn every wage offer the merchant has made in stage 1. Thus, a sales representative knows the wages he may receive as well as the wages that the merchant may pay to the other sales representative. Each sales representative then can decide whether to promote his product or not (see Figure II on the last page).

Once the sales representatives have decided on their promotion effort, the probabilities of sale of the products are determined (as described above). According to these probabilities, the computer decides randomly whether *no*, *exactly one*, or *both products* are sold.

Diagram of the experiment:

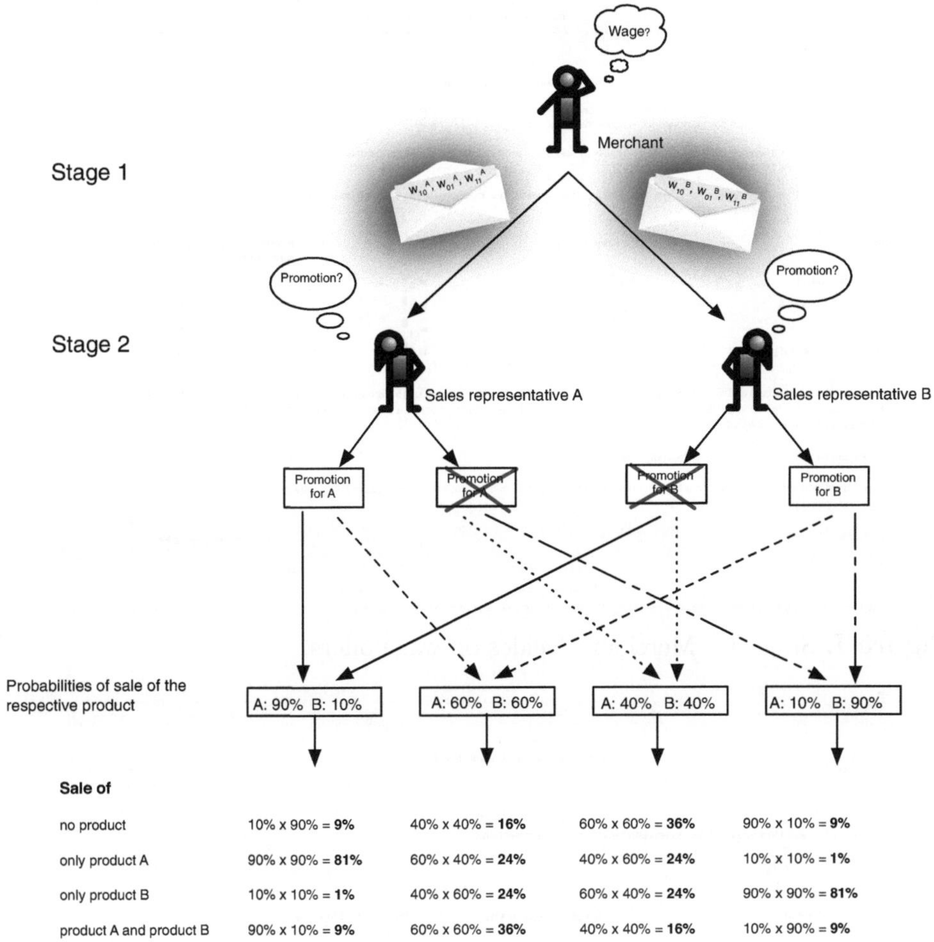

The profits are as follows:

Sale of	Merchant's profit	Sales rep. A's profit	Sales rep. B's profit
no product	$0 - w_{00}^{A} - w_{00}^{B} = 0$	$w_{00}^{A} - PC = 0 - PC$	$w_{00}^{B} - PC = 0 - PC$
only product A	$15 - w_{10}^{A} - w_{10}^{B}$	$w_{10}^{A} - PC$	$w_{10}^{B} - PC$
only product B	$15 - w_{01}^{A} - w_{01}^{B}$	$w_{01}^{A} - PC$	$w_{01}^{B} - PC$
both products	$30 - w_{11}^{A} - w_{11}^{B}$	$w_{11}^{A} - PC$	$w_{11}^{B} - PC$

Your payoff:

In addition to the (possibly negative) profit realized in the experiment you get 4 € and the resulting amount is paid out to you in cash.

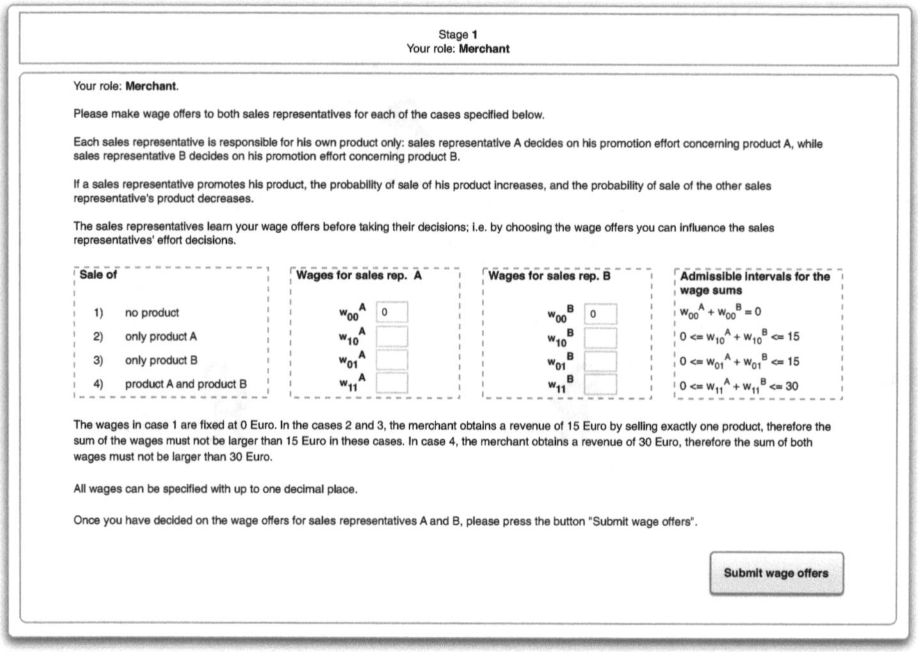

Figure I. Stage 1 – Merchant decides on wage offers.

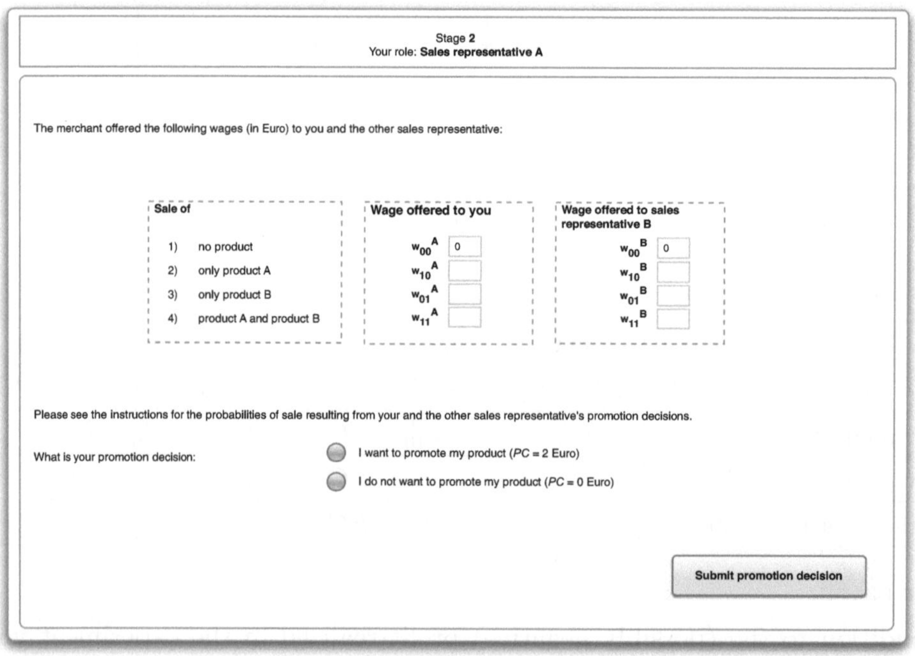

Figure II. Stage 2 – Sales representatives A and B decide on promotion.

The following instructions were handed out to the participants in the treatment with two agents and without conflict ($\gamma = 0$):

Experimental instructions

In this experiment, you can earn money. Your payoff depends on your decisions and on other participants' decisions.

During the whole experiment communication is not allowed. If you have a question, please raise your hand out of the cabin. All decisions are anonymous; i.e., no participant ever learns the identity of a person who has made a particular decision. The payment is conducted anonymously, too; i.e., no participant learns what the payoff of another participant is.

In this experiment, you will either be a merchant with a probability of one-third or a sales representative with a probability of two-thirds. Every merchant is matched with two sales representatives (sales representative A and sales representative B). As soon as the experiment starts, you will learn whether you have been assigned to the role of a merchant or to the role of a sales representative.

The merchant can sell exactly one unit of a product A via sales representative A and exactly one unit of a product B via sales representative B. The merchant receives a revenue of 15 € for each product sold. He can pay his sales representatives wages depending on the number of products sold.
(Suppose that the costs the merchant had to incur when purchasing the products are not relevant in this experiment. Furthermore, the merchant does not have to bear any stockkeeping costs if product A or product B is not sold.)

Each sales representative (sales representative A and sales representative B, respectively) can decide whether he wants to promote his product (product A and product B, respectively). If no sales representative promotes his product, the probability of sale of each product is 40%. If a sales representative promotes his product, the probability of sale of his product increases by 50 percentage points. Each sales representative can decide whether to promote his product or not. The resulting probabilities of sale depend on whether *no sales representative*, *one sales representative*, or *both sales representatives* promote their respective products:

- If no sales representative promotes his product, then each product will be sold with a probability of 40%.
- If sales representative A promotes his product and sales representative B does not promote his product, then product A will be sold with a probability of 40% + 50% = 90%, and product B still will be sold with a probability of 40%.
- If sales representative B promotes his product and sales representative A does not promote his product, then product B will be sold with a probability of 40% + 50% = 90%, and product A still will be sold with a probability of 40%.
- If both sales representatives promote their respective product, then product A and product B will be sold with a probability of 40% + 50% = 90% each.

Sales rep. A	Probability of sale of product A
does not promote product A	40%
promotes product A	90%

Sales rep. B	Probability of sale of product B
does not promote product B	40%
promotes product B	90%

If a sales representative promotes his product, he has to incur promotion costs PC = 2 €. If a sales representative does not promote his product, he does not have to incur promotion costs (PC = 0 €).

The merchant cannot observe whether his sales representatives decide to promote their products or not. Thus, the merchant cannot condition his wage offers on the sales representatives' promotion decisions but only on the number of products sold. A sales representative also cannot observe the promotion decision of the other sales representative.

In detail, the experiment proceeds as follows:

The experiment consists of only a single period.
This period consists of two stages.

Stage 1 – Merchant decides on wage offers

The merchant offers his sales representatives wages depending on the number of products sold. There are four possible cases. For each case, the merchant can specify one wage:

1. neither product A nor product B are sold
→ wage w_{00}^A for sales representative A and w_{00}^B for sales representative B
2. only product A but not product B is sold
→ wage w_{10}^A for sales representative A and w_{10}^B for sales representative B
3. only product B but not product A is sold
→ wage w_{01}^A for sales representative A and w_{01}^B for sales representative B
4. both products A and B are sold
→ wage w_{11}^A for sales representative A and w_{11}^B for sales representative B

As the merchant obtains no revenue in case 1, the wages w_{00}^A and w_{00}^B are fixed at 0 €. In the cases 2, 3, and 4, the merchant has to set the wages w_{10}^A and w_{10}^B, w_{01}^A and w_{01}^B, w_{11}^A and w_{11}^B for his sales representatives A and B (see Figure I on the last page).
(All wages can be specified with up to one decimal place. Please use points instead of commas as decimal separators.)

Stage 2 – Sales representatives A and B decide on promotion

The sales representatives A and B learn every wage offer the merchant has made in stage 1. Thus, a sales representative knows the wages he may receive as well as the wages that the merchant may pay to the other sales representative. Each sales representative then can decide whether to promote his product or not (see Figure II on the last page).

Once the sales representatives have decided on their promotion effort, the probabilities of sale of the products are determined (as described above). According to these probabilities, the computer decides randomly whether *no*, *exactly one*, or *both products* are sold.

Diagram of the experiment:

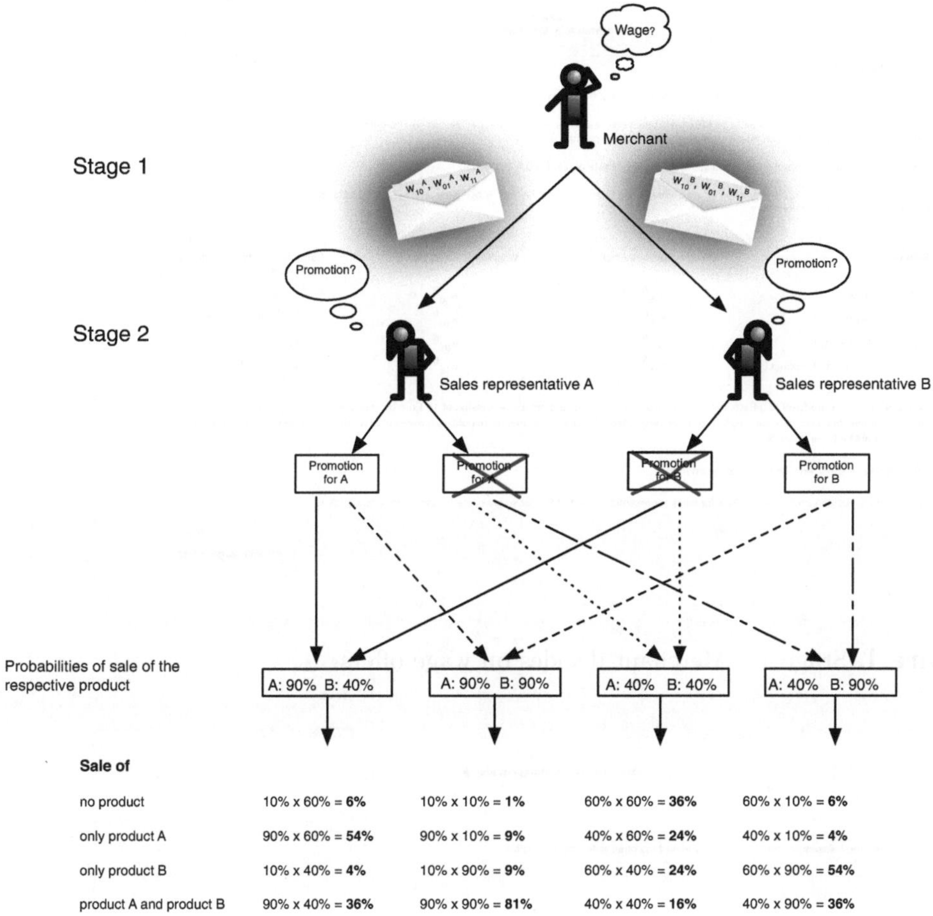

The profits are as follows:

Sale of	Merchant's profit	Sales rep. A's profit	Sales rep. B's profit
no product	$0 - w_{00}^A - w_{00}^B = 0$	$w_{00}^A - PC = 0 - PC$	$w_{00}^B - PC = 0 - PC$
only product A	$15 - w_{10}^A - w_{10}^B$	$w_{10}^A - PC$	$w_{10}^B - PC$
only product B	$15 - w_{01}^A - w_{01}^B$	$w_{01}^A - PC$	$w_{01}^B - PC$
both products	$30 - w_{11}^A - w_{11}^B$	$w_{11}^A - PC$	$w_{11}^B - PC$

Your payoff:

In addition to the (possibly negative) profit realized in the experiment you get 4 € and the resulting amount is paid out to you in cash.

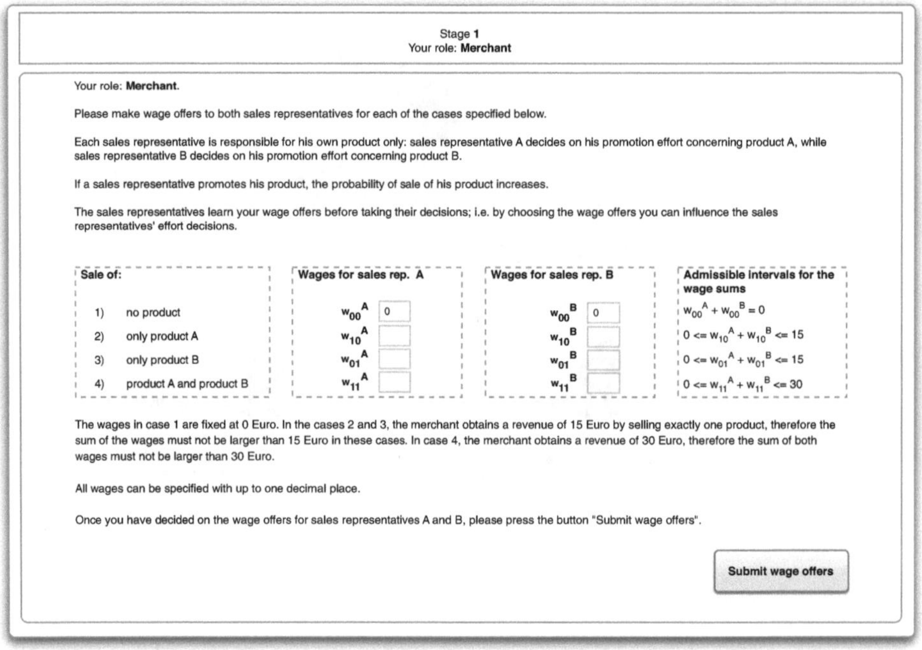

Figure I. Stage 1 – Merchant decides on wage offers.

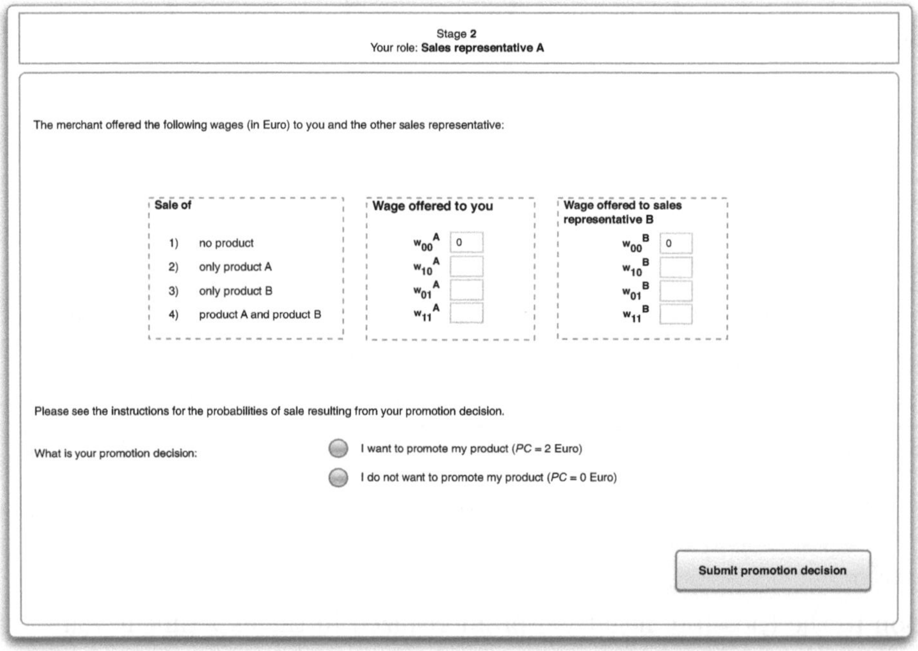

Figure II. Stage 2 – Sales representatives A and B decide on promotion.

7

Behavioral Biases and Cognitive Reflection

7.1 Introduction

Only recently, researchers have started to investigate the impact of cognitive ability on judgment and decision making. Frederick (2005) introduces the cognitive reflection test (CRT) which is a simple, three-item test to measure a person's mode of reasoning and cognitive ability.[1] Frederick (2005) shows that people with high CRT scores are generally more patient and more willing to gamble in the domain of gains.[2] In a related study, Oechssler, Roider, and Schmitz (2009) replicate the findings regarding time and risk preferences and in addition they study the relationship between cognitive abilities and the conjunction fallacy, conservatism, and anchoring.[3] One central result is that

[1]The CRT has recently also been used to assess the decision making processes of professional groups such as judges and financial planners, see Guthrie, Rachlinski, and Wistrich (2007) and Nofsinger and Varma (2007).

[2]Using other measures of cognitive ability, Brañas-Garza, Guillen, and del Paso (2008) and Slonim, Carlson, and Bettinger (2007) also study whether there are relations between cognitive abilities and risk or time preferences.

[3]See also Bergman et al. (2010), who analyze the anchoring effect and find that the amount of anchoring decreases but does not vanish with higher cognitive ability.

E. I. Hoppe-Fischer, *Essays on Contract Design and Incentive Provision*,
Edition KWV, https://doi.org/10.1007/978-3-658-24133-9_7

individuals with low cognitive abilities tend to be significantly more affected by behavioral biases.

In the present study, we investigate whether the incidence of further behavioral biases is related to cognitive abilities. Specifically, we study the base rate fallacy, overconfidence, and the endowment effect. Moreover, we replicate the finding of Oechssler, Roider, and Schmitz (2009) related to the conservatism bias in order to investigate an interesting question that was brought up in their paper. Are people that exhibit the conservatism bias (i.e., overweight the base rate) less susceptible to the base rate fallacy (i.e., to underweight the base rate)? We observe the contrary. In particular, we find that individuals with lower cognitive abilities are significantly more likely to exhibit both, the base rate fallacy and the conservatism fallacy. With regard to overconfidence, we find that subjects with higher CRT scores have a significantly more precise self-assessment. Finally, test scores do not affect the occurrence of the endowment effect which is striking in both, low and high CRT groups.

7.2 Experimental design

The experiment was conducted in July 2009.[4] Using ORSEE (Greiner, 2004), we recruited the participants from the subject pool of the Cologne Laboratory for Economic Research. In total, 414 students from the University of Cologne participated in the experiment. Following several socio-demographic questions (concerning gender, age, field of study, and length of study), the subjects had to fill in a questionnaire consisting of three questions building the CRT and several questions related to the behavioral biases mentioned in the introduction.[5] Participants were given 15 minutes to fill in the questionnaire and the experimenter stopped the experiment after the time was

[4]It was run after the (unrelated) principal-agent experiment described in Chapter 6.

[5]Subjects found a calculator, a pen, and a piece of paper in their cabin.

over.[6] Subjects were paid 0.40€ for each CRT question they answered correctly. Moreover, for the decision problems related to the base rate fallacy and conservatism, they received 0.40€ if their answer did not deviate more than 15 percentage points from the correct answer. Regarding overconfidence, subjects had to answer five general knowledge questions and they had to assess how many of these they answered correctly. For each correct answer (including the assessment question) they received 0.20€. Finally, with regard to the endowment effect, subjects could receive additional 0.20€ or, alternatively, take a highlighter home. In total, subjects earned between 0€ and 2.80€, and the average payoff was 1.24€. Moreover, 180 subjects left the lab with a brand new highlighter. The experiment was programmed and conducted with z-Tree (Fischbacher, 2007).

7.3 Cognitive reflection test

To measure cognitive ability, we use the three-item cognitive reflection test (CRT) that was introduced by Frederick (2005). The three questions are designed such that they have an intuitive but wrong answer that comes to mind quickly and a correct answer that is easy to understand when explained. Hence, the test is supposed to measure a person's ability to engage in cognitive reflection and thus to resist reporting the spontaneous but wrong answer. In particular, the three questions read as follows.

1. A bat and a ball together cost 110 cents. The bat costs 100 cents more than the ball. How much does the ball cost? (spontaneous answer: 10 cents; correct answer: 5 cents)

2. If it takes 5 machines 5 minutes to make 5 widgets, how long would it take 100 machines to make 100 widgets? (spontaneous answer: 100 minutes; correct answer: 5 minutes)

[6]Note that only three participants did not complete the questionnaire within the given time limit so that our analysis is based on 411 completed questionnaires.

3. In a lake, there is a patch of lily pads. Every day, the patch doubles in size. If it takes 48 days for the patch to cover the entire lake, how long would it take for the patch to cover half of the lake? (spontaneous answer: 24 days; correct answer: 47 days)

In our sample, 13 % of the subjects answered none of the questions correctly, 24 % knew the correct answer to one question, 27 % to two questions, and 36 % answered all three questions correctly. On average, the subjects answered 1.84 of the CRT questions correctly.[7]

Table 7.1 shows the distribution of the answers to the CRT questions. For each question, the majority of the subjects gave the correct answer. Among the subjects who did not submit the correct answer, the intuitive answer was given most frequently.

Question	Correct	Intuitive	Other
Bat and ball	56.7 %	39.9 %	3.4 %
Widgets	58.9 %	28.2 %	12.9 %
Lily pads	68.9 %	16.1 %	15.1 %

Table 7.1. Distribution of answers to the CRT questions.

7.4 Results

The central results of our study are summarized in Tables 7.2 and 7.5. Depending on their CRT score, we divide the participants in two groups. The "low" group consists of individuals who answered zero or one of the questions correctly, while the "high" group consists of participants that gave the correct

[7] There is a strong gender difference: male subjects have an average score of 2.12, while female subjects have an average score of 1.61 only. The difference is highly significant ($p < 0.0001$, two-sided Mann-Whitney U test). This gender difference has also been found in other studies using the CRT, e. g. Frederick (2005) and Oechssler, Roider, and Schmitz (2009).

answer to two or three questions.[8] We refer to subjects in the "high" group as the more *analytical* decision takers, while we describe subjects in the "low" group as relatively *intuitive* decision takers.

		CRT group		
Category	Item	low	high	p-value
Base rate fallacy	Avg. prob. stated (correct prob.: 9%)	77.4%	61.5%	$p \approx 0.0002$
Conservatism	Avg. prob. stated for urn A (correct prob.: 97%)	56.8%	60.1%	$p \approx 0.056$
Overconfidence	% overconfident	60.7%	57.4%	$p \approx 0.056$
	% correct self-assessment	23.2%	32.4%	
	% underconfident	16.1%	10.2%	

Table 7.2. Behavioral biases by CRT group.

7.4.1 Base rate fallacy

When people are asked to judge the probability of an event, they often have to take into account information about the base rate probability and they also have to consider specific evidence about the case at hand (Tversky and Kahneman, 1982). In such a context, they exhibit the base rate fallacy if they follow the representativeness heuristic and neglect the base rate probability.

In analogy to the mammography problem in Eddy (1982), subjects in our study faced the following problem: "In a city with 100 criminals and 100,000 innocent citizens there is a surveillance camera with an automatic face recognition software. If the camera sees a known criminal, it will trigger the alarm with 99 % probability; if the camera sees an innocent citizen, it will trigger the alarm with a probability of 1 %. What is the probability that indeed a criminal was filmed when the alarm is triggered?" The correct answer

[8] This categorization was used by Oechssler, Roider, and Schmitz (2009). We also considered the categorization of Frederick (2005) who assigned subjects with zero correct answers to the "low" group and those with three correct answers to the "high" group. However, with regard to our data this would imply not to analyze more than 53 % of the observations. Note that the latter categorization would not change our results qualitatively.

is $\approx 9\,\%$, but in both CRT groups, a large fraction of the subjects stated a probability larger than 90 %. These subjects exhibit the base rate fallacy since they do not or barely consider the low base rate of criminals in the population. However, compared to the low CRT group, subjects in the high CRT group are considerably less susceptible to this bias and state the correct probability more often (see Figure 7.1).[9]

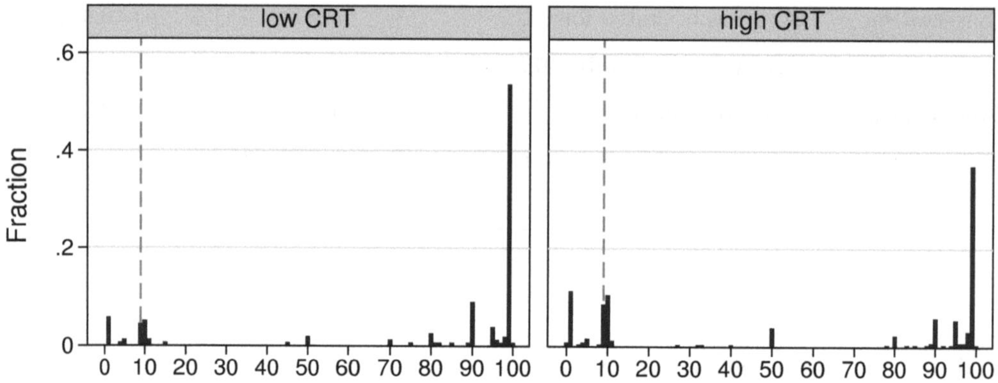

Figure 7.1. Distribution of probabilities stated for the base rate fallacy problem. The dashed line indicates the correct answer.

It is also striking that the average CRT score of subjects who correctly take into account the small base rate is considerably larger than the average CRT score of subjects who exhibit the base rate fallacy (see Table 7.3).

Prob. stated	Average CRT score	n
0–10 %	2.16	115
11–90 %	1.74	76
91–100 %	1.72	220

Table 7.3. Average CRT scores for categorized answers to the base rate fallacy problem.

[9]In the high CRT group, 19.1 % of the subjects answered 9 % or 10 %, while in the low CRT group, this answer is stated in only 9.7 % of the cases ($p = 0.01$, two-sided χ^2 test). Moreover, the average probability assessed in the high CRT group equals 61.5 %, which is significantly smaller than 77.4 %, the average probability assessed in the low CRT group.

7.4.2 Conservatism bias

While people that exhibit the base rate fallacy underweight base rates, there are also situations where base rates are overweighted relative to sample evidence. In such situations, subjects are too conservative in adapting prior probabilities to new evidence, and hence this fallacy is called conservatism bias. In order to test whether the tendency to exhibit this fallacy is related to a person's CRT score, we confronted the subjects with the following problem that was first studied by Edwards (1968): "There are two urns; each one contains ten balls. Urn A contains 7 red and 3 blue balls, while urn B contains 3 red and 7 blue balls. One urn is randomly chosen by flipping a fair coin. 12 balls are now drawn from this urn with replacement. The result is the following: 8 red and 4 blue balls were drawn. What is the probability that the randomly drawn urn is urn A when observing this result (8 red and 4 blue balls)?" The correct answer is 97 %, but many subjects (34 % in the low CRT group and 28 % in the high CRT group) simply entered the base rate of 50 % as their answer (see Figure 7.2).

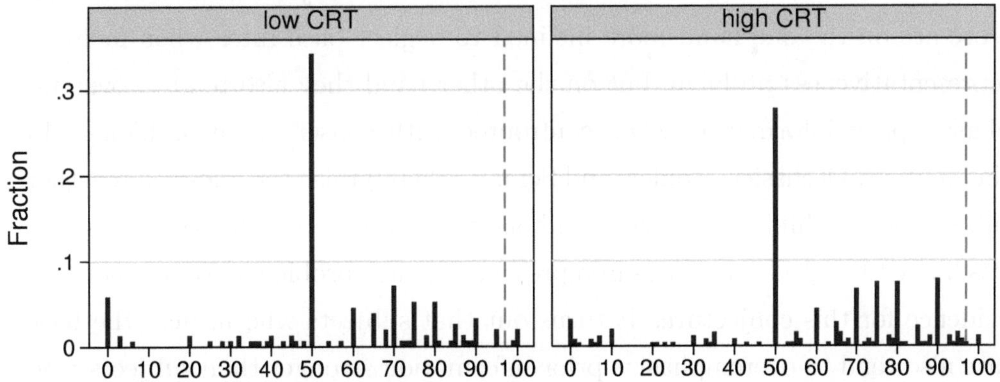

Figure 7.2. Distribution of probabilities stated for the conservatism problem. The dashed line indicates the correct answer.

The average answer in the low CRT group is 56.8 %, while it is 60.1 % in the high CRT group. The fact that the intuitive decision takers' average answer is closer to the base rate than the analytical decision takers' average answer shows that the former group is more heavily affected by the conservatism fallacy than the latter group. Again, it is remarkable that subjects whose answer is close to the correct one have a larger CRT score on average (see Table 7.4). This indicates that more reflection and analytical reasoning is helpful to prevent falling for the bias.

Prob. stated	Average CRT score	n
0–49 %	1.68	70
50 %	1.73	124
51–89 %	1.90	171
90–100 %	2.20	46

Table 7.4. Average CRT scores for categorized answers to the conservatism problem.

7.4.3 Overweighting and underweighting of base rates

The results in Sections 7.4.1 and 7.4.2 show that subjects with a low CRT score are on the one hand more inclined to neglect base rates when facing a representativeness problem, but on the other hand they also tend to overemphasize prior information when confronted with conservatism problems. In this context, Oechssler, Roider, and Schmitz (2009) raise the question whether subjects who exhibit a conservatism bias (i. e., who overweight base rates) are less likely to neglect base rates in representativeness problems. We cannot find evidence for this conjecture. It turns out that subjects who neglect the base rate also tend to overemphasize prior information stronger than subjects who are not susceptible to that bias.[10] It seems to be simply the framing of these

[10] For this specific question, we restricted our analysis to a subset of subjects who, for each bias, either clearly exhibited the bias or stated the correct answer. Concerning the base rate neglect problem, subjects exhibit this fallacy when their answer is $\geqslant 90\,\%$, while they do not if their answer is 9 % or 10 %. Concerning the conservatism problem, subjects overemphasize prior information when their answer equals 50 %, while they do not if their answer is $\geqslant 90\,\%$. There are 100 subjects who neglect the base rate of which 76 also

problems which leads low CRT subjects to focus more heavily on very salient pieces of information and not to process all available information correctly.

7.4.4 Overconfidence

We asked the subjects five questions related to general knowledge. After answering the questions, they were also asked to estimate the number of general knowledge questions they had answered correctly.[11] Within each CRT group, we divided the participants into three subgroups. Subjects were classified as being overconfident (underconfident) when the estimated number of correct answers was larger (smaller) than the actual number, and otherwise they were classified as assessing the number of right answers correctly.

Compared to the low CRT group, relatively more subjects in the high CRT group assessed their number of right answers correctly (see Table 7.2). The difference is statistically significant. While the more intuitive decision takers are relatively less successful in assessing the right number of correct answers, there is no clear tendency that they are more overconfident than the analytical decision takers (in the low CRT group, the share of subjects being overconfident and also the share of underconfident subjects is larger than in the high CRT group).

overweight prior information, while of the 30 subjects who do not neglect the base rate, only 18 overweight prior information (two-sided χ^2 test, $p = 0.086$).

[11] (1) What is the distance between earth and sun in astronomical units? a) 587; b) 1; c) 4553; d) 14. (2) How many inhabitants does the Saarland (a German federal state) have? a) 2,132,000; b) 1,670,000; c) 1,037,000; d) 890,000. (3) In which year did Albert Einstein die? a) 1955; b) 1947; c) 1961; d) 1938. (4) Who is the author of "Wilhelm Tell"? a) Johann Wolfgang von Goethe; b) Friedrich Schiller; c) Friedrich Hölderlin; d) Theodor Fontane. (5) Which metropolitan area has the largest number of inhabitants? a) Shanghai; b) Istanbul; c) Los Angeles; d) Moscow. (6) What do you think: how many of the preceding questions have you answered correctly?

7.4.5 Endowment effect

In experimental economics, it is often observed that subjects' willingness to pay differs substantially from their willingness to accept (see e. g. Horowitz and McConnell, 2002). This phenomenon is often explained by the endowment effect (Kahneman, Knetsch, and Thaler, 1991). In our experiment, half of the subjects found a yellow 'Stabilo Boss' highlighter on the desk in their cabin (scenario 1) while the other half of the subjects was given the opportunity to buy such a highlighter from the experimenter when leaving the laboratory (scenario 2). At the end of the questionnaire, subjects in scenario 1 faced the following decision: "From now on, the yellow highlighter on your desk belongs to you. You can decide between the following alternatives: (1) I take the highlighter home when leaving the laboratory; (2) When the payment is conducted, I sell the highlighter to the experimenter at a price of 0.20€. In case 2, 0.20€ are added to your profit realized in the experiment." In contrast, subjects in scenario 2 saw a bowl with highlighters when entering the lab and at the end of the questionnaire they were confronted with the following decision: "When the payment is conducted, you can buy a yellow 'Stabilo Boss' highlighter at a price of 0.20€. (1) I want to buy a yellow highlighter; (2) I do not want to buy a yellow highlighter. In case 1, you will receive 0.20€ less."

Overall, we find very strong evidence for the endowment effect. When the highlighter is in the cabin (scenario 1), 64.6 % of the subjects decided to take the highlighter home, while only 22.9 % of the subjects decided to buy it when the payment is conducted (scenario 2). This difference is highly significant ($p < 0.0001$, two-sided χ^2 test). However, higher cognitive ability does not reduce the susceptibility to the endowment effect (see Table 7.5).[12]

Taken together, is subjects' performance on the CRT a good predictor for their susceptibility to behavioral biases? While we have found strong evidence

[12]Note that the endowment effect is the stronger, the larger is the difference in buying decisions between the two scenarios. In the high CRT group this difference is 42.8 %, while it is 40.4 % in the low CRT group.

that this is indeed the case for the base rate fallacy and the conservatism bias, the susceptibility to the endowment effect does not vary with the CRT score. Hence, our results suggest that the CRT has strong predictive power only for biases that may arise in problems for which there exists a correct solution and where analytical skills are helpful to derive this solution.

	CRT group		
	low	high	p-value
Scenario 1	61.0 %	67.0 %	$p \approx 0.38$
Scenario 2	20.6 %	24.2 %	$p \approx 0.55$

The p-values result from a two-sided χ^2 test.

Table 7.5. Endowment effect: Fraction of subjects buying the highlighter per scenario and CRT group.

To conclude, it is important to take bounded rationality into account when modeling human behavior. In particular, the design of institutions and incentive schemes might benefit from a fruitful interaction between laboratory experiments and contract theory. In future research, it seems to be challenging and very interesting to incorporate the experimentally observed behavioral aspects of human decision making into theoretical studies on contract design and incentive provision.

References

Abeler, J., A. Falk, L. Götte, and D. Huffman (2009), Reference Points and Effort Provision, *American Economic Review*, forthcoming.

Aghion, P., M. Dewatripont, and P. Rey (1994), Renegotiation Design with Unverifiable Information, *Econometrica* 62, 257–282.

Aghion, P., M. Dewatripont, and P. Rey (2002), On Partial Contracting, *European Economic Review* 46, 745–753.

Aghion, P., M. Dewatripont, and P. Rey (2004), Transferable Control, *Journal of the European Economic Association* 2, 115–138.

Aghion, P., D. Fudenberg, R. Holden, T. Kunimoto, and O. Tercieux (2009), Subgame-Perfect Implementation under Value Perturbations and the Hold-Up Problem, Discussion Paper.

Aghion, P. and J. Tirole (1994), The Management of Innovation, *Quarterly Journal of Economics* 109, 1185–1209.

Aghion, P. and J. Tirole (1997), Formal and Real Authority in Organizations, *Journal of Political Economy* 105, 1–29.

Akerlof, G. (1982), Labor Contracts as Partial Gift Exchange, *Quarterly Journal of Economics* 97, 543–569.

Bardsley, N., R. Cubitt, G. Loomes, P. Moffatt, C. Starmer, and R. Sugden (2010), *Experimental Economics: Rethinking the Rules*, Princeton: Princeton University Press.

E. I. Hoppe-Fischer, *Essays on Contract Design and Incentive Provision*,
Edition KWV, https://doi.org/10.1007/978-3-658-24133-9

Bennett, J. and E. Iossa (2006a), Building and Managing Facilities for Public Services, *Journal of Public Economics* 90, 2143–2160.

Bennett, J. and E. Iossa (2006b), Delegation of Contracting in the Private Provision of Public Services, *Review of Industrial Organization* 29, 75–92.

Bentz, A., P. A. Grout, and M. L. Halonen (2005), What Should Governments Buy from the Private Sector - Assets or Services? Discussion Paper.

Bergman, O., T. Ellingsen, M. Johannesson, and C. Svensson (2010), Anchoring and Cognitive Ability, *Economics Letters* 107, 66–68.

Bernheim, B. D. and M. D. Whinston (1998), Incomplete Contracts and Strategic Ambiguity, *American Economic Review* 88, 902–932.

Besley, T. and M. Ghatak (2001), Government versus Private Ownership of Public Goods, *Quarterly Journal of Economics* 116, 1343–1372.

Bolten, J. E., R. S. Leonard, M. V. Arena, O. Younossi, and J. M. Sollinger (2008), Sources of Weapon System Cost Growth, *RAND Corporation.*

Bolton, P. and M. Dewatripont (2005), *Contract Theory,* Cambridge, MA: MIT Press.

Bolton, G. and A. Ockenfels (2000), ERC: A Theory of Equity, Reciprocity, and Competition, *American Economic Review* 90, 166–193.

Bös, D. (1991), *Privatization: A Theoretical Treatment*, Oxford: Oxford University Press.

Bös, D. and G. De Fraja (2002), Quality and Outside Capacity in the Provision of Health Services, *Journal of Public Economics* 84, 199–218.

Brañas-Garza, P., P. Guillen, and R. L. del Paso (2008), Math Skills and Risk Attitudes, *Economics Letters* 99, 332–336.

Brandts, J. and G. Charness (2010), The Strategy versus Direct-Response Method: A Survey of Experimental Comparisons, Discussion Paper.

Brüggen, A. and F. Moers (2007), The Role of Financial Incentives and Social Incentives in Multi-Task Settings, *Journal of Management Accounting Research* 19, 25–50.

Brüggen, A. and M. Strobel (2007), Real Effort versus Chosen Effort in Experiments, *Economics Letters* 96, 232–236.

Cambridge Economic Policy Associates (2005), Public-Private Partnerships in Scotland – Evaluation of Performance, Final Report.

Camerer, C. F. (2003), *Behavioral Game Theory: Experiments in Strategic Interaction*, Princeton: Princeton University Press.

Charness, G. and M. Dufwenberg (2006), Promises and Partnership, *Econometrica* 74, 1579–1601.

Charness, G. and M. Dufwenberg (2010), Hidden Information, Participation, and Communication, *American Economic Review*, forthcoming.

Charness, G. and M. Rabin (2002), Understanding Social Preferences with Simple Tests, *Quarterly Journal of Economics* 117, 817–869.

Che, Y.-K. and D. B. Hausch (1999), Cooperative Investments and the Value of Contracting, *American Economic Review* 89, 125–147.

Che, Y.-K. and S.-W. Yoo (2001), Optimal Incentives for Teams, *American Economic Review* 91, 525–541.

Chen, B. and Y. S. Chiu (2010), Public-Private Partnerships: Task Interdependence and Contractibility, *International Journal of Industrial Organization* 28, 591–603.

Chiappori, P. A. and B. Salanié (2003), Testing Contract Theory: A Survey of Some Recent Work, in: *Advances in Economics and Econometrics*, Econometric Society Monographs, Eighth World Congress, Vol. 1, ed. by M. Dewatripont, L.P. Hansen, and S.J. Turnovsky, Cambridge, UK: Cambridge University Press, 115–149.

Chong, E., F. Huet, and S. Saussier (2006a), Auctions, Ex-post Competition, and Prices: The Efficiency of Public-Private Partnerships, *Annals of Public and Cooperative Economics* 77, 521–554.

Chong, E., F. Huet, S. Saussier, and F. Steiner (2006b), Public-Private Partnerships and Prices: Evidence from Water Distribution in France, *Review of Industrial Organization* 29, 149–169.

Chung, T.-Y. (1991), Incomplete Contracts, Specific Investments, and Risk Sharing, *Review of Economic Studies* 58, 1031–1042.

Coase, R. H. (1937), The Nature of the Firm, *Economica* 4, 386–405.

Crémer, J. and F. Khalil (1992), Gathering Information Before Signing a Contract, *American Economic Review* 82, 566–578.

Crémer, J., F. Khalil, and J.-C. Rochet (1998a), Contracts and Productive Information Gathering, *Games and Economic Behavior* 25, 174–193.

Crémer, J., F. Khalil, and J.-C. Rochet (1998b), Strategic Information Gathering Before a Contract Is Offered, *Journal of Economic Theory* 81, 163–200.

Dana, Jr., J. D. (1993), The Organization and Scope of Agents: Regulating Multiproduct Industries, *Journal of Economic Theory* 59, 288–310.

De Palma, A., L. Leruth, and G. Prunier (2009), Towards a Principal-Agent Based Typology of Risks in Public-Private Partnerships, IMF Working Paper.

Department of Transportation (2003), An Evaluation – Major Highway Program, Report 3–13.

Dewatripont, M., I. Jewitt, and J. Tirole (2000), Multitask Agency Problems: Focus and Task Clustering, *European Economic Review* 44, 869–877.

Dewatripont, M. and J. Tirole (1999), Advocates, *Journal of Political Economy* 107, 1–39.

Dufwenberg, M. and G. Kirchsteiger (2004), A Theory of Sequential Reciprocity, *Games and Economic Behavior* 47, 268–298.

Dufwenberg, M., A. Smith, and M. Van Essen (2010), Hold-Up: With a Vengeance, *Economic Inquiry*, forthcoming.

Economist Intelligence Unit (2005), Business 2010: The Public Sector.

Eddy, D. M. (1982), Probabilistic Reasoning in Clinical Medicine: Problems and Opportunities, in: *Judgement under Uncertainty: Heuristics and Biases*, ed. by D. F. Kahneman, P. Slovic, and A. Tversky, Cambridge, UK: Cambridge University Press, 249–267.

Edlin, A. S. and B. E. Hermalin (2000), Contract Renegotiation and Options in Agency Problems, *Journal of Law, Economics, and Organization* 16, 395–423.

Edlin, A. S. and S. Reichelstein (1996), Holdups, Standard Breach Remedies, and Optimal Investment, *American Economic Review* 86, 478–501.

Edwards, W. (1968), Conservatism in Human Information Processing, in: *Formal Representation of Human Judgement*, ed. by B. Kleinmutz and R. B. Cattell, New York: Wiley, 17–52.

Ellingsen, T. and M. Johannesson (2004a), Promises, Threats, and Fairness, *Economic Journal* 114, 397–420.

Ellingsen, T. and M. Johannesson (2004b), Is There a Hold-Up Problem? *Scandinavian Journal of Economics* 106, 475–494.

European Investment Bank (2004), The EIB's Role in Public-Private Partnerships.

Evans, R. (2008), Simple Efficient Contracts in Complex Environments, *Econometrica* 76, 459–491.

Ewerhart, C. (2006), The Effect of Sunk Costs on the Outcome of Alternating-Offers Bargaining between Inequity-Averse Agents, *Schmalenbach Business Review* 58, 184–203.

Fehr, E., O. Hart, and C. Zehnder (2009), Contracts, Reference Points, and Competition – Behavioral Effects of the Fundamental Transformation, *Journal of the European Economic Association* 7, 561–572.

Fehr, E., O. Hart, and C. Zehnder (2010), Contracts as Reference Points – Experimental Evidence, *American Economic Review*, forthcoming.

Fehr, E., G. Kirchsteiger, and A. Riedl (1993), Does Fairness Prevent Market Clearing? An Experimental Investigation, *Quarterly Journal of Economics* 108, 437–459.

Fehr, E. and K. M. Schmidt (1999), A Theory of Fairness, Competition, and Cooperation, *Quarterly Journal of Economics* 114, 817–868.

Fehr, E. and K. M. Schmidt (2004), Fairness and Incentives in a Multi-Task Principal-Agent Model, *Scandinavian Journal of Economics* 106, 453–474.

Fehr, E. and K. M. Schmidt (2006), The Economics of Fairness, Reciprocity, and Altruism – Experimental Evidence and New Theories, in: *Handbook of the Economics of Giving, Altruism, and Reciprocity,* ed. by S.-C. Kolm and J. M. Ythier, Amsterdam: Elsevier, 615–691.

Fischbacher, U. (2007), z-Tree: Zurich Toolbox for Ready-Made Economic Experiments, *Experimental Economics* 10, 171–178.

Flyvbjerg, B. (2004), Procedures for Dealing with Optimism Bias in Transport Planning, British Department for Transport, Guidance Document.

Francesconi, M. and A. Muthoo (2006), Control Rights in Public-Private Partnerships, Discussion Paper.

Frederick, S. (2005), Cognitive Reflection and Decision Making, *Journal of Economic Perspectives* 19, 25–42.

Friedman, D. and A. Cassar (2004), *Economics Lab: An Intensive Course in Experimental Economics*, New York: Routledge.

Friedman, D. and S. Sunder (1994), *Experimental Methods: A Primer for Economists*, Cambridge, UK: Cambridge University Press.

Gilbert, R. J. and M. H. Riordan (1995), Regulating Complementary Products: A Comparative Institutional Analysis, *Rand Journal of Economics* 26, 243–256.

Gilroy, L. C., R. W. Poole, Jr., P. Samuel, and G. Segal (2007), Building New Roads through Public-Private Partnerships: Frequently Asked Questions, Reason Foundation, Policy Brief 58.

Greiner, B. (2004), An Online Recruiting System for Economic Experiments, in: *Forschung und Wissenschaftliches Rechnen 2003. GWDG Bericht 63*, ed. by K. Kremer and V. Macho, Göttingen: Ges. für Wiss. Datenverarbeitung, 79–93.

Grimsey, D. and M. K. Lewis (2004), *Public-Private Partnerships*, Cheltenham: Edward Elgar.

Grossman, S. J. and O. D. Hart (1986), The Costs and Benefits of Ownership: A Theory of Vertical and Lateral Integration, *Journal of Political Economy* 94, 691–719.

Gul, F. and W. Pesendorfer (2007), The Canonical Space for Behavioral Types, Discussion Paper.

Guriev, S. (2003), Incomplete Contracts with Cross-Investments, *B. E. Journal of Theoretical Economics* (Contributions) 3, Article 5.

Güth, W., S. Huck, and W. Müller (2001), The Relevance of Equal Splits in Ultimatum Games, *Games and Economic Behavior* 37, 161–169.

Guthrie, C., J. J. Rachlinski, and A. J. Wistrich (2007), Blinking on the Bench: How Judges Decide Cases, *Cornell Law Review* 93, 1–44.

Hackett, S. H. (1993), Incomplete Contracting: A Laboratory Experimental Analysis, *Economic Inquiry* 31, 274–297.

Halonen-Akatwijuka, M. (2010), Organizational Design, Technology, and the Boundaries of the Firm, *Economica* 77, 544–564.

Halonen-Akatwijuka, M. and E. Pafilis (2009), Reputation and Ownership of Public Goods, University of Bristol, CMPO Working Paper 09/211.

Hart, O. D. (1995), *Firms, Contracts, and Financial Structure*, Oxford: Oxford University Press.

Hart, O. (2003), Incomplete Contracts and Public Ownership: Remarks, and an Application to Public-Private Partnerships, *Economic Journal* 113, C69–C76.

Hart, O. (2008), Reference Points and the Theory of the Firm, *Economica* 75, 404–411.

Hart, O. (2009), Hold-Up, Asset Ownership, and Reference Points, *Quarterly Journal of Economics* 124, 267–300.

Hart, O. and B. Holmström (2010), A Theory of Firm Scope, *Quarterly Journal of Economics* 125, 483–513.

Hart, O. and J. Moore (1988), Incomplete Contracts and Renegotiation, *Econometrica* 56, 755–785.

Hart, O. D. and J. Moore (1990), Property Rights and the Nature of the Firm, *Journal of Political Economy* 98, 1119–1158.

Hart, O. and J. Moore (1999), Foundations of Incomplete Contracts, *Review of Economic Studies* 66, 115–138.

Hart, O. and J. Moore (2007), Incomplete Contracts and Ownership: Some New Thoughts, *American Economic Review* 97, 182–186.

Hart, O. and J. Moore (2008), Contracts as Reference Points, *Quarterly Journal of Economics* 123, 1–48.

Hart, O., A. Shleifer, and R. W. Vishny (1997), The Proper Scope of Government: Theory and an Application to Prisons, *Quarterly Journal of Economics* 112, 1127–1161.

Hermalin, B. E. and M. L. Katz (1993), Judicial Modification of Contracts between Sophisticated Parties: A More Complete View of Incomplete Contracts and Their Breach, *Journal of Law, Economics, and Organization* 9, 230–255.

Hirao, Y. (1993), Task Assignment and Agency Structures, *Journal of Economics and Management Strategy* 2, 299–323.

HM Treasury (2003), *PFI: Meeting the Investment Challenge*, Norwich: HMSO.

Holmström, B. and P. Milgrom (1991), Multitask Principal-Agent Analyses: Incentive Contracts, Asset Ownership, and Job Design, *Journal of Law, Economics, and Organization* 7, 24–52.

Hoppe, E. I. and D. J. Kusterer (2009), Conflicting Tasks and Moral Hazard: Theory and Experimental Evidence, Discussion Paper.

Hoppe, E. I. and D. J. Kusterer (2011), Behavioral Biases and Cognitive Reflection, *Economics Letters*, forthcoming.

Hoppe, E. I. and P. W. Schmitz (2010a), Public versus Private Ownership: Quantity Contracts and the Allocation of Investment Tasks, *Journal of Public Economics* 94, 258–268.

Hoppe, E. I. and P. W. Schmitz (2010b), Public-Private Partnerships versus Traditional Procurement: Innovation Incentives and Information Gathering, CEPR Discussion Paper 7681.

Hoppe, E. I. and P. W. Schmitz (2010c), The Costs and Benefits of Additional Information in Agency Models with Endogenous Information Structures, *Economics Letters* 107, 58–62.

Hoppe, E. I. and P. W. Schmitz (2011), Can Contracts Solve the Hold-Up Problem? Experimental Evidence, *Games and Economic Behavior*, forthcoming.

Horowitz, J. K. and K. E. McConnell (2002), A Review of WTA/WTP Studies, *Journal of Environmental Economics and Management* 44, 426–447.

Huberman, G. and C. Kahn (1988), Limited Contract Enforcement and Strategic Renegotiation, *American Economic Review* 78, 471–484.

Innes, R. D. (1990), Limited Liability and Incentive Contracting with Ex-ante Action Choices, *Journal of Economic Theory* 52, 45–67.

Iossa, E. and D. Martimort (2008), The Simple Micro-Economics of Public-Private Partnerships, Discussion Paper.

Iossa, E. and D. Martimort (2009), The Theory of Incentives Applied to PPPs in the Transport Sector, in: *The Handbook of Transportation Economics*, ed. by A. De Palma, R. Lindsey, E. Quinet, and R. Vickerman, Cheltenham: Edward Elgar.

Itoh, H. (1994), Job Design, Delegation, and Cooperation: A Principal-Agent Analysis, *European Economic Review* 38, 691–700.

Kaeser, H. U. (2008), Abandon Ships, CSIS Discussion Paper.

Kahneman, D., J. L. Knetsch, and R. H. Thaler (1991), Anomalies: The Endowment Effect, Loss Aversion, and Status Quo Bias, *Journal of Economic Perspectives* 5, 193–206.

Keser, C. and M. Willinger (2000), Principals' Principles when Agents' Actions Are Hidden, *International Journal of Industrial Organization* 18, 163–185.

Keser, C. and M. Willinger (2007), Theories of Behavior in Principal-Agent Relationships with Hidden Action, *European Economic Review* 51, 1514–1533.

Kessler, A. S. (1998), The Value of Ignorance, *Rand Journal of Economics* 29, 339–354.

Khalil, F., D. Kim, and D. Shin (2006), Optimal Task Design: To Integrate or Separate Planning and Implementation? *Journal of Economics and Management Strategy* 15, 457–478.

Kosar, K. R. (2006), Privatization and the Federal Government: An Introduction, CRS Report for the Congress.

Koszegi, B. and M. Rabin (2006), A Model of Reference-Dependent Preferences, *Quarterly Journal of Economics* 121, 1133–1165.

Laffont, J.-J. and D. Martimort (2002), *The Theory of Incentives: The Principal-Agent Model*, Princeton: Princeton University Press.

Laffont, J.-J. and J. Tirole (1991), Privatization and Incentives, *Journal of Law, Economics, and Organization* 7, 84–105.

Laux, C. (2001), Limited-Liability and Incentive Contracting with Multiple Projects, *Rand Journal of Economics* 32, 514–526.

Levine, D. K. (1998), Modeling Altruism and Spitefulness in Experiments, *Review of Economic Dynamics* 1, 593–622.

Lewis, T. R. and D. E. M. Sappington (1997), Information Management in Incentive Problems, *Journal of Political Economy* 105, 796–821.

Lyon, T. P. and E. B. Rasmusen (2004), Buyer-Option Contracts Restored: Renegotiation, Inefficient Threats, and the Hold-Up Problem, *Journal of Law, Economics, and Organization* 20, 148–169.

MacLeod, W. B. (2002), Complexity and Contract, in: *The Economics of Contracts: Theory and Applications*, ed. by E. Brousseau and J.-M. Glachant, Cambridge, UK: Cambridge University Press, 213–240.

Martimort, D. (2006), An Agency Perspective on the Costs and Benefits of Privatization, *Journal of Regulatory Economics* 30, 5–44.

Martimort, D. and J. Pouyet (2008), To Build or not to Build: Normative and Positive Theories of Public-Private Partnerships, *International Journal of Industrial Organization* 26, 393–411.

Maskin, E. and J. Moore (1999), Implementation and Renegotiation, *Review of Economic Studies* 66, 39–56.

Maskin, E. and J. Riley (1984), Monopoly with Incomplete Information, *Rand Journal of Economics* 15, 171–196.

Maskin, E. and J. Tirole (1999), Unforeseen Contingencies, Property Rights, and Incomplete Contracts, *Review of Economic Studies* 66, 83–114.

Masten, S. E. and S. Saussier (2002), Econometrics of Contracts: An Assessment of Developments in the Empirical Literature of Contracting, in: *The Economics of Contracts: Theory and Applications*, ed. by E. Brousseau and J.-M. Glachant, Cambridge, UK: Cambridge University Press, 273–292.

Melese, F. (2005), Privatizing Public Hospitals: A Win-Win for Taxpayers and the Poor, Reason Foundation, Policy Brief 41.

Monbiot, G. (2002), Very British Corruption, *Guardian*, January 22.

Myerson, R. B. (1981), Optimal Auction Design, *Mathematics of Operations Research* 6, 58–73.

Mylovanov, T. and P. W. Schmitz (2008), Task Scheduling and Moral Hazard, *Economic Theory* 37, 307–320.

Nofsinger, J. R. and A. Varma (2007), How Analytical Is Your Financial Advisor? *Financial Services Review* 16, 245–260.

Nöldeke, G. and K. M. Schmidt (1995), Option Contracts and Renegotiation: A Solution to the Hold-Up Problem, *Rand Journal of Economics* 26, 163–179.

Nöldeke, G. and K. M. Schmidt (1998), Sequential Investments and Options to Own, *Rand Journal of Economics* 29, 633–653.

OECD (2008), *Public-Private Partnerships - In Pursuit of Risk Sharing and Value for Money*, Paris: OECD Publishing.

Oechssler, J., A. Roider, and P. W. Schmitz (2009), Cognitive Abilities and Behavioral Biases, *Journal of Economic Behavior & Organization* 72, 147–152.

Ohlendorf, S. (2009), Expectation Damages, Divisible Contracts, and Bilateral Investment, *American Economic Review* 99, 1608–1618.

Pitchford, R. (1998), Moral Hazard and Limited Liability: The Real Effects of Contract Bargaining, *Economics Letters* 61, 251–259.

Prendergast, C. (1999), The Provision of Incentives in Firms, *Journal of Economic Literature* 37, 7–63.

Public Accounts Select Committee (2000), The PFI Contract for the New Dartford and Gravesham Hospital, Twelfth Report.

Rabin, M. (1993), Incorporating Fairness into Game Theory and Economics, *American Economic Review* 83, 1281–1302.

Renda, A. and L. Schrefler (2006), Public-Private Partnerships. Models and Trends in the European Union. Study Requested by the European Parliament's Committee on Internal Market and Consumer Protection.

Rogerson, W. P. (1992), Contractual Solutions to the Hold-Up Problem, *Review of Economic Studies* 59, 777–793.

Roider, A. (2004), Asset Ownership and Contractibility of Interaction, *Rand Journal of Economics* 35, 787–802.

Salanié, B. (1997), *The Economics of Contracts*, Cambridge, MA: MIT Press.

Samuel, P. (2005), Should States Sell their Toll Roads? Reason Foundation, Policy Study 334.

Schmidt, K. M. (1996a), The Costs and Benefits of Privatization: An Incomplete Contracts Approach, *Journal of Law, Economics, and Organization* 12, 1–24.

Schmidt, K. M. (1996b), Incomplete Contracts and Privatization, *European Economic Review* 40, 569–579.

Schmitz, P. W. (2001), The Hold-Up Problem and Incomplete Contracts: A Survey of Recent Topics in Contract Theory, *Bulletin of Economic Research* 53, 1–17.

Schmitz, P. W. (2002), On the Interplay of Hidden Action and Hidden Information in Simple Bilateral Trading Problems, *Journal of Economic Theory* 103, 444–460.

Schmitz, P. W. (2005), Allocating Control in Agency Problems with Limited Liability and Sequential Hidden Actions, *Rand Journal of Economics* 36, 318–336.

Schmitz, P. W. (2006), Information Gathering, Transaction Costs, and the Property Rights Approach, *American Economic Review* 96, 422–434.

Schuster, J. M. (1998), Neither Public nor Private: The Hybridization of Museums, *Journal of Cultural Economics* 22, 127–150.

Schweizer, U. (1999), *Vertragstheorie*, Tübingen: Mohr Siebeck.

Segal, I. (1999), Complexity and Renegotiation: A Foundation for Incomplete Contracts, *Review of Economic Studies* 66, 57–82.

Segal, I. and M. D. Whinston (2002), The Mirrlees Approach to Mechanism Design with Renegotiation (with Applications to Hold-Up and Risk Sharing), *Econometrica* 70, 1–45.

Sevilla, J. (2005), Accountability and Control of Public Spending in a Decentralized and Delegated Environment, *OECD Journal on Budgeting* 5, 7–21.

Shapiro, C. and R. Willig (1990), Economic Rationales for the Scope of Privatization, in: *The Political Economy of Private Sector Reform and Privatization*, ed. by E. N. Suleiman and J. Waterbury, Boulder: Westview Press, 55–87.

Shleifer, A. (1998), State versus Private Ownership, *Journal of Economic Perspectives* 12, 133–150.

Slonim, R., J. Carlson, and E. Bettinger (2007), Possession and Discounting Behavior, *Economics Letters* 97, 215–221.

Texas Center for Policy Studies (2002), Privatization of Water and Wastewater Services.

Tirole, J. (1999), Incomplete Contracts: Where Do We Stand? *Econometrica* 67, 741–781.

Tirole, J. (2001), Corporate Governance, *Econometrica* 69, 1–35.

Tversky, A. and D. F. Kahneman (1982), Evidential Impact of Base Rates, in: *Judgement under Uncertainty: Heuristics and Biases*, ed. by D. F. Kahneman, P. Slovic, and A. Tversky, Cambridge, UK: Cambridge University Press, 153–160.

Vickerman, R. (2004), Maintenance Incentives under Different Infrastructure Regimes, *Utilities Policy* 12, 315–322.

Vickers, J. and G. Yarrow (1988), *Privatization: An Economic Analysis*, Cambridge, MA: MIT Press.

Von Siemens, F. A. (2009), Bargaining under Incomplete Information, Fairness, and the Hold-Up Problem, *Journal of Economic Behavior & Organization* 71, 486–494.

Watson, J. (2007), Contract, Mechanism Design, and Technological Detail, *Econometrica* 75, 55–81.

Wickelgren, A. L. (2006), The Limitations of Buyer-Option Contracts in Solving the Hold-Up Problem, *Journal of Law, Economics, and Organization* 23, 127–140.

Williamson, O. E. (1975), *Markets and Hierarchies: Analysis and Antitrust Implications*, New York: Free Press.

Williamson, O. E. (1985), *The Economic Institutions of Capitalism*, New York: Free Press.

Yescombe, E. R. (2007), *Public-Private Partnerships*, Oxford: Elsevier.

MIX
Papier aus verantwortungsvollen Quellen
Paper from responsible sources
FSC® C105338

If you have any concerns about our products,
you can contact us on
ProductSafety@springernature.com

In case Publisher is established outside the EU,
the EU authorized representative is:
Springer Nature Customer Service Center GmbH
Europaplatz 3, 69115 Heidelberg, Germany

Printed by Libri Plureos GmbH
in Hamburg, Germany